INDIAN SELF-RULE

INDIAN SELF-RULE

First-Hand Accounts of
Indian-White Relations from Roosevelt to Reagan

EDITED BY KENNETH R. PHILP

*With Forewords by Floyd A. O'Neil, Alvin M. Josephy, Jr.,
and E. Richard Hart*

UTAH STATE UNIVERSITY PRESS
LOGAN, UTAH
1995

Copyright © 1986 by the Institute of the American West

All rights reserved. This book, or parts thereof,
may not be reproduced in any form without written permission
of the publisher.

published by
Utah State University Press — Logan, Utah
1995

Reprinted by arrangement with Howe Brothers

LIBRARY OF CONGRESS CATALOGING-IN-PUBLICATION DATA

Indian self-rule: first-hand accounts of Indian-white relations from
 Roosevelt to Reagan / edited by Kenneth R. Philp
     p.   cm.
 Originally published: Salt Lake City, Utah: Howe Bros., 1986.
 Contains papers which evolved from the Conference on Indian Self-
 Rule, sponsored by the Institute of the American West and held in
 Sun Valley, Idaho from Aug. 17–20, 1983.
 Includes biographical references and index.
 ISBN 0-87421-180-8
 1. Indians of North America — Government relations — 1934–
 2. Indians of North America — Politics and government. 3. Indians of
 North America — Social conditions. 4. United States. Indian
 Reorganization Act. 5. Self-determination, National — United States.
 I. Philp, Kenneth R., 1941–   . II. Conference on Indian Self-Rule
 (1983: Sun Valley, Idaho)
 E93.1466   1994
 323.1'197073'0904 — dc20   94-36862
                                                                      CIP

Photographs on pages 2, 14, 26, 27, 110, and 261 are by Charlotte Lloyd Walkup
(formerly Charlotte Tuttle Westwood). Page 187 is by Benjamin Reifel from
Charlotte Lloyd Walkup's collection. Pages 111, 186, and 260 are by E. Reese-
man Fryer. The title page photograph of the Navajo Tribal Council in session
at Window Rock, Arizona, is by Milton Snow from E. Reeseman Fryer's collec-
tion. Photographs are courtesy of Ms. Walkup, Mr. Fryer, and the Institute of
the American West Collection, Special Collections, University of Utah.

Preface

This publication evolved from a historic conference that met at the Elkhorn Inn in Sun Valley, Idaho, from August 17 to 20, 1983. The theme of this conference was "Indian Self-Rule: Fifty Years Under the Indian Reorganization Act." Participants came from all over the nation. They included Indian spokesmen, past and present federal policy makers, anthropologists, historians, political scientists, and other scholars. An atmosphere of excitement permeated the conference. An audience of four hundred people listened attentively to keynote addresses and panel sessions that analyzed the legacy of the IRA on Indian life.

The Conference on Indian Self-Rule provided a rare opportunity for communication between different groups of people. It was the most important gathering of persons to evaluate the Indian Reorganization Act since a symposium sponsored by the American Anthropological Association in 1953. On each day of the conference keynote speakers and panelists carefully examined a different period of federal Indian policy which has affected tribal progress toward self-rule: (1) the Indian New Deal, 1928–1945; (2) the Termination Era, 1945–1960; (3) the policy of Self-Determination, 1960–1976; and (4) the impact of the IRA on Indian America from 1977 to the present.

The Conference on Indian Self-Rule was the ninth in a series of summer conferences sponsored by the Institute of the American West, a non-profit educational institution founded in 1975 as the humanities division of the Sun Valley Center for the Arts and Humanities. E. Richard Hart, the director of the Institute, Alvin M. Josephy, Jr., president of the Institute's National Council, and Vine Deloria, Jr., a nationally-known author, formulated early plans for the 1983 program

[v]

that commemorated the fiftieth anniversary of the Indian Reorganization Act. They were assisted by two former Commissioners of Indian Affairs, Louis Bruce and Robert L. Bennett. Members of the National Council that played a major role in organizing the conference were Floyd A. O'Neil, Suzan Shown Harjo, and Alfonso Ortiz.

The Institute of the American West obtained financial support for the conference from a variety of sources. The following groups and individuals deserve special thanks and recognition: the Association for the Humanities in Idaho; the Atlantic Richfield Foundation; the Gannett Foundation; KWSU-TV of Pullman, Washington; the National Endowment for the Humanities; and the Sun Valley Center for the Arts and Humanities. Generous contributions also were received from Mrs. Damaris D. W. Ethridge, numerous individuals, and an anonymous donor.

A portfolio of limited edition prints by five distinguished Native American artists was commissioned by the Institute of the American West for the Conference on Indian Self-Rule. It included works by David P. Bradley, N. Scott Momaday, Jaune Quick-to-See Smith, Darren Vigil, and R. Lee White. Proceeds from the sale of this portfolio helped fund the conference.

Financial assistance from the above organizations and individuals made it possible for the Institute of the American West to provide more than one hundred fellowships that enabled people from different parts of the United States to attend the conference. More importantly the Institute was able to bring the conference proceedings to national, regional, and local audiences by circulating a news tabloid on the themes of the conference, promoting radio and television programming, and conducting oral interviews with former government administrators and Indian leaders who played a significant role in the past half-century of federal-Indian relations. Interviewers were Gregory C. Thompson, Kathryn MacKay, Marjane Ambler, and John R. Alley.

A complete set of transcribed conference proceedings, including the oral interviews and other materials, have been deposited in the Special Collections Department of the Marriott Library at the University of Utah. These valuable documents will be available for future historical research on federal Indian policy since the New Deal. Cassette copies of the keynote addresses and panel sessions were recorded by the

National Public Radio affiliate KUER-FM 90 at Salt Lake City. These cassettes can be purchased from the University of Utah. Selma Thomas of Seattle, Washington produced and directed a video for broadcast on Public Broadcasting Service stations. Finally, John R. Alley and the editorial staff at Howe Brothers merit acknowledgement for their assistance in the publication of this book.

Contents

Dr. Henry Roe Cloud casting the first vote on the Winnebagos' Indian Reorganization Act constitution.

oKVBHVoo4ITA

Indian Self-Rule: First-Hand Accounts of Indian-White Relations from Roosevelt to Reagan

Walden Aisle F Bay 09   Item 1801

Thank you for buying from **Seattle Goodwill Industries** on Amazon Marketplace.

Ship To

Linda Thurston
15 Powers Ct
Alameda, CA 94501-2414

Order Details

Order ID	112-8272419-7351430
Order Date	6/18/2018 5:20:29 PM
Shipping Service	Standard
Buyers Name	Linda Thurston

SKU / Listing ID	Title / Condition	Location / Comments
oKVBHVoo4ITA	Indian Self-Rule: First-Hand Accounts of Indian-White 1801 Relations from Roosevelt to Reagan	Walden - Aisle F - Bay 09 - Item 1801

439684665514722   Good

Price: $3.95   Shipping: $3.99

May have some shelf-wear due to
normal use.

Code: 9780874211801
ASIN: 0874211808

**Seattle Goodwill Industries strives to have each and every customer 100%
satisfied with their purchase. If for any reason you are not 100% satisfied please
email us at onlinebooks@seattlegoodwill.org with your concerns.**

If we need to make something right, we will, <u>Guaranteed!</u>

Thanks for buying on Amazon Marketplace. To provide feedback for the seller please
visit http://www.amazon.com/feedback.

Foreword to the New Edition

During the decade following the conference that produced *Indian Self-Rule*, several of the participants passed from the scene. A surprising number, though, are still living and actively performing many of the same roles that they had in 1983. The durability of the scholarship in this book is also revealing. Many of the observations made at the conference are still in vogue, very much a part of current thinking. Continuity in concerns and thought about and by American Indians was noted by the participants then, and it is still evident.

Subsequent scholars have drawn a great deal from this work and have quoted from it extensively. Few books have appeared that incorporate the range of American Indian voices that this one contains. While there are a great number of non-Indian voices in it as well, the Indian perspectives predominate. Although the subjects covered within the book are today still being discussed in Indian country, there have been at least two major changes. One is that water rights, always important but sometimes overlooked, are now stressed far more than ever before. A second, distinctly more current area of concern is the issue of American Indian gambling. Gambling involves constitutional questions and contributes to as well as reflects the changing lifestyle and economics of Indian tribes. Attention toward many other topics covered in *Indian Self-Rule* has continued to increase. The issue of the extent and specific nature of Indian governments' jurisdiction is certainly one such subject. Jurisdiction is particularly well covered in Part IV of the book. The comments included there, made more than a decade ago, remain remarkably up-to-date.

[1]

The uses of *Indian Self-Rule* have been many. Perhaps the greatest number of copies have been sold at colleges and universities as textbooks for teaching American Indian history and culture. Its value for that purpose is still significant. The book also achieved a certain notoriety because of the varied new source material — the reflections and comments of its contributors — it provided on recent Indian history. Many of those individuals had been involved with the nuts and bolts of Indian affairs during the presidential administrations of Roosevelt, Truman, Eisenhower, Kennedy, Johnson, Nixon, Ford, or Reagan. Charlotte Walkup, E. Reeseman Fryer, Robert L. Bennett, Robert Burnette, Russell Jim, Rupert Costo, Helen Peterson, and Gerald One Feather are but a few of those who participated in the changes brought about in American Indian life during the reforms of FDR's presidency. In a way, the 1983 meeting represented a final hurrah for many of these important historical actors. When they looked back across half of a century to tell us first hand what they and their contemporaries were attempting and to reflect on the consequences of those actions, they provided remarkable documentation of a turbulent time.

It is important that this book be republished. It is needed in the classroom, and it continues to be one of the best sources for first-hand observations by American Indians about their own past.

FLOYD A. O'NEIL
American West Center
University of Utah

Foreword

Especially when one is young, fifty years—half a century—seems
like a long, long time. Exactly fifty years before I was born in 1915,
Abraham Lincoln had just been murdered and the American Civil War
was ending. The white men's wars with Red Cloud, Crazy Horse, Cap-
tain Jack, Chief Joseph, Geronimo, and many other Native American
patriots were still in the future. I was eleven years old before the nation
observed the fiftieth anniversary of "Custer's Last Stand" in an atmosphere something like that of a day of mourning and rededication,
a 1926 Memorial Day on June 25. I was old enough then to thrill to
"The Flaming Frontier," Hollywood's super-epic salute (with an inter-
mission) to the martyred cavalry leader at the Little Bighorn, and to
the white actor, Richard Dix, coated in makeup, playing the role of
"The Vanishing American" (both films helped to form false and stereo-
typic images of Indians for me and many other non-Indians). Lincoln,
Appomattox, Custer, cavalry, and Indians, they were ancient history
to me, visions of long, long before I was born.

Now we are looking back together at a half century since the
passage of the Indian Reorganization Act in 1934 (I was in college
then), and although to younger people, it must now seem a very long
time ago, it strangely does not seem so to me. During those fifty years,
of course, many events occurred and many changes came to Native
Americans, to Indian-white relations, and to relations between Indians
and the federal and state governments. But, in many of the most basic
matters concerning the status and well-being of America's Native
American population, the more that things changed, the more they
stayed the same, so that I see the fifty years as a period of compressed

[3]

time in which numerous wheels spun and few, if any, of the fundamental issues of Indian affairs of 1934 were solved.

John Collier, Dillon Myer, William Zimmerman, Glenn Emmons, and many others have come and gone. At times, it seems like they were here only last week, for the issues over which they contested in the name of Indians are still with Indians. Rupert Costo, Barney Richard, Sam LaPointe, Thomas Sam, Max Bigman, Joseph Bruner, John Snake, Ray Claymore, and many others seem closer to us than the 1930s. Those among them who are still alive could be—and in fact, often are—saying today just what they said in the 1930s.

Indians still do not possess the same freedoms enjoyed by their fellow Americans. Indians still do not enjoy meaningful self-government, self-determination, or sovereignty. The Bureau of Indian Affairs still lays the dead hand of patronizing (usually smirking) bureaucratic authority over reservation matters far beyond the parameters of its trust and treaty obligations. Reservation and tribal natural resources and other properties are still victimized by theft, cheating, and fraud. Indian religion is still not respected and protected. Discrimination and prejudice are still rampant in many states. Indian health, education, housing, and sanitation are still underfunded and largely neglected. Indian unemployment and poverty are still a national scandal. Indeed, even the ration system is back—disguised today to hungry reservation victims of cutbacks and lack of opportunity as commodity distribution programs.

The scene is not good, and one must wonder what has happened in all those fifty years through which one has lived—years filled with zigs and zags in policies, with National Congress of American Indians and National Tribal Chairmen's Association resolutions, with National Indian Youth Council and American Indian Movement activism, with task forces, Bobby and Ted Kennedy educational investigations, and a battery of unending studies. There were changes, as stated, to be sure, and some were undoubtedly for the good. But which ones, and what did they accomplish?

It is time to ask questions, to seek what Indians wanted and expected fifty years ago, twenty-five years ago, and today. Fifty years ago, relatively few Native Americans like Rupert Costo asserted the right of Native Americans to speak and act for themselves. In those days of John Collier and Oliver LaFarge, most whites deemed Indians "children" or "incompetents," unable to know what was best for themselves. Yes, that was the way it was only fifty years ago, but how many whites, including those still in government, continue to think the same way today? Less than twenty-five years ago, in Chicago, an Indian conference demanded the right *to participate with whites* in deciding policies and programs for Indians. How much has changed since then? Today—well, who *is* in the Indians' driver's seat: Native Americans or the secretary of the interior?

In this book and in the Institute of the American West conference on "Indian Self-Rule" that preceded it, it was hoped these fifty years would be carefully examined, drawing not alone on the studies and perspectives of Indian and non-Indian historians and students, but on the memories and reminiscences of participants, again both Indian and non-Indian, in the historic events and processes of that era. To assess what was good and what was bad, what was hoped for and what was frustrated, what was planned and what went wrong, what seemed right and what proved a mistake, what should be kept and what discarded, all these contributors had to ask—and try to answer—a multitude of questions.

Did the planners and writers of the IRA hold up the promise of real self-government, of self-determination and the sovereignty of the tribes? If so, where was it killed, how, and by whom? What were the roles of the Felix Cohens and of Congress, and how judge them? What were the feelings of the tribes about the IRA in 1934? Who were right and who were wrong? What were the enduring good and bad things about the IRA?

In later periods, what were—and are—the lasting adverse impacts of the termination policy, of relocation, of other events of the late Truman and Eisenhower years? How do we assess, from the tribes' points of view, the Indian Claims Commission? Then came the Kennedy and Johnson Administrations, the Area Redevelopment Act and the Office of Economic Opportunity, the proliferation of non-BIA programs and "Indian desks" in Washington that brought new funds to reservations, the Indian Civil Rights Act, the Red Power movement and years of activism, the resurgence of traditionalism and the reassertion of Indian pride on and off the reservations. What about the long, torturous travail of contracting, landmark legal decisions, the energy crisis, and, finally, Reaganomics?

The context, too, is broad, for the changes and wheel spinning have not only been political and economic. What has happened in Indian education and health (contract and tribal schools for instance, and the move of Indian health in 1955 out of the BIA for better or worse), to Indian art, literature, music, and other cultural expressions? What, indeed, in an age of accelerated Indian assimilation and acculturation with perhaps fifty thousand young Indians in white-run colleges, universities, and graduate schools, has happened to tribal cultures, Indian values, and Indian spiritual beliefs and lifeways? All of these are only a few of the areas and subjects worthy of being discussed and questioned.

It is, for certain, a long time, as hairs grey and infirmities appear, from 1934 until today. But perhaps with the help of those who lived through the last fifty years, we will realize that it was all only yesterday and is still very much with us, affecting not only today but tomorrow and the next fifty years as well. Our own years, after all, stemmed from the days of our parents and are, in turn, bequeathed to the years of our children and grandchildren. This is an opportunity to let them know.

ALVIN M. JOSEPHY, JR.
President, National Council,
Institute of the American West

When Europeans arrived on the North American continent, they found hundreds of tribes occupying a vast and verdant country. Although the invaders quickly recognized the wealth of natural resources, their religious bigotry and cultural ethnocentrism prevented them from recognizing the cultural, spiritual, and intellectual riches possessed by the Native Americans. For three hundred years prior to the drafting of the United States Constitution, Europeans confronted the American Indians, usually attempting to expropriate the tribes' territories, often fighting them and trying to convert them to Christianity and materialism, and rarely, if ever, attempting to understand or learn from them. Despite this pattern, during that same three centuries, a foundation of law to deal with Indian tribes was built. Though it seems incredible to us today, Spanish legal scholars argued whether Indians were human and entitled to some rights just like other people. Similarly, the French, British and English were able to establish certain basic codes of law that dealt with Indian-European relations.

By the time the United States Constitution was ratified, the framers had quite a history of precedents from which to draw in order to set down the method by which the new country was to deal with tribes. There were even those among the whites who knew enough to examine the Indian experience, as well, before drafting that remarkable document. The Iroquois Confederacy, it has been argued, was one model that the framers of democracy used. The authors of the Constitution could have gone much farther than they did in guaranteeing the rights of Indian tribes (the same for other non-whites and females), but they did make a start. They concluded that tribes were sovereign entities and that they held their natural resources in common. The Constitution prohibited states from legislating laws over Indians and reserved for the federal government the right to govern Indian trade. The federal government became a trustee for Indian rights and resources. But as Felix Cohen stated in his *Handbook of Federal Indian Law*, "Perhaps the most basic principle of all Indian law, supported by a host of decisions . . . is the principle that *those powers which are lawfully vested in an Indian tribe are not, in general, delegated powers, granted by express acts of Congress, but rather inherent powers of a limited sovereignty which has never been extinguished.*"

In 1984, it will have been one hundred and fifty years since the Indian Trade and Intercourse Act refined federal policy, legitimized removal of tribes from their ancestral lands, and suggested that the relationship of the federal government to the tribes was a "paternal one." The federal government had a condescending and paternalistic attitude towards tribes and committed innumerable unconscionable acts against Indian peoples (including the occasional campaign to exterminate them), but during the period up until the Grant administration, the government, when it did make a formal, honorable effort to deal with tribes, signed treaties with them as sovereign nations. Ratified by Congress, a treaty becomes the most legally binding kind of agreement this country is capable of making.

During the first century of federal Indian affairs in the United States, a very corrupt and mismanaged bureaucracy, the Indian Office, grew to have considerable autocratic control over tribes' relations. As part of a "reform" movement in the 1870s the government decided not only to cease making treaties with tribes, but to change the whole course of Indian policy. It became government policy to assimilate all Indians into what was thought to be the mainstream of American life. Although Indians had already lost millions upon millions of acres of land to the new republic, pressures were great to take from tribes what had been left them through treaties, acts, and executive orders. In the 1880s, the policy of assimilation took shape in what came to be called the Dawes Act. This piece of legislation, formally called the General Allotment Act and passed on February 8, 1887, was to "Provide for the Allotment of Lands in Severalty to Indians on the Various Reservations . . . ." In essence, the act was meant to force Indians to cease their tribal ways, to become individual farmers on small plots of lands, and thus to open the remainder of U.S. Indian reservations to non-Indian use.

During the last decade of the nineteenth century and the first decades of the twentieth century, the government used all of its might to force Indian peoples to give up their tribal identity—their languages, cultures, arts, spirituality, and knowledge. Even today most tribal elders can recall a childhood when Bureau of Indian Affairs officials forced them to attend white schools where their native tongue was forbidden on penalty of punishment (often violent). Elders can recall how native religion was suppressed and condemned as pagan and backward. Indians were warned to give up any thoughts of tribalism and told their only chance in the United States was to act like whites. Bureau officials demanded that traditional dancing and singing cease. On some reservations in the West, BIA agents became petty dictators, demanding that Indians use passes to visit doctors, leave the reservation, or be out after curfew. Pregnant women were forced to dig out the roots of cottonwood trees as punishment for playing cards on Sunday. Children knelt for hours on wooden rods because they had spoken a single word of their native tongue. Religion was suppressed, tribal resources were stolen or swindled away, and Indian people lived in scandalous poverty. In the early twentieth century conditions on some reservations became a blight on the democracy.

It was exactly one hundred years after the Indian Trade and Intercourse Act that Congress enacted the Wheeler-Howard Act, also

known as the Indian Reorganization Act (IRA). The Meriam Report
of 1928, John Collier's crusading, and Felix Cohen's scholarly legal
work all helped lead to its passage. The bibliography at the end of this
publication lists quite a number of additional sources that shed light on
the years surrounding the passage of the act and on the motivations of
those who pressured it through. Among those sources are Kenneth
Philp's *John Collier's Crusade for Indian Reform*, Graham Taylor's
The New Deal and American Indian Tribalism, and Lawrence Kelly's
new book, *The Assault on Assimilation*.

In reading about the IRA, one overriding fact should be remembered. At the time it was passed, the first and most important thing
about the IRA, to the people who passed it, was that it would negate
the Dawes Allotment Act. Indeed, the Indian Reorganization Act
begins, in the first section, by saying, ". . . hereafter no land of any
Indian reservation, created or set apart by treaty or agreement with the
Indians, Act of Congress, Executive order, purchase, or otherwise, shall
be allotted in severalty to any Indian."

Those Indians and non-Indians who opposed the act and preferred traditional governments were sharply attacked by Collier and his
allies. A 1938 publication entitled *The New Day for the Indians:
A Survey of the Working of the Indian Reorganization Act of 1934* and
sponsored by F. W. Hodge, Ruth Benedict, Ales Hrdlicka, A. V. Kidder,
Oliver La Farge, Jay B. Nash, and a number of other Collier supporters, charged that opponents of the IRA included

> People who resist any change in the historic policy which succeeded in
> diminishing Indian landholding. . . .
>
> Those who resist the assistance being given by the present administration to
> Indians in taking back the use of their own lands and range from whites,
> and preventing further land losses.
>
> Property holders and local officials who do not want to see land added to
> reservations taken off the local tax roles.
>
> Those who deplore giving Indians the right to control their own domestic
> relations, customs and the like.
>
> Those who oppose a policy that looks toward the Indian as a relatively
> permanent, distinct (though not segregated) element in our population
> and culture.
>
> Those who also oppose giving authority to Indian tribes to assert their prop-
> erty rights through independent suits.

Those who insist on confusing modern cooperative forms of enterprise with Communism.

Those who dislike a policy which changes government employees from masters of Indians to collaborators with Indians.

And finally, those Indians and whites who have used Indian misfortunes and disagreements to collect fees for their own support.

Under the present regime Indian Service opposition to fee-chasing among Indians has constantly provoked intemperate attacks from the racketeering interests whose incomes have been jeopardized.

At that time, in 1938, 189 tribes had accepted the IRA and 77 tribes had rejected it. Clearly, the administration was attempting to force the policy on tribes, whatever their objections.

The IRA and "Indian New Deal" were part of a broader reform movement under the Roosevelt administration, which resulted in such environmentally oriented acts as the 1934 Taylor Grazing Act. The movement to protect overgrazed lands led to the stock reduction program in the Southwest, a program that turned the Navajos against Collier and the IRA and has affected that tribe's attitude towards federal programs ever since.

The Indian New Deal was also supposed to give Indians new educational and economic opportunities and to provide tribes with an avenue for creating representative and effective tribal governments. One of the purposes of this book, the conference from which it resulted, and the overall Institute of the American West project is to assess to what degree the IRA has helped tribes, during the last fifty years, move towards more self-rule. The roots and effect of the later termination and self-determination policies also are examined here by some of those who are best qualified to discuss the subjects—those who battled against termination and for self-determination.

If we are surprised at the number of about-faces—the twists and one hundred and eighty degree turns that federal Indian policy has taken in the last hundred years—that is all the more reason to attempt to understand the dilemmas facing tribes today. How could it take our elected officials more than two centuries to come upon the policy of self-determination, in "the land of the free"? And yet it was not until 1975 that Public Law 93-638, the "Indian Self-Determination and Educational Assistance Act," was passed—legislation designed to give Indians the chance to control more of Indian affairs. Under this act tribes began to take over some functions of the Bureau of Indian Affairs in a process known as "638 contracting."

The late 1970s and 1980s have brought new problems for tribes, or a resurgence of old problems. During the Kennedy and Johnson years, a flood of federal funds helped lower the unemployment rate on reservations to its lowest percentage in history, but when federal funds began to dry up, many of the industries that had been attracted to reservations began to disappear. During the Carter administration, unemployment and associated economic problems began to increase. Under the Reagan administration, unemployment has reached crisis proportions. Education and health care have also suffered in the past three years.

Both the Carter and the Reagan administrations have publicly stated support for the policy of self-determination, but in the 1980s there are a number of fundamental questions about what that means. Is health care a trust responsibility of the federal government? Dr. Everett Rhoades, a Kiowa physician who was chosen in 1982 to head the Indian Health Service, suggested in June of this year that health care is a trust responsibility of the federal government. Is education a trust responsibility? President Ronald Reagan says, "No." When he vetoed an admendment to the Tribally Controlled Community Colleges Act, he specifically reported that support for tribal colleges and Indian students was *not* a trust responsibility. Are tribal governments and reservations sovereign? Former Secretary James Watt's publication "Preparing Indian Tribes . . . for Economic Self-Sufficiency in the 21st Century" includes a statement affirming the "government-to-government relationship" of tribes to the federal government, but at the same time there are persistent charges that the Interior Department will not approve reservation severance taxes or tribal constitutional amendments, and that the BIA continues to drag its feet in approving tribal economic development plans.

More important was Secretary Watt's public posture and his rhetoric concerning tribes and tribal governments. Accusing tribes of "socialism," he said he would like to "liberate" them, but was meeting resistance. Ironically, he said, "We have terrible schools on the Indian reservations and we've tried to change that. Congress won't." The attack by Watt on tribal governments was particularly unsettling since he must be aware that IRA governments were designed by the federal government itself and patterned after the U.S. Constitution. His rhetoric seemed to include carefully chosen words reminiscent of the termination period. When the secretary of the interior first met with the National Tribal Chairmen's Association, he reportedly told the congregation of leaders, "If your agenda is to play political hardball, to get news headlines, if you're going to scream and yell about getting someone fired, then why should I deal with you." Sioux leaders have charged that Watt's publicizing of eagle killings was an unfair attack on Indians, an attack that may have been inspired by Indian leaders' criticism of Watt.

There are other reasons why this administration reminds Indians of termination. By law Indians are supposed to be consulted before decisions that affect them are made. In late 1982, when the National Advisory Council on Indian Education (appointed by President James E. Carter) complained that the government was closing Indian boarding schools without first consulting the affected tribes, President Reagan fired all fourteen council members. The Association on American Indian Affairs has added:

> The Association is . . . especially concerned about the current Administration's practice of attempting to use the budget process to settle basic questions of public policy. Programs that have been the subject of national debate have been terminated, or termination has been attempted, through the practice of not requesting monies for them in the President's budget. Examples of this include vital programs for Indian tribes in jobs, child welfare, health, and schools.

The President's public emphasis on volunteerism and private sector support for reservation industry is also reminiscent of the policies of the Eisenhower administration. The Reagan administration budgeted money to encourage new industry on reservations, but in amounts no greater than Collier budgeted fifty years ago (when populations were less and the dollar was worth more).

On the heels of his veto of the Eastern Indian Land Settlement Act, President Reagan proclaimed "American Indian Day" and encouraged Americans to observe May 13, 1983, by engaging in "appropriate ceremonies and deeds and to reaffirm their dedication to the ideals which our first Americans subscribe." The ideals which Indians are reaching for today include energy independence, conscionable employment levels, adequate health care, fair educational opportunities, and political self-rule. As United States citizens, Indian and non-Indian, it is our obligation to understand these ideals and the issues associated with them. (Unemployment on reservations has reached 50 percent, 60 percent, and even 80 percent in some areas, levels which would not be countenanced in any other segment of the U.S. population.)

The contemporary significance of the IRA can perhaps best be seen in Alaska today. Native leaders have been struggling, since 1971, to survive the consequences of the Alaska Native Claims Settlement Act. A number of organizations have been formed, including the Alaska Federation of Natives and the Inuit Circumpolar Conference, which was organized in 1977 and which, every three years, brings together representatives of Inuit peoples from Alaska, Canada, and Greenland in order to defend and preserve the culture and rights of the Inuit, as well as the Arctic environment. There are nearly seventy IRA native Alaska communities, and another thirty who have requested approval of IRA constitutions. The Alaska Federation of Natives, with a grant from the Alaska Humanities Forum, recently sponsored a conference for Alaska IRA councils. Because native leaders believe that the 1971 act did not extinguish rights guaranteed under the IRA, at that recent meeting a new organization was formed. This new group, called the United Tribes of Alaska, has a membership of IRA Alaskan tribes intent on preserving those rights promised by the Indian Reorganization Act. The battle for sovereignty for Alaskan native communities will not end quickly.

A broad spectrum of assessments of the IRA can be evoked from non-Indian and Indian critics. Certainly, from an Indian point-of-view the act was inspired, written and passed by whites, without much consultation with Indian leaders. But from the non-Indian point-of-view it was a dramatic improvement over the assimilationist policies followed under the Dawes Allotment Act. A half century later, the history of the IRA, its implementation, and the policies which grew out of it are of immediate relevance to current issues.

E. Richard Hart,
Former Director
Institute of the American West

Mr. Munnell, author of the Consolidated Chippewa constitution, and Mr. Murrell, interpreter at the Chippewa meeting on the Indian Reorganization Act, in 1936 or 1937.

INTRODUCTION

The Indian Reorganization Act Fifty Years Later

Kenneth R. Philp

In January 1984, Francis Paul Prucha wrote an excellent article on "American Indian Policy in the Twentieth Century" for the *Western Historical Quarterly*. He indicated that historians and other people, for the most part, have failed to see American Indians as communities that have evolved over time. To correct this problem, Prucha has suggested that scholars should explore in greater depth the recent history of Indian-white relations and federal Indian policy.

According to Prucha, there are several topics that need illumination. Scholars should focus their research on the accomplishments of individual Indians, the urbanization of Indians, the Indian policies of other federal agencies besides the Bureau of Indian Affairs, and the increasingly sophisticated way that tribes have interacted with the federal government. Furthermore, we need to look at how Indian groups have used lawyers and created tribal mechanisms to better manage their destiny, at the economic history of reservation communities, and at the contradiction that exists between federal recognition of tribal automony and the federal paternalism associated with honoring the government's trusteeship responsibility.

This book addresses many of the issues raised by Prucha. It provides an assessment, from different disciplinary perspectives, of the Indian progress toward self-rule during the years since the passage of the Indian Reorganization Act. It is also enriched by the viewpoints of Indian people and former government officials who helped formulate and administer federal Indian policy.

[15]

In my judgment, this book will be indispensable to both scholars and students who want to learn more about the contours of recent Indian history. I also hope that the substance of this volume will be carried by a strong breeze out of the halls of academia into the world at large. If it is, Indians, federal and state policy makers, and the general public should better understand the complex development of Indian history and the issues of tribal sovereignty, self-determination, and the trusteeship obligation of the United States government.

It seemed unnecessary to follow the usual format of an introduction and merely summarize the contents of this book. What follows instead is an overview of federal Indian policy since the New Deal. It is intended to place the themes of the Conference on Indian Self-Rule and this book in historical perspective.

The fiftieth anniversary of the presidency of Franklin Roosevelt provides us with an opportunity to examine an important turning point in American Indian history. One of Roosevelt's many legacies was to openly repudiate the Dawes General Allotment Act of 1887. This legislation had shattered Indian homelands and created a class of 100,000 landless people. President Roosevelt not only condemned this tragedy, he brought about a fundamental change in Indian-white relations. Beginning in 1933, the federal government abandoned its effort to assimilate Indians for a policy that emphasized tribal sovereignty and self-determination.

The central purpose of land allotment had been to exterminate the Indians' group life and cultural heritage. The federal government worked toward this goal by sending Indian students to boarding schools, where an all out attempt was made to force them into mainstream society. A strategic offensive also was mounted against Indian land. Reservations were opened up to white settlement after tribesmen received title to 160 acre homesteads. Between 1887 and 1933, the Indians lost over 87 million acres of land under the provisions of the Dawes Act.

The appointment of John Collier as Indian commissioner in 1933 reflected President Roosevelt's determination to set Indian affairs on a new course. Collier was a well-known advocate of Indian rights and a brilliant critic of land allotment. The commissioner believed that the land allotment system had violated tribal sovereignty and the vested rights that Indians had obtained in previous treaties for the cession of large areas of their traditional homelands. Collier stressed that the government had a legal and moral obligation to recognize the bilateral contractual relationship with Indians that existed before 1871 when Congress had prohibited treaty making.

Collier honored this legal and moral obligation by restructuring federal Indian policy. He was the architect of the Indian Reorganization Act of 1934. This legislation offered the Indians a tribal alternative to assimilation. The IRA set up mechanisms to encourage cultural pluralism and tribal self-government, and it increased federal assistance for the economic development of reservation communities.

The IRA was designed to protect and increase the amount of land set aside for Indian homelands. It ended future land allotment, extended trust restrictions on Indian land until otherwise directed by Congress, permitted the voluntary exchange of restricted allotments and heirship land to consolidate checkerboard reservations, and restored to tribal ownership remaining surplus land created by the Dawes Act. The IRA directed the secretary of the interior to initiate conservation measures on Indian land and authorized an annual appropriation of $2 million for the acquisition of new tribal real estate.

The major thrust of the IRA was to encourage the process of tribal self-government. Indians were allowed to hold positions in the Indian Bureau without regard to civil service laws. An annual appropriation of $250,000 was authorized to help tribes establish constitutions, bylaws, and charters of incorporation for business purposes. Tribal councils that adopted constitutions could employ legal counsel, prevent the leasing or sale of land without tribal consent, and negotiate with federal or state governments for public services.

Other important provisions of the IRA included federal aid for economic reconstruction and education. Congress authorized a $10 million revolving credit fund to stimulate economic development on reservations and an annual appropriation of up to $250,000 for tuition and scholarships to increase Indian enrollment at vocational schools, high schools, and colleges. The IRA recognized the importance of mutual consent in Indian-white relations by allowing tribes the right to accept this legislation in a special referendum.

Officials in the Roosevelt administration implemented other policies that were directly related to the Indian Reorganization Act. They started economic recovery on reservations by bringing Indians under most of the New Deal relief programs and by creating a separate Indian Civilian Conservation Corps. Commissioner Collier issued two policy statements that guaranteed Indian religious freedom and curtailed missionary activity at boarding and day schools. And he used the Johnson-O'Malley Act to provide federal funds for states where Indians had enrolled in public schools. An Indian Arts and Crafts Board also was established in the Interior Department.

The Indian Bureau, in cooperation with the Justice Department, asked Felix S. Cohen, a legal scholar, to compile a list of statutes, treaties, and judicial decisions that dealt with Indian rights. Cohen published his research in the *Handbook of Federal Indian Law*. This volume presented legal and moral arguments that defended the concepts of Indian sovereignty, political equality, tribal self-government, and federal jurisdiction in Indian affairs.

The ultimate success of these reforms depended on whether tribes voted for and made use of the Indian Reorganization Act. A total of 258 elections were held. They did not apply to the Indians of Oklahoma or the Natives of Alaska, who were automatically blanketed in under most sections of the IRA in 1936. Over two-thirds of the eligible tribes voted to accept the IRA. This represented only 40 percent of the Indians who cast ballots, because large tribes such as the Navajos, who opposed stock reduction, voted against the measure. Ninety-two out of 258 tribes or approximately 36 percent wrote constitutions; 72 tribes or 28 percent agreed to draft charters of incorporation for business purposes.

There were many reasons why the Indians did not overwhelmingly endorse the IRA. Suspicion toward the federal government remained strong because of the previous record of broken treaties and promises. Many Indians feared that the IRA would encourage segregation and increase the power of paternalistic federal bureaucrats over their lives. They were more concerned with settling claims against the government and securing federal recognition of their treaty rights than participating in IRA tribal governments controlled by the Indian Bureau.

Indians were disappointed because the IRA did not provide for complete self-determination. By 1940, over 60 percent of the employees of the Bureau were Indians, but they still did not hold critical policy-making positions. Most of the decisions made by IRA tribal councils were subject to administrative review by superintendents and the secretary of the interior. The federal government continued to control tribal trust fund expenditures, per capita payments, and the leasing and other use of tribal property.

Tribal factionalism made it difficult to administer the IRA. Internal disunity was caused by wide variations in acculturation, mixed- versus full-blood rivalry, and religious and cultural differences. IRA constitutions frequently led to bitter disputes over who would control newly established tribal councils. Many Indians, especially those in the Southwest, disliked IRA tribal governments because they threatened local village autonomy or traditional ways of running tribal affairs. Tribal governments also were the vehicle for implementing unpopular conservation measures that led to the slaughter of sheep, goats, and horses to prevent overgrazing.

All of this is not to say that IRA tribal governments were unsuccessful. They made significant political progress, and tribal councils generally showed good judgment in controlling their resources. Tribal councils used IRA loans and tribal funds to purchase land, livestock, and farming and fishing equipment. Group action through IRA corporations and cooperatives increased the utilization of Indian resources. Over one hundred additional cattle associations were set up, and the number of Indian-owned cattle increased dramatically. Agricultural production increased fourfold. Tribes also set up trading stores and arts and crafts guilds to promote the sale of their pottery, blankets, and silver jewelry.

As impressive as these achievements were, most tribes experienced difficulty in developing their reservation resources. The $10 million revolving credit fund was too small to permanently end Indian poverty. Many tribes were denied access to this fund when the Solicitor's Office in the Interior Department ruled that a tribe had to vote for the IRA and draft a constitution and business charter before it could borrow money. Between 1934 and 1945, Congress funded $4.2 million in loans because only 28 percent of the tribes that voted for the IRA decided it was worthwhile to draft business charters in the midst of the Great Depression. The credit fund revolved one and one-half times, which enabled the Indian Bureau to advance $6.6 million to tribal enterprises and credit associations.

A significant increase in Indian-owned land was critical to the IRA policy of encouraging community life and tribal sovereignty. In 1934, the National Resources Board indicated that to make the Indians self-supporting Congress would have to spend over $103 million to acquire 25 million acres of additional agricultural and grazing land. Congress refused to implement this costly recommendation. Pressured by white economic interests, it agreed to spend about $5 million under the IRA's land acquisition program.

This money, along with tribal funds and special congressional legislation, allowed the Indian Bureau to purchase 4 million acres of new tribal land. Unfortunately, most of this property was submarginal land that had little economic value. During the Second World War, Congress ended the IRA policy of acquiring more land for tribes. This decision and the lack of adequate credit had disastrous economic consequences. By 1945, Indian farm families had a net annual income of $501. This was only slightly better than 1928 when the Institute of Government Research issued its famous report on Indian poverty.

Another shortcoming of the IRA was that it failed to solve the problems associated with land allotted before 1933. The continued restrictions on the sale of allotted land under the IRA threatened indefinite government supervision over many competent individuals. Indians found that it was all but impossible to obtain loans from private sources to make improvements on their property. Over 45,000 Indians were heirs to 6 million acres of allotted land that had been divided by inheritance into small unproductive parcels. It cost the Indian Bureau over $1 million annually to administer this property. The IRA permitted the voluntary consolidation of this land into tribal ownership, but most Indians refused to give up private control over their real estate.

Indian political self-determination and economic progress under the IRA depended to a large degree on the success or failure of the Indian Bureau's educational program. Willard Beatty, the director of Indian education during the New Deal, closed boarding schools and encouraged Indian students to attend government day schools or nearby public schools. He developed a progressive education curriculum aimed at solving rural problems on reservations. Beatty also began a bilingual education program to promote Indian literacy. But he found it impossible to retain control over Johnson-O'Malley funds, and public schools refused to create special Indian programs in their districts.

Beatty's innovations in the field of Indian education did not lead to increased congressional support. The IRA's $250,000 annual authorization for Indian tuition and scholarships was not fully funded. Only a few hundred Indians attended college during the New Deal. More importantly, Congress refused to spend the money needed for new Indian educational facilities after it closed boarding schools. Consequently, thousands of Indian children were denied an education. And no serious efforts were made to train adult Indians in the sophisticated administrative skills needed to make the IRA function properly.

The reconstruction of Indian affairs during the Roosevelt years was part of a larger effort to develop a sense of pan-Indianism throughout the Western Hemisphere. Commissioner Collier believed that Indians in the United States needed to collaborate with other tribal groups in the New World in their quest for social justice. He hoped that international contacts between tribes would lead to a broad cultural renaissance and strengthen the Indians' claim to tribal sovereignty.

On April 14, 1940, representatives of nineteen American republics and their Indian delegates met at Patzcuaro, Mexico. The delegates at Patzcuaro made recommendations patterned after the framework of the Indian Reorganization Act. They suggested that all American governments help Indians maintain their separate group identity by providing them with needed land, credit, and technological assistance. They also signed a treaty that created a permanent Inter-American Indian Institute that was required to meet every four years to discuss common Indian problems.

A shift in sentiment away from the Indian New Deal began during the Second World War. The war not only disrupted pan-Indian reform in the Western Hemisphere, it encouraged a sense of national unity and social consensus that led to a renewed emphasis on integrating minority groups. More than 40,000 Indians migrated to urban areas to find war-related jobs. Another 25,000 served with distinction in the armed forces.

Many of these individuals permanently left their reservations because they had become disillusioned with the operation of the Indian

Reorganization Act. It had failed to provide enough land and credit to support a growing population, and many individuals did not want to remain farmers. The IRA also had led to the growth of a centralized Indian Bureau to provide expanded social services. This development had led to some social progress, but it also contradicted earlier promises that the federal government would respect tribal sovereignty and the right to self-determination.

After 1945, Congress responded to the Indians' dislike of federal paternalism and their desire to be independent. Indian Bureau programs were dismantled, and Congress, without Indian consent, passed termination legislation that ended federal wardship over several tribes. The government also lifted restrictions on more than 2.5 million acres of Indian allotments and heirship land. This decision was part of a broader policy that encouraged Indians to leave their reservations and relocate to more prosperous cities.

Termination had tragic consequences. It led to the sale of valuable Indian land and hampered tribal self-determination and economic development under the Indian Reorganization Act. The Indian Bureau curtailed the use of IRA credit funds and relied on private enterprise to establish industries on or near reservations. Tribal economic development languished because the private sector of the economy was unable or unwilling to solve the problem of poverty and employment on reservations. Only five hundred new industrial jobs were created during the Eisenhower years. This failure helps explain why over 35,000 Indians decided to move to urban centers under the Indian Bureau's relocation program. Once they left their reservations, Indians were cut off from federal services. They also encountered cultural isolation and found it difficult to obtain decent jobs or adequate housing.

By 1960, most Indians were aware that termination had simply given Congress an excuse to ignore their treaty rights and end vital federal services. During the next two decades, Indian opposition to termination intensified. Both Indians and federal officials began to reexamine the positive legacy of the Indian New Deal. The presidential administrations of John F. Kennedy, Lyndon B. Johnson, and Richard M. Nixon generally followed the principles behind the Indian Reorganization Act. They renewed the federal commitment to tribal self-determination and the development of reservation economic resources.

In 1969, President Johnson created the National Council on Indian Opportunity in the Office of the Vice-President. A few years later, President Nixon established the American Indian Policy Review Commission to study the Indians' unique relationship to the federal government.

This new direction in Indian affairs was led by Indian commissioners such as Philleo Nash, Robert Bennett, Louis Bruce, and Benjamin Reifel. These men had begun their careers by working for the government during the New Deal. Some of the many policy initiatives during their tenure included expanding the IRA credit fund, encouraging Indian preference for employment at all levels within the Indian Bureau, and working closely with the National Tribal Chairmen's Association. Self-determination was emphasized by allowing Zuni Pueblo and the Miccosukees of Florida to direct Indian Bureau programs on their reservations.

Congress also was influenced by the long shadow cast by the Indian New Deal. It reaffirmed the concepts behind the Indian Reorganization Act in several important pieces of legislation. The Indian Civil Rights Act of 1968 strengthened the New Deal policy of guaranteeing Indian religious freedom and giving tribes jurisdiction over civil and criminal law on their reservations. The Indian Financing Act of 1974 consolidated several loan funds and increased money available for tribal business enterprises. The most far-reaching reform was the Indian Self-Determination and Educational Assistance Act of 1975. It provided aid to Indian students and encouraged the Indians to manage their own schools. Tribal councils were given a significant role in setting policy goals and administering federal programs that affected them.

Congress did not fund the IRA land acquisition program on an annual basis, but it did provide additional tribal land for Taos Pueblo, the Havasupais, and the Warm Springs Indians. The Alaska Native Claims Settlement Act of 1971 guaranteed Native American ownership of 44 million acres of land and created a $1 billion fund to be used by 225 corporations set up by village communities. Congress also returned several terminated tribes to federal trust status.

The Inter-American Indian Institute, required by treaty to meet every four years, did not receive the attention it deserved from either tribal communities or the federal government. But Indians did understand the international dimension of their struggle for social justice. Twenty-three western tribes formed the Council of Energy Resource Tribes modeled after the Organization of Petroleum Exporting Countries. Indian activists also presented a resolution to the International Human Rights Conference in Geneva, Switzerland, calling on the United Nations to turn its attention to the plight of Native Americans.

Today, the federal government, as it did in the 1950s, has repudiated the philosophy behind the Indian New Deal. Former Secretary of the Interior James Watt has labeled Indians as social misfits and characterized their homelands as examples of the failure of socialism. The commitment to Indian education has waned with the abrupt closing of ten off-reservation schools and President Ronald Reagan's veto of a bill allocating funds for Indian community colleges. The Reagan administration dismissed 17,000 claims of Indians who had been illegally deprived of their rights or property, until it was overruled by a federal judge in Washington, D.C. Cutbacks in federal programs have battered reservation economies. Since 1980, average unemployment on reservations has increased from 40 percent to almost 80 percent. The question of Indian water rights also has not been resolved.

Widespread public criticism forced President Ronald Reagan to issue a statement on January 24, 1983 concerning federal Indian policy. The president repudiated termination and pledged to uphold the Indian Self-Determination Act. He admitted that without healthy reservation economies the concept of self-government had little meaning. The president, however, offered little real hope for the future. Instead, he followed the discredited economic policies of the 1950s by insisting that tribes would have to reduce their dependence on federal revenue and rely on private enterprise to provide money for capital investment. It remains unclear how the withdrawal of federal funds and services, and cutbacks in Indian education will automatically solve Indian social problems.

Times and circumstances do change, but it is important to understand and appreciate the fundamental historical developments of the recent past. For Native Americans, these developments have their roots in the Indian Reorganization Act. They include a sincere respect for mutual consent and the bilateral relationship in Indian affairs, recognizing the value of a pluralistic society, and the need for direct federal financial commitment to insure educational opportunity, self-determination, and the economic well-being of all Indian people.

PART ONE

The Indian New Deal

Winnebago basket makers in front of their home near the Winnebago Agency, Nebraska.

The Pine Ridge, South Dakota, Agency office in 1936.

28

I was one of those who first translated the Indian Reorganization Act to our people in Bannock and Shoshone. I have waited fifty years to see this legislation work and to see it enforced by the Interior Department. Now it seems to me the whole intent of the government was to play games with our lives in order to steal our lands and resources. We had high hopes at first.

I am now discouraged. There is no separation of powers under the tribal set up. There are no separate judicial, legislative, and executive branches of tribal government. For this reason, I believe we were intentionally set up to fail. The checks and balances of these three powers are taken for granted in the white man's world. To the reservation Indian, these guarantees of freedom do not exist. As an example, the reservation Indian has no grievance recourse but to a tribal court. All other non-Indian citizens can go to the highest court in the land, the Supreme Court. How many of you who live off the reservation would like to end your grievance with the city court?

Back then, we were told to tell our people that our tribal self-government would be based on a foundation of law. This has not happened. Lacking a foundation of law, we are now a pitiful people. Our tribal governments are now compared to dictatorships in the banana republics of South America.

Who is responsible? The Interior Department has failed to act as a responsible trustee. As a result, basic tribal laws are flagrantly violated. The tribal politicians have learned how to be deceitful to be elected, to practice nepotism, to outlaw those opposed to their practices, and to violate any law they wish to gain their end.

Edward Boyer, a member of the
Ft. Hall Shoshone-Bannock tribe.

Of late years, somewhat of a cult has developed around John Collier. He is perceived as the hero of Indian rights, a warrior in the struggle for recognition of such rights. He is not our hero.

Collier was vindictive and overbearing. He tolerated no dissent, neither from his staff nor from the tribes. He was a rank opportunist in politics, at once espousing and then rejecting one or another proposal.

He did not hesitate to use informants and the FBI against Indian opponents. He habitually tampered with the truth in his dealings with Indians.

Rupert Costo, Cahuilla, president of the
American Indian Historical Society

I think that this legislation [the Indian Reorganization Act] has worked out very well for our reservation. We have six council men, a chairman, and a chartered livestock association. The IRA revolving credit fund enabled many of our younger tribal members to obtain loans and get started in the cattle business. In the early 1930s, we did not have enough irrigation water. Tribal leaders persuaded the government to build a storage dam . . . and we gained access to plenty of water.

Arthur Manning, Shoshone-Paiute leader,
former council member on the
Duck Valley Reservation

Collier's work as Commissioner of Indian Affairs is probably the most impressive achievement in the field of applied anthropology that the discipline of anthropology can claim. Collier reversed a policy of tribal disintegration that had been accepted as a national goal for over one hundred years and established a new political, economic, and social status for America's Indian minority. . . .

Collier succeeded in preserving Indian identity from complete absorption in the "melting pot" by creating a system of autonomous tribal entities within the political and economic superstructure of American society as a whole. He pursued this policy because it offered the best chance of preserving Indian tribal identity: Indian "grouphood" as he put it.

Wilcomb E. Washburn, Smithsonian Institution

CHAPTER ONE

The Indian New Deal: An Overview

Floyd A. O'Neil

I plan to discuss the Indian New Deal in terms of four topics: origins, founding the New Deal, the Indian Reorganization Act, and the end of John Collier's career in the Bureau of Indian Affairs. Some of the things I will note will be in the form of questions rather than answers. A reason for our discussions here is to create a crucible of ideas where divergent interpretations may find a proper colloquy.

The Indian New Deal has become one of those contested areas in the interpretation of American history. The participants in our consideration of Indian self-rule will have heated discussions and even downright disagreements. But it is hoped, by those of us who were fortunate enough to help with the planning of this project, that we may also expect to shed some light. It is my personal hope that this work will not be known in the future as the dark and bloody ground of partisanship, but that fire may be struck and light indeed shed among scholars and friends.

In 1887, Congress passed the General Allotment or Dawes Severalty Act. This legislation made the allotment of land to individual Indians and the break up of tribal landholdings the official policy of the United States. That policy, which dominated the Indian world for the next half century, had disastrous consequences. The general public, however, was slow in realizing it. The policy was designed to assimilate the Indians into the general population and to make them into farmers. During that time, farming was still the largest single vocation within the United States.

To those of us who truly hate to farm, it is almost inconceivable how far the philosophy of Jeffersonian agrarianism had penetrated into the American psyche. The remnants of that psyche still exist in rural America even though the farming population has declined to significantly below three percent of the population. Many things were wrong with the Dawes Severalty Act. One was that the Indians had been moved to the most meager available lands and then simply told to farm these lands. Secondly, at the very moment that the United States was creating farms and insisting that Indians live upon them, there was already an agricultural crisis based on overproduction. Furthermore, that over-production was created by the most efficient and productive set of farmers in the world. They enjoyed, as well, the richest and best land the country offered. To expect that the Indian farmer could compete in such an economic world, above and beyond simply subsisting, was faulty and short sighted.

A more important factor than this, and the hardest one for those reforming Indian America to comprehend, was simply that most Indians did not want to farm. This was especially true on the Northern Plains and in the Far West where farming was considered undignified and confining. Many Indian people did endure, despite the folly of the Dawes Severalty Act. Their success at farming was a monument to their ability.

Another characteristic of the era that lasted from 1887 to 1934 was the presence of reformers. They were responsible, in part, for the passage of the Dawes Severalty Act. These doctrinaire and highly motivated reformers were prominent citizens from the East. They were invariably dedicated Christian folk.

Reformers who associated with the churches dominated American Indian affairs after the Civil War. The Grant peace policy, instituted in large part by the Quakers, employed honest Christian men as agents of the federal government among the Indians. These men were an interesting lot, although the experiment did not last a long time; but those who were looking for reform found the Indian Bureau to be a remarkably appropriate target. Helen Hunt Jackson's *A Century of Dishonor* was only one small incident in the long road of Indian reform that stretched from the Civil War to the time of the Indian Reorganization Act.

In 1882, an organized group of zealous, hard-working reformers founded the Indian Rights Association in Philadelphia. In certain instances, this association did defend and champion Indian rights. Nevertheless, it almost seems, when reading the correspondence of those remarkable people, that there was an inherent right of reformers that had to be taken into account by the federal government. By 1905, the commissioner of Indian affairs was one of this organization's own, Francis Leupp, which attests to how powerful and influential it had become.

There were a number of underlying suppositions held by the leaders of the Indian Rights Association. They were (1) that farming was superior to hunting, (2) that alcohol was evil, (3) that idleness was the ultimate evil, and (4) that Christianity was a magic elixir that would change people and, therefore, the Christian religion should take a very strong position in American Indian life and assume a strong proselytizing stance. Essential to this view of Christianity was the idea that the existence of tribes was evil. Therefore, only as individual men who loved property and sought it could Indians ever really be assimilated successfully into the general population. And, of course, assimilation was absolutely necessary.

Reformers also believed that education would magically bring Indians into the mainstream of civilization in the United States. As a result, during the period of the Dawes Severalty Act, there was a great expansion of the education establishment within the Bureau of Indian Affairs. Commissioners such as Thomas Jefferson Morgan made Indian education one of their leading policies and priorities.

It is interesting to look back upon that educational system. When I was a child growing up on an Indian reservation, the 1930s was considered, by comparison with earlier decades, a very good time to be in an Indian school. Beatings were less frequent, and children of tender years were not removed without their parents' consent to Indian schools at a far distance.

The word *assimilation* was not an abstract, remote concept. Rather, it was an active philosophy, with tremendous power to break up families and even to take the lives of children. For the death rate of Indian children was much higher than that of the general population. Whether you read the records of the Indian school at Fort Lewis, Colorado or the Teller Institute at Grand Junction, Colorado or the Stewart Indian school at Carson City, Nevada or a great number of others, the sad stories of sending the children's bodies home are characteristics of the correspondence which have always left me depressed.

During these very difficult times of adjustment, the American Indians protested, but with very little success. So, most of the tribes turned inward and went back to their old ways of celebrating ceremonies and living as nearly as they could the communal life that they had known and loved. Many books have described this tragic era.

By the year 1920, the people of the United States had a change of heart about Indian life. This change was caused, in part, by a back-to-nature movement. The founding of national parks, where people could go to be alone and commune with nature, reminded many Americans of the lives that Indian people had been forced to give up.

When looking at the literature of the period, one is always struck at how often words such as wilderness, campfire, trail, and forest are used in late nineteenth century and early twentieth century America. The founding of the Boy Scouts and the Girl Scouts symbolized this new orientation. America had started to think of the West more as an area of beauty and opportunity, rather than as an awesome space to be seized and subdued.

At the beginning of the century the American Indian was considered the vanishing American. But after the founding of the Indian Health Service, it soon became apparent that the vanishing Americans were not vanishing; for those who administered Indian affairs noted increases in population. A burgeoning group of artistic and literary American romantics also began to see the Indian in a far more favorable light than a generation earlier. By 1920, there was a more modest view, a more moderate view, of the American Indian than there had been previous to this time. It was precisely in that year that a new man came onto the scene of American Indian affairs and life.

Before I deal with the career and the personality of John Collier, it should be noted that he appeared at a time when America itself was being transformed. The era from 1887 to 1920 could be characterized as a period of certitude. While there were political storms, both Theodore Roosevelt and Woodrow Wilson were progressives, both of the parties sought ends that were very similar. There seemed to be a greater unanimity in what society wanted, needed, and honored. This was not true for the period following World War I. The nation turned its back on the sterner themes. Change was pervasive, but I leave this theme to Frederick Lewis Allen and to other historians who have described this era so very well.

But the progressivism of Theodore Roosevelt and of Woodrow Wilson did not die. It was only wounded. Some of the reformers even maintained a form of zeal. One of these reformers was John Collier. He was a dedicated man whose name and spirit will be honored and attacked, praised and villified in this book.

Most of the time, a leader sees a direction in history and aims for that direction. In a few instances, it is almost impossible to see the shape of history without the influence of one dynamic leader. Such a case in the modern world is Martin Luther. While Collier was no Luther, many of the changes affecting American Indians in the near past are hard to separate from his profound influence.

John Collier was an urban reformer with a much wider, more comprehensive view of the world than that held by most Americans involved in politics during his time. Furthermore, he had instincts for reform. His experiences while studying in France and Europe, at Columbia University, and in New York City, all led this Atlanta-born reformer to see the world a little differently than most of his contemporaries. Collier's early professional life was beset with successes and failures that reflected his unique personality. He was a brilliant, impatient, caustic, and dedicated man.

In 1920, Collier made a famous trip to Taos Pueblo at the urging of Mabel Dodge Luhan. There, he discovered a utopian Red Atlantis. Collier had worked in the areas of the eastern slums, where he came to know the difficulty in establishing a community that was responsive, embracing, and functioning. He seemed to have found it all at Taos. And, furthermore, he had found it with a people who were remarkably peaceful, or at least he viewed them that way. Because of his career as a reformer in urban areas, Collier had a greater and deeper respect for human culture and ethnicity than most public figures of his time. At one point, he became involved in a famous fight over a congressional bill to quiet the title to lands non-Indians occupied within Pueblo Indian reservations. It was no accident that the secretary of the interior, Albert

Fall, was a New Mexican and that the bill had been introduced by his fellow New Mexican, Holm Bursum. Early in his career with the Indians, Collier took the posture that the integrity of Indian life and of Indian lands should be absolutely protected. His defense of the Indians' land might not have gotten him into trouble with United States officials and with other reformers, but his insistence that Indian culture and religion should be respected was an issue made of hotter metal. Collier was to find out just how searing such a notion could be.

Collier plunged into opposition to the Bursum Bill with great zeal. It was an opportunity for him to gain notoriety. His attendance at the November, 1922 meeting of the All Indian Pueblo Council assured his place at the center of the fray. He also joined artists and writers who signed a protest against the Bursum Bill. One of Collier's most important roles was that of propagandist, and he was good at his job. The older reformers in the Indian Rights Association were slower to respond, and a natural anxiety grew between the old group and the rambunctious Collier. That anxiety quickly generated distrust and later generated hatred. One should hasten to say that Collier was only a part of the opposition to the Bursum Bill, but he clamored to head the movement, which he found very much to his liking.

The defeat of the Bursum Bill was so consumingly a part of his life that Collier looked for a way to make the defense of Indians a part of his own career. This was accomplished in 1923 when Collier and his friends and supporters founded the American Indian Defense Association. Even though the organization had a rocky start, due partly to Collier's incessant scheming, it was soon a viable organization. The influence of that group was to be an irritant to the federal Indian establishment in the succeeding years.

In his position at AIDA, Collier may have found his most appropriate role. He was at home as an abrasive, captious critic. He displayed these qualities in articles contributed to the surviving journals of the Progressive Era such as *Sunset* magazine. He was also appointed to the Committee of 100, a committee to investigate Indian affairs. There, he did not distinguish himself, and for that matter, neither did anyone else. For a new order was needed and an old order held the line.

As the 1920s progressed, there was a competition, none too friendly, between the Indian Rights Association and the AIDA to become the most important single voice in advising about Indian affairs. In terms of total power, the Indian Rights Association held the upper hand. In terms of moving in the direction that history was flowing, Collier and the AIDA were nearer to the path of reform that the nation would soon follow.

One of the issues where Collier was certainly more attuned to the mind of America and to the direction America was going than his rivals was in the area of Indian religious freedom. Lawrence Kelly's new book sheds light on this interesting theme. One might observe that the times were appropriate for the issue of religious freedom. The people of the United States had revolted from the churches and their control as never before. Sidney Ahlstrom wrote of this change in his religious history of the American people.

> A greatly diminished hold on the country's intellectual and literary leadership was another important sign of change. This meant in turn that ministerial candidates were turning to other vocations. Nor were they dissuaded from this decision by the assorted hypocrites and boobs that marched through Sinclair Lewis's *Elmer Gantry*. Dr. Arrowsmith's vocation seemed a more effective means of saving Main Street from babbittry. Offended as much by the obsurantism of the Fundamentalists as by the cultural accommodations of the churches, intellectuals, young and old, were leaving the church—with H. L. Mencken piping the tune and providing the laughs.

In the era before 1920, the churches of America were very powerful, and in no other operation of the federal government was their presence felt more than in the Indian Bureau. All of those who have read American Indian history know of the churches' peace policy, their school contracts, and their ability to act as an unofficial arm of the federal government in Indian country. If one studies the details of maps of western Indian reservations, one sees that it was the Christian churches who first obtained patents to the land on Indian reservations, and in most cases they still own these spots.

If one looks at the rosters of the Indian Rights Association, the Lake Mohonk Conference, and other Indian service organizations, we find churchmen and churchwomen involved in these organizations in large numbers. As the Indian Rights Association gained power, even more church oriented people joined their ranks. These groups had a great say about who would be commissioner of Indian affairs and who would occupy a great number of other jobs as well. When it came to policy, their hope of Christianizing and civilizing the Indians gave them a theological justification for their acts. But this assimilation policy was to clash with the more tolerant view of American Indian culture and religion that had been adopted by John Collier and his cohorts.

Encouraged by people such as Herbert Welch of the Indian Rights Association, Commissioner Charles Burke moved during the 1920s toward crushing Indian dancing and other ceremonials. Collier and the AIDA made a concerted effort at thwarting these attempts to bully the Indians into giving up their ancient religion and ceremonial practices.

The Indian Rights Association claimed to have material that suggested that Indian ceremonials contained lewd, lascivious acts, as well as other acts of debauchery that would shock the American public. Welch and his associates should have investigated more closely before attacking these ceremonials as inappropriate for Indian America in the 1920s. Welch and his associates were uninformed; they also misinterpreted Indian ceremonies. Debauchery and licentiousness were not, as we know, at the center of these ceremonies.

In our examination of this religious struggle, we must consider as well the larger issue: did religious freedom exist in the United States? Absolute freedom of religion had not existed in the territories of the United States since the case of *Reynolds vs. the United States*, handed down in 1879, but in such areas under federal jurisdiction, how far could the federal government intervene in Indian religions without outraging the Constitution? Collier and his friends had long maintained that a literal interpretation of the Constitution was necessary and proper, and that Indian religion was to be considered religion in the same sense as Christianity and Judaism.

When I was growing up, I remember the horror tales about various agents who attempted to suppress Indian dances during the 1920s. The degree of heat and emotion generated in the Indian tribes by the federal government's posture was always surprising.

American Indian policy showed strain as the Coolidge administration left office. An investigation of American Indian life had produced the Meriam Report, which showed just how deplorable were the living standards of the Indian people. Its startling revelations prepared Herbert Hoover, the succeeding President, to seek better means of handling American Indian policy. Herbert Hoover, of course, was a very capable administrator. He looked to those on whom he could rely to implement changes that would quell the criticism of the government in its dealings with American Indians.

Hoover appointed Ray Lyman Wilbur, a former president of Stanford University, as the secretary of the interior. Charles Rhoads was named commissioner of Indian affairs. That Hoover chose men whom he knew and respected for these positions is worth noting. It was a high priority of Hoover, Wilbur, Rhoads, and his assistant, J. Henry Scattergood, to implement reforms that would improve the condition of Indians in the United States. The amount of money spent upon the Indians increased significantly during Hoover's administration. But the Hoover administration was unable to change things substantially. Rhodes and Scattergood were both close associates of the hierarchy of the Indian Rights Association. In implementing the kind of reform that was needed, they were not dramatic enough. They merely laid the groundwork for more thoroughgoing reform under a new administration.

One should hasten to the Rhoads-Scattergood-Wilbur-Hoover group's defense by saying that the new president, when he came to office in 1929, had only a short period of time in which to get his administration under way. The stock market crash and the ensuing depression soon made their roles extremely difficult ones to perform. In spite of the depression, they were able to get additional money for Indian affairs. And indeed, one might argue that, ironically, conditions in *Indian* America were better at the end of the Hoover administration than at the beginning.

Collier welcomed Hoover's appointments and even indicated that he thought they could implement the needed reforms of the Indian Bureau, but the period of friendship between them did not last very long. Collier once again became an abrasive, attacking critic. The Hoover administration, like its predecessor, had to contend with a fractious, critical voice that was always aimed at the government and its Indian policy.

After Hoover lost the election in 1932, Franklin Rooesvelt came to office with a candidate in mind for the commissioner of Indian affairs post. He was Harold L. Ickes, a Chicago man who also owned a home in Arizona and whose wife was a knowledgeable writer on Indian topics in the American Southwest. Ickes was an impressive man: he became the secretery of the interior. Ickes had known Collier for a long time, but it was not a chain reaction that made Collier the commissioner of Indian affairs designee in the Roosevelt administration. Rather, it was a series of communications to Roosevelt and later to Ickes asking that Collier be made commissioner that probably led to his appointment. Collier did not have difficulty getting the approval of the United States Senate for the appointment. He did have difficulty in getting his name approved by Franklin Roosevelt, because many people expressed support for other candidates.

The New Deal for the American Indians began before the passage of the Indian Reorganization Act. Indian persons were employed to improve reservation lands that had been eroded and to work on deforested areas. Much of the work was coordinated by the Emergency Conservation Work Agency. That agency was more commonly known as the Indian C.C.C. It became a truly large program. Over 25,000 people were recruited from the Indian tribes and were employed principally in conservation work. They worked in nearly seventy-five camps in fifteen western states.

The same good things could be said for the C.C.C. and its contribution to Indian families that could be said about the C.C.C. and non-Indian families. It reduced radically the number of young men who would be forced into vagabondage in those desperate times. Although American Indian men did not take up a life as tramps and wandering hoboes as often as non-Indians, these were still desperate times for them. They found employment in the C.C.C. much to their liking.

Soon after his appointment, Secretary Ickes issued an order that ended the sale of allotments and the issuance of fee patents. Collier, true to his attitudes about a multi-cultural society in America, issued an order terminating the federal program of Americanization for Indians. Collier directed that the cultural history of Indians was to be considered, in all respects, equal to that of any non-Indian group and declared that it was desirable that Indians be bilingual. But his commitment to the idea of maintaining and nourishing American Indian culture went even further when he claimed that Indian arts should be prized, nourished, and honored. His own administration reflected this, for he was able to implement programs to aid Indian art.

In another action taken by Collier, many Indian students were transferred from boarding schools to community day schools. These boarding schools often contained a residue of the Christianizing assimilationist philosophy. The commissioner also forbade the officers of the federal government to require Indian students to attend Christian worship service at these schools. With his concept of cultural pluralism firmly in mind, he asked Congress to discontinue the appropriations to suppress traffic in peyote. Congress obliged him.

It is interesting, too, that the 1934 Johnson-O'Malley Act was a major feature of his administration. The Johnson-O'Malley Act, like the Indian Reorganization Act, is still very much with us as operative American law. Under the terms of the Johnson-O'Malley Act, the federal government could contract with states and territories to provide education to Indians who were under federal supervision. The Bureau also could contract for medical and social welfare services.

The Indian Reorganization Act of 1934 allowed Congress to spend $250,000 annually for the expenses involved in organizing chartered corporations on Indian reservations. Operated by tribal councils that had established a constitution and by-laws, these corporations could employ legal counsel, prevent the leasing or sale of land without tribal consent, and negotiate with federal or state governments for public services. The IRA also created a $10 million revolving credit fund that was used to promote tribal economic development. Collier thought of the IRA as temporary legislation, yet it is now in its fiftieth year.

As John Collier and his staff began implementing the Indian Reorganization Act, they ran into many more troubles than they expected. One of the difficulties was that the Bureau staff had been built up over the past half century. These people, in the main, were firmly dedicated to the idea of assimilation. Collier's orders forbidding the assimilationist posture confused and angered many within the Bureau of Indian Affairs.

There was an additional problem. Some American Indians had espoused the idea of being progressive men and women, as they often called themselves. Among them was the chairman of the Navajo tribe. Collier ran into great difficulties on the Navajo reservation. He found it impossible to get the Navajos to enroll under the aegis of the Indian Reorganization Act. Today they still are not organized under the law passed in 1934.

Collier and his men had a difficult time enrolling many of the tribes under the IRA. Many Indians were fearful that the establishment of an IRA tribal council would be detrimental to their interest because it would be controlled by the federal government. A large number of people had taken up farming, adopted white ways, and were well on the road to assimilation. They felt that this was a step backwards. Indian Bureau statistics said that 181 tribes voted for the IRA, while 77 tribes rejected it. The number of tribes, however, does not tell the whole story. While those who voted for the IRA had an aggregate population of 130,000 Indian people, those who rejected it had an aggregate population of somewhere between 85,000 and 90,000 persons.

The ratification process was fraught with great fear and difficulty. There were struggles between mixed-bloods and full-bloods. There was a great deal of lobbying by the BIA and Collier's men for adoption; there also was a great deal of covert lobbying against it by the older Bureau employees who feared they might lose their jobs. A great number of the churches and the older reform groups such as the Indian Rights Association also worked against it. The lobbying back and forth caused this to be a very confusing time. Some of the confusion has been reduced by a new book by Graham D. Taylor, *The New Deal and American Indian Tribalism.*

I lived on an Indian reservation during the 1930s. Even though I was a child, I vividly remember the struggle over whether to adopt the IRA. When I questioned my father concerning it, he simply explained that there was a New Deal for non-Indians and a New Deal for Indians. This answer, from today's vantage point, appears too simplistic.

S. L. Tyler in his *History of Indian Policy* has listed some of the criticisms of the Indian Reorganization Act. It

was put into effect too rapidly. Neither the Congress nor the Indians were adequately informed concerning it nor prepared for it. Bureau personnel needed better training for application of provisions contained in IRA, some of which were quite foreign to their past experience and to their personal philosophy concerning the Indians. . . . The philosophy of the IRA itself was violated in that the Indians did not play a truly significant part in preparing [tribal constitutions]. As a result the meaning of these instruments of government was often quite foreign to them.

Many good tribal governments were replaced by less capable ones.

Indian Service administrators conceived of the Indian Reorganization Act as for the good of the Indians. They failed to realize that the community life patterns of some Indian tribes were not compatible with its principles. Successful programming had to be done at the community level with Indian participation. Probably because of administrative difficulties some of the education features of the IRA were not practiced, such as a tribal review of Bureau budgets. Promise and performance, plans and achievements, tended to be very different.

There were other problems. The funding level of the IRA was never very high. It was hoped that democratic government would relieve some of the political struggles within Indian communities; in many cases it simply exacerbated them. I am always astounded when I deal with writings about Indian factionalism, because fighting in Washington, D.C., between political factions, is called politics, but fighting over some of the same issues on Indian reservations is called factionalism. Perhaps there is more than a smidge of racism inherent in our lexicon as we deal with the Indians.

The Indian Reorganization Act cannot be separated from its chief proponent, John Collier. The commissioner was capable of using forceful administrative methods that he deplored in other people. For example, he coerced some tribes into ratifying the IRA. A long list of Collier's indiscretions could be cited.

But we should not stop until we have had a moment to evaluate some of the good things the Indian Reorganization Act accomplished. One of the good things that it accomplished was the physical conservation of Indian land, soil, water, and vegetation. The conservation of Indian resources left a salutary legacy for the present. There was an overall endeavor to help the Indians go to work. The halting of Indian land losses and the reabsorption of certain lands into the reservations (even though these have been called submarginal lands, I notice that oil and other valuable things are taken from them now) were important to Indian reservations then and still will be in the future.

Under the leadership of both W. Carson Ryan and Willard Beatty, the two principal educators who worked under Collier, Indian education improved. Although some argued that moving Indian students out of the old Indian boarding schools and into the public schools was harmful, by and large, an increased devotion to the *idea* of education resulted.

It is interesting to observe, as I look back over those years, the kind of heat that Collier created on the reservations. Those teachers, who had worked for their churches and taught at the Indian boarding schools, despised Collier almost beyond belief. I had never heard anyone accused of being in league with the devil until I heard a school teacher claim that Collier was. She was challenged by the son of a tribal council member. This student said that his father believed that Collier was a good friend of the American Indian. This confrontation seemed to send our teacher into a tizzy.

Those teachers were incredible. I remember one of the hymns we were required to sing in the school. It was from an old Protestant hymnal, and maybe you will recognize the words. The Indian children at the Fort Duchesne School were required to sing it, too. It went:

> Let the Indian and the Negro,
> Let the rude barbarian hear,
> Of the glories of the kingdom . . .

These lyrics did not wash with the Indian students. When they would not sing those words, the teacher would become incensed. It was one of my first experiences in watching the politics of acculturation at work. It was then, and still is, fascinating.

At this point I should note something. Collier was attacked more on issues affecting the establishment and maintenance of an advantaged Christian group on reservations than on any other subject. To those historians who have attacked Collier for his too rapid change I would urge them to modesty. The freedom of religion issue was still very much alive in Collier's time. One need only look at the frenzied opposition to Indian dances less than a decade before the advent of the Indian Reorganization Act to see the power of these Christian churches and the Christianization issue that seemed to be inherent in his opposition. It is small wonder, that, in 1968, when I was doing a long series of oral interviews with reservation people, that I was told by one of the Ute elders to never trust Christians, because they wanted the minds of Indian children, were inquisitive about Indian sex habits, and did not answer to anybody.

One should try, as an analyst, to remove that Christian element from the opposition to Collier to see how much of it would have been left on other than religious grounds. Perhaps this would help us attain a better and more moderate interpretation of Collier and his period. During the 1920s, Collier took the opposite point of view to that of the Bureau, its leaders, and the Indian Rights Association. In the 1930s, they took the opposite role and delighted in attacking him in a way that indicates an element of revenge. Neither side looks very pure.

The Indian Reorganization Act should be looked at in another way. The Indians of the United States needed a system that had more integrity and validity in the eyes of the federal government. One need not search very far in the letters in the National Archives from Indian people in 1925 and 1945 to see that there was far more familiarity between the Indians in the field and the bureaucrats in Washington in 1945 than in 1925. We should search to see if the Bureau had a less paternalistic attitude toward the Indians over whom they held great control.

In recent years there have been complaints that the Indian Reorganization Act was defective. It did not give the Indian enough individual freedom. The secretary of the interior and the commissioner of Indian affairs also had ultimate control over policy. This has been viewed as an unrealistic invasion of Indian rights and liberties. These criticisms should not prevent us from carefully defining what we mean by the idea of a dependent domestic nation. If that idea describes a relationship to the federal government, does it not imply that the federal government has a responsibility? If wardship continues, what does wardship mean?

If this presentation sounds a little too much like I am defending John Collier, I am not. There would have been reform whether there was a Collier or not, because the policy of allotment and assimilation had failed. Furthermore, those who had influenced Indian affairs from without—the reformers—and those who saw the Indian as their special concern became less and less credible as American society changed and they did not.

Collier could be petty. Let me read you a line or two from a letter written to Rupert Costo, who was the official representative of the Cahuilla Tribe. This was part of Collier's answer to Costo, who had filed for expenses:

> Since you were not authorized in advance by the Commissioner of Indian Affairs as a delegate, and such requirement is absolutely necessary under existing legislation, before you can be compensated and further, since your tribe has no tribal funds to its credit from which such allowance can be made, the office is not in a position to consider any claim you may file for such allowance.

In other words, if you were working toward adoption of New Deal programs you got Bureau money. If you were not, you had to pay your own way.

Scholars have long pointed toward the use of politics to get the IRA adopted on Indian reservations, but they had not paid the same amount of attention to the opposition and how it came about. Who sponsored it? Who financed it? That, to me, would be as interesting a topic as the other, and while it has been partly dealt with by several scholars, it certainly has not been covered to the point of my satisfaction. Church records must be examined carefully. We must remember the advice of the Ute elder to never trust a Christian.

World War II had a very heavy impact upon the Indian Reorganization Act and the administration of Collier. Furthermore, in the last four years of his administration, he lost credibility as his abrasive personality alienated more and more people. By the end of his administration, congressional leaders had abandoned him and his programs.

The role of Indians in World War II indicated to some congressmen that the Indians could be integrated into society. As this new view of assimilation grew, the old enemies of Collier worked harder against his programs. In truth, his programs looked jerry-built and were inappropriate to the thinking of the moment. Indian poverty continued. Only when Indians migrated to urban areas did their economic status greatly improve.

In recent times there has been an orgy of criticism of the Indian Reorganization Act. Some of this criticism has used remarkable amounts of presentism. This is both unfair to the participants and bad history. Perhaps the New Deal era, Collier, and his men deserve better than they have received. For instance, who has researched the evolution of American Indian law in those few years when Felix Cohen worked intimately with John Collier? Furthermore, there has been no great groundswell in the various tribes of the United States to replace the Indian Reorganization Act. Historians, anthropologists, sociologists, lawyers, and others have complained about the IRA, in recent years, in a way that would have been considered nonsensical in 1940. And, in spite of all that criticism, we are examining the first fifty years of the administration of the IRA. With such survival in evidence, we ought to reexamine the strident criticisms while we reconsider this historic period.

CHAPTER TWO

Federal Indian Policy, 1933-1945

Rupert Costo, Benjamin Reifel, Kenneth R. Philp,
Dave Warren, Alfonso Ortiz

*Conditions were deplorable on the San Carlos Reservation before the
Indian Reorganization Act. There was no economic development of any
kind. I heard about the IRA when the superintendent came to our CCC
camp and explained the contents of this legislation. I remember that a
prominent Indian stood up and said, "This is what we have been waiting
for. The white man has driven us around like cattle for many years. We
need to take advantage of the opportunity to form our own government and
run our own business." I think the IRA was the best thing that ever happened to Indian tribes. It gave them the right to self-government. For
many years, the San Carlos Apaches held a celebration on June 18 to com-
memorate the birth of this legislation.*

Clarence Wesley, San Carlos Apache leader

*Clearly, the Indian Reorganization Act achieved none of its central
policy objectives. Foremost among these were the promises of "complete
economic independence" and "self-determination" for Indian tribes. Indian
people remain far removed from either goal a half century later. In the
end, as in the beginning, the IRA was sacrificed to John Collier's own gods
of "organization"—most particularly in the form of "the help . . . the
knowledge and the enthusiasm . . . of the expert." Also, it was undermined
corrosively by the pragmatic assimilationist philosophy of the 1928 Meriam
Report and its adjunct advocacy of termination.*

Hank Adams, Assiniboine activist and writer

[47]

Rupert Costo

I want to thank the Institute of the American West for the opportunity to join you in this most important discussion and to express my
views on the Indian Reorganization Act of 1934. The IRA was the last
great drive to assimilate the American Indian. It was also a program to
colonialize the Indian tribes. All else had failed to liberate the Indians
from their land: genocide, treaty-making and treaty-breaking, sub-
standard education, disruption of Indian religion and culture, and the
last and most oppressive of such measures, the Dawes Allotment Act.
Assimilation into the dominant society, if by assimilation we mean the
adoption of certain technologies and techniques, had already been
underway for some hundred years. After all, the Indians were not and
are not fools; we are always ready to improve our condition. But assimilation, meaning fading into the general society with a complete loss of
our identity and our culture, was another thing entirely, and we had
fought against this from the first coming of the white man.

This type of assimilation would be the foregone conclusion of the
Indian Reorganization Act. Colonialization of the tribes was to be
accomplished through communal enclaves subject to federal domination through the power of the secretary of the interior. Now this view of
the IRA is not held by practically all of the historians who write the
history of the IRA era.

The record shows otherwise. All one must do is to read and study
the hearings held in the Congress, the testimony of Indian witnesses, the
evidence of life itself, the statements of the Indian commissioner, and
the practically identical tribal constitutions adopted by, or forced upon,
the Indians under the IRA. In these constitutions the authority of the
secretary of the interior is more powerful than it was before the so-called
New Deal. No wonder the Indians called it the Indian Raw Deal.

The IRA did not allow the Indians their independence, which was
guaranteed in treaties and agreements and confirmed in court decisions. It did not protect their sovereignty. Collier did not invent self-
government: the right of Indians to make their own decisions, to make
their own mistakes, to control their own destiny. The IRA had within it,
in its wording and in its instruments, such as the tribal constitutions,
the destruction of the treaties and of Indian self-government.

There are those who believe that most of the Indians who opposed the IRA were members of allotted tribes who had been economically successful with their allotments. This is a simplistic response, and one that displays a serious lack of understanding of Indian affairs and history. Allotments certainly did not originate with the Dawes Act. They also were established in treaties. The Dawes Act did, however, force Indians into the allotment system, with a guarantee that they would have to sell their land, either through taxation or by sheer physical force. Those who survived created what they had always wanted, an estate for themselves and their children, a type of insurance against being moved again like cattle to other lands and the chance to make a decent living on their own land.

The Quapaw of Oklahoma were bitterly opposed to the IRA. They said:

> We have a treaty with the United States, describing by metes and bounds the size and shape of our allotments, and it states that its purpose is to provide a permanent home for the nation. And the United States agrees to convey the same by patent to them and their descendants, and this is according to article 2 of the Treaty of 1833.

In hearings before the House of Representatives, the Flathead made a similar statement. They agreed that the tribe might have the power to make contracts through the IRA, but instead of new legislation they believed it would be better to insist on sovereign rights and treaty rights.

On May 17, 1934, in hearings before the Senate, the great Yakima nation, in a statement signed by their chiefs and councilmen, said, "We feel that the best interests of the Indians can be preserved by the continuance of treaty laws and carried out in conformity with the treaty of 1855 entered into by the fathers of some of the undersigned chiefs and Governor Stevens of the territory of Washington." Now these are only a few examples of some of the testimony given by Indian witnesses and by most of the tribes. Many refused to even consider the IRA and rejected it outright.

But the commissioner of Indian affairs reported to the House of Representatives on May 7, 1934, that "I do not think that any study of the subject with all of the supporting petitions, reports, and referendums could leave any doubt that the Indian opinion is strongly for the bill." He then proceeded with this outright falsification of the facts, saying,

"In Oklahoma I would say quite overwhelmingly they favor the bill." Both Congressmen Roy Ayres of Montana and Theodore Werner of South Dakota disputed those statements. They showed that Collier was falsifying the facts.

During April 1934, the tribes that had bitterly opposed the IRA attended some of the ten meetings held by the commissioner of Indian affairs throughout the country. Here, as evidence shows, they were subjected to Collier's manipulations. In May, they came before the House of Representatives and completely reversed themselves. In fact, they gave a blanket endorsement to the Indian Reorganization Act. The congressmen, in shocked disbelief, prodded them again and again. Finally they asked, "If the proposed legislation is completely changed into an entirely different act would you then also endorse it?" The Indian delegates, according to many of their tribesmen and tribeswomen said, without any authority of their people, "Yes. Even then we would endorse it." In short, at least two of the tribal delegates gave a blanket endorsement of the IRA in advance of the final legislation. How did this happen? I can tell you how it happened. They received promises that were never kept. They received some special considerations and they felt the arm of the enforcer ordering them to accept or be destroyed. That was Collier's way, as I very well know.

In California, at Riverside, forty tribes were assembled. All but three voted against the proposed bill. Collier then reported that most of the California tribes were for the proposed bill. The historical record was falsified, and his falsification was swallowed whole by Kenneth Philp who also stated in his book that "several mission Indians, led by Rupert Costo, agreed with an unsigned three-page circular sent around the reservation which claimed Collier's ideas were 'communistic and socialistic.'" The implication is that this was a sneaky, underhanded job. The truth is that there was a complete cover letter with that circular, signed by me and my tribe. We were outraged at the provisions of the proposed bill.

It is a curious fact that, in all the ten meetings held with Indians over the country, in not one meeting was there a copy of the proposed legislation put before the people. We were asked to vote on so-called explanations. The bill itself was withheld. We were told we need not vote but the meetings were only to discuss the Collier explanations.

In the end, however, we were required to vote. And I suppose you would call all this maneuvering self-rule. I call it fraud. The Hupa Indians of northern California had two petitions on this proposed bill. One was to be signed by those supporting it; the other, by those who opposed it. In neither case had anyone seen the actual bill, but they rejected it on a massive scale on the basis of the explanations alone.

The Crow rejected the IRA and stated for the record in a letter to Senator Burton K. Wheeler, one of the sponsors of the bill, "That under the Collier-chartered community plan, which has been compared to a fifth-rate *poor farm* by newspapers in Indian country, the Indian is being led to believe that they, for the first time in history, would have self-government." But according to the bill, any plans the Indians might have for such self-government would have to be first submitted to the interior secretary or commissioner of Indian affairs for supervision and approval. Self-government to this extent was already accomplished through the tribal councils and tribal business committees, which, by the way, were organized and functioning long before Collier manifested his great interest in the Indians in general.

Now at these councils, Indians discuss matters they consider of vital interest and initiate measures for better management of their affairs, but no action may become effective without the approval of the commissioner of Indian affairs, or the secretary of the interior. Where is the advantage of an almost similar system bearing John Collier's name? Can we say that this power of the interior was forced upon the commissioner in the final proposed bill? No, not at all. His original bill contained not less than thirty-three references making it obligatory for the interior secretary to approve vital decisions of the tribes.

It is a matter of record that in California Indians were afraid to come to meetings for fear of losing their jobs if they showed disapproval of the Collier proposed bill. On the second day of the Riverside meetings, the Collier enforcers would not allow us to speak, and according to one report of an Indian organization, "they almost threw Rupert Costo out." Another element of the Collier enforcer policy is found in the warning to civil service employees in the BIA by Interior Secretary Ickes that they would be dismissed if they spoke out against Bureau policies on the proposed bill. All this is a matter of record. It can be shown in official hearings, correspondence, and data.

A resolution by the senators in New York stated their opposition to the bill. It warned that the proposed bill absolutely revoked the right of free citizens enacted in 1924 by Congress. The objection was published in the Senate hearings on May 17, 1934. The Seneca scornfully dubbed the proposed Indian court, which did not pass, as "ridiculous." To this opposition was added the position of the Oneida at Senate hearings. They said, in a resolution to Senator Wheeler published on April 17, 1934, that

> The Oneida nation firmly adheres to the terms of the Treaty of Canandaigua between our nation, our confederacy, and the U.S. of November 11, 1794, that the laws of the U.S., the acts of Congress, and the customs and usages of the Oneida nation are the controlling provisions of Oneida basic law, and/or the federal officials, the exponents of such basic law and the guides for the sachems, chiefs, headmen and warriors.

And they added this statement: "Any acts of the state of Wisconsin through its officers, courts, or legislature contrary to the above are without sanction of law and repugnant to the nation of Oneida Indians." They had some courage then, you know.

Now let us travel forward in time to the present and see what has happened to the Indian nations that approved the Indian New Deal. The Blackfeet fight for water rights is a classic example of domination of the interior secretary to the utter damage of the tribe. The federal government has ordered a survey of their water resources despite the fact that they have already had a survey which gave them their rights. The new survey robs them of their water rights. This is a matter of record, as well.

The White Mountain Apache have water, but the state and the federal government, with the active help of the federal agencies and the Bureau of Indian Affairs, are still attempting to limit their water rights and then erode those rights altogether. The few Yavapai Apache of Arizona, in the Orem Dam issue, had finally won their case so that the Orem Dam would be built elsewhere than on their reservation. This dam would have flooded their entire reservation. I have to tell you that this issue has again come up, and the Yavapai must still fight against the flooding of their land. This tribe was one of the first to accept the Indian Reorganization Act, and this is Dr. Carlos Montezuma's tribe. They have not gained one single thing from the IRA.

Added to the injustice of interior secretary domination and the power of the Bureau of Indian Affairs is the disgraceful corruption existing in the BIA and other agencies having to do with Indian affairs. Agents of these agencies regularly violate tribal laws. Remember the Osage roll that was falsified while head rights were actually sold to non-Indians. Remember the tragedy of illegal cutting of timber, and the illegal trespassing on Indian lands by whites who ran their cattle over Indian land. They have been known to even run their cattle over Indian cemeteries, as they did in California until we stopped them. It takes a little guts, you know.

Continued corrupt practices go on all the time, and the tribes are in a posture of constant vigilance, ready to do battle against the corrupt agency representatives and the violation of their simplest rights. Let us talk about self-government. Let us talk about self-rule, if you will. Here is a very late example. The Ute tribe of the Uintah-Ouray Agency recently passed an ordinance setting aside the Hill Creek area as a wilderness and cultural resources protection area. The tribe is concerned because non-Indian interests have requested permission from the Bureau of Indian Affairs to develop mineral sites at Hill Creek. What do you think happened? The Phoenix area director of the BIA, James Stephens, has rescinded the tribe's July 14, 1983 ordinance. I deeply appreciate and strongly approve the statement made in the August 1983 edition of the Institute of the American West's tabloid by Russell Jim of the Yakima tribe. He pointed to the lack of specific standards of judgment regarding trust responsibility on the part of the federal government toward the Indian tribes. He said, in part, that until a true definition of trust responsibility is formulated to preserve and protect the indigenous people of this land our treaties and rights will gradually be eroded, and by that erosion the mainstream of society will interpret that we accept the eventual genocide of a people.

There is a real need to investigate the sources of material on the Indian Reorganization Act. I have evidence that John Collier deliberately and wantonly falsified records, changed decisions, and made inaccurate reports to the Congress. We will investigate it as we are doing even now.

Finally, what of the future? We have survived and we will prevail, believe it! The Indians have no other place to go. We have never known any other land. This is our land and with the help of our God we will continue to surmount and conquer even the so-called legacy of the Collier Indian New Deal.

BENJAMIN REIFEL

While I was a boy growing up on the Rosebud Indian Reservation, we had the most sickening poverty that one could imagine. Tuberculosis was a killer of Indians. The people on the Pine Ridge Reservation and at Oglala were eating their horses to survive. Impoverishment was everywhere.

I remember going to Oglala in 1933 as a farm agent. The superintendent of the reservation, a gentleman by the name of James H. McGregor, looked to me almost as a son. After I graduated from college with a degree in agriculture, he recommended that the commissioner appoint me to be a farm agent. The reason he wanted me to be farm agent was because, in this particular district on the Pine Ridge Reservation, all of the 1,300 people, except two or three mixed-blood families, had conducted their business with a farm agent who was a graduate of Carlisle by the name of Jake White Cow Killer. He talked Sioux and Lakota in all of his communications with these people. He was a member of the village in that area. McGregor wanted someone who could speak the language.

I was only twenty-five years of age, and the old timers would come in to have their dances. They could have dances only on Saturday night. Bert Kills Close to Lodge came in and said, "I want to get permission to have a dance tonight for our group in the village." I had just received a copy of a telegram signed by John Collier, Commissioner of Indian Affairs. It said, "If the Indian people want to have dances, dances all night, all week, that is their business." So I read it to him. Bert sat there, stroked his braids, looked off in the distance, and he said in Lakota, "Well, I'll be damned." The interesting part of it was, if they did not have the dance Saturday night, they would have a dance a month later, because they felt they were on their own. The Indian policemen were not going to police anybody, and it was just too much for them to have self-determination about their own dances.

Speaking of the benefits of the Indian Reorganization Act, we now have more young men and women in universities and colleges. Some of them are represented here. When I was in college in 1928, I could count the number of Indian students, at least from our reservation, on the fingers of your hand. Now they are in the hundreds and up to the thousands at universities and colleges around the country. We also have community colleges on five or six of our reservations.

The Flandreaux Santee Sioux Indian Tribe is made up of a group of about a hundred families that came into the Dakotas during the massacre in Minnesota. They homesteaded along with the whites around the Flandreaux Indian School. When the Indian Reorganization Act was finally passed, they got a leader and they went to us for assistance. They accepted the act and drafted a constitution, by-laws, and a charter. They also took advantage of the Indian land purchase provisions, and they bought farms around there. And then housing was made available under a rehabilitation program for the people who were needy. They got houses on their forty-acre tracts. Last month, under the Supreme Court decision for the Seminoles, they could have bingo. So they are now making good money playing bingo, and the state cannot touch them. This is because the Indian people have rights under the trust responsibility.

But getting back to the Indian Reorganization Act, there was in 1934 an Indian congress at Rapid City to discuss the Wheeler-Howard bill. Walter V. Woehlke, John Collier, and Henry Roe Cloud, a Winnebago Indian, were there. Henry Roe Cloud was probably one of the few Indians at the time that had a doctor's degree. I was quite impressed with him. Henry Roe Cloud had recently been appointed the first Indian to be the superintendent of the Haskell Institute.

And I remember Rev. Joseph Eagle Hawk, one of the dear friends of mine in the community. He was a fine gentleman and a Presbyterian minister. Speaking of Indians not having a right to express themselves, we held this meeting at Rapid City for three or four days. I took leave to go up there because I wanted to see what it was all about. When Roe Cloud finished explaining part of the bill, Rev. Joe Eagle Hawk got up and said to Roe Cloud:

> You know, when we used to ship cattle to Omaha, Nebraska, they would go down to the slaughter house and they had a goat and they would lead a goat

> through the slaughter. The cattle would follow the goat in, the goat's life would be saved, and all the cattle would be killed. I think that is what you are, this Judas goat.

And he said that before the commissioner. I was impressed.

One of the things discussed at Rapid City was establishing some kind of official constitutional tribal government. When I grew up as a kid on the reservation, we had general tribal councils. What did they talk about when they came together? They passed a resolution asking the secretary of the interior, or the federal government, to allow them to have an attorney to represent them in their claims. When they had any tribal monies in place, the congressmen, about election time, would come around and say we will get you a per capita payment. They would then get a per capita payment, because at that time our Indian people, since 1921, even before that in South Dakota, were entitled to vote in the general election. If there was some of the tribal land to be leased, the general tribal council would come together and pass a resolution.

When I was a kid, there was also an old fellow called Chief High Bald Eagle. In those days we had an Indian trader store and a post office with counters and cages. Old High Bald Eagle was sitting up there with his legs crossed. He must have been about eighty or ninety years old; he looked like two hundred to me. We were having what we called a Scattergood dam constructed not too far away from our home. They were having a big tribal council meeting, and someone said to High Eagle in our language, "Why are you not up there at that big meeting?" He said, "When I was a young man years ago, when things were really important, then our leaders got together. But now, when a child gets constipated just about August eating chokecherries and it gets so his bowels are all stuck up, they have to have a council meeting on it." That is about as important as I thought the council meetings were on the Rosebud Reservation. That was also true at Pine Ridge. So I was impressed with Collier's idea that Indians would get together and form some kind of governmental operation where they would democratically elect their own people and select their own leaders.

I was also concerned over the years about the tribal courts. Tribal court judges were appointed by the superintendent or the Indian agent. There was no appeal from them. Before the Indian Reorganization Act came along, I remember my brother was thrown in jail because he lived close to where there was a big fight going on and they thought he was a part of it. My younger brother came in where I was working in a store, and he said, "Hey, our brother George is in jail." So what did I do? I knew the superintendent lived near by because I was a close friend of his son. I went over there, and he said, "What happened, Ben?" Well, I told him what happened, and he wrote out a little note which I gave to Andrew Night Pipe, who was the chief of police. Andrew Night Pipe unlocked the door and let my brother go home. That was the sort of thing that was going on, and I felt we needed a better judicial system.

I was really impressed with the original draft of the so-called Wheeler-Howard bill. In it was a section where there would be a circuit court that would move from one reservation to another. Funds would be provided for this court to operate. Under the federal system, there would be the right of appeal from the local court just like any other court. There would be none of this business that goes on where the judges are appointed by the superintendent or the tribal council. The revised bill was cut from forty or fifty pages to just about eleven pages. The court system and several other things were taken out.

After the Rapid City meeting, I asked the superintendent for permission to talk about the bill with the people; he agreed. But he felt that there was a little red tinge to all of this, because one of the remarks he made to me was "I do not mind the little red schoolhouses as long as they are not red on the inside." Nevertheless, he was very supportive of my going out and explaining this bill. Of course, there were those on the reservation who were very opposed to it. And there were those who were for it. Think of me, only twenty-five years old, getting up there arguing with the old timers such as American Horse. I do not know who all the rest of them were. I felt that this was something we could support.

Conditions have improved. Tribal councils have been organized. They are fighting among themselves, but as Floyd O'Neil said, this is no different than Congress. In South Dakota, some tribal councils cannot even write checks, because they are tied up in fussing over who is going to be in control. That is no different than in California where the governor was not going to make payments to employees. The legislative body would not go along. It took the Supreme Court of the

United States or the federal court to order them to make payments to the employees.

When I was a student at Harvard, I took a course from Arthur Schlesinger, a history professor. He said, "You must remember, that we have spent two hundred years becoming a constitutional democratic government." A while back, we celebrated our two hundredth anniversary. Our tribal councils organized under the Indian Reorganization Act, or even if they are not under the IRA, are trying to develop a democratic process among their systems in spite of tremendous poverty. If we had 80 percent or 90 percent poverty in the United States, no president would last even the four-year term that he has. You can believe that. Conditions are better from the standpoint of health, from the standpoint of food getting into the families' mouths, and from the standpoint of getting a little better education. But it is just as bad, if not worse, today from the standpoint of unemployment. That is the sad aspect of the current situation in the United States. And whether you have an IRA constitution and by-laws or not, the 80 percent to 90 percent Indian impoverishment is the same clear across the country.

KENNETH R. PHILP

Rupert Costo's remarks are, in many respects, well taken. John Collier constantly talked about tribal self-government, Indian sovereignty, and Indian rights. But there was always a credibility gap between what he talked about and the way he treated individual Indians. The original Wheeler-Howard bill, that long forty-eight page document, which in many ways was the strongest statement ever made by the government reaffirming Indian sovereignty, was drawn up before consultation with Indian leaders. Later on, Indian congresses were held. Those were not congresses where people just approved of things. I do not know of any commissioner that has gone out and held those kinds of congresses. They were a reaffirmation of the Indian general will. They were very important congresses.

My assessment of the Indian New Deal has become more negative over the years. The policy of termination grows out of many of the failures of the New Deal. One of the shortcomings of the New Deal was that it did not get widespread Indian support. One of the reasons that occurred was because the Indian Reorganization Act was a white-imposed reform program. Another reason it did not gain much support was because of the success of the policies associated with the Dawes Act and the success of the Christian reform movement of the nineteenth century. What Collier encountered in the 1930s, contrary to his romanticized image of Indians, was a group of articulate, educated tribal leaders. They believed that they could run their own affairs without the IRA. When Collier refused to pay attention to these people, they organized their own pan-Indian groups. In Oklahoma, there was a great deal of opposition to Collier by Christian Indians. They organized a group called the American Indian Federation which was very successful in opposing New Deal programs. In Alaska there was a group of Indians called the Native American Brotherhood. They opposed New Deal efforts to create reservations in Alaska. Most of these people stressed the individual work ethic, Americanization, and assimilation as a valuable kind of thing.

Somewhere we need to draw clearer lines from Indian opposition to the New Deal to the advent of termination. Congress, in many ways, was listening to Indians when it began termination after 1945. This was what many Indians, from the time of Carlos Montezuma, wanted. They called for the abolition of the BIA throughout the 1930s.

I do not see how one can view the New Deal as being assimilationist. It was assimilationist only in the sense that, if Indians acquired economic knowledge through their own tribal businesses and acquired political savvy in IRA tribal councils, they would be able to relate better to mainstream society. The adoption of white imposed constitutions also encouraged the process of assimilation. Collier challenged the hegemony of missionaries. Felix Cohen's *Handbook of Federal Indian Law* stressed Indian sovereign rights. Indian dances were encouraged during the New Deal. Collier had a poetic insight into Indian culture and wanted to preserve it.

Collier was not an assimilationist. In fact, he was criticized by both Indians and whites for promoting segregation and Jim Crow Indian policies. The New Deal stressed that reservations were permanent homelands. That is not assimilation. That is something quite different. The New Deal began a federal land purchase program to acquire real estate for reservations. If you have assimilation in your mind, there is no sense acquiring new real estate for tribes.

Collier saw the international dimension of Indian social justice. He created the Inter-American Indian Institute. He wanted Indians all over the hemisphere to get together and meet to reaffirm their sovereignty and fight together for social justice.

I would agree, however, that one can criticize Collier for being paternalistic and domineering. His treatment of Joseph Bruner, who led the American Indian Federation, was incredible. He treated this man with great disdain. Bruner was right in terms of fighting for the right of Indians to be consulted and listened to in the formulation of policy. His organization, the American Indian Federation, discredited itself by joining up with the German-American Bund and other fascist groups. I do not think you justify some of the things Bruner did by saying that the New Dealers played dirty tricks, therefore, it was justifiable for Indians to do dirty tricks.

Dave Warren

I am going to address the question of the Indian Reorganization Act and its implications for culture as it related to educational policy and programs. Reform is always attached to the personality and the psychological workings of an individual who is willing to take a stand in behalf of whatever he believes to be in the just cause. This is not something we need to dwell on, except that we are dealing with a whole era which is built upon the personality of John Collier. It raises all kinds of interesting philosophical questions.

Floyd O'Neil mentioned already that perhaps we did not need a John Collier. The simple fact of the matter was that this was the end of an era set in motion by the Dawes Severalty Act. It was the opening of a new era, which was not only specific to the Indian community but general across the country in terms of education. The progressives and progressive educationist associations were having their day in trying to reform American education to make it more valuable and meaningful to the general American community. It is by no accident that we find an interesting convergence of the progressive educationists working with John Collier, in the person of Willard Beatty.

In looking for something to begin with and for us all to consider, I wanted to find out what Collier's own view of education was, within a general framework of whatever he thought his reforms were all about. I found this somewhat lengthy passage which I would like to share with you. Interestingly enough, it was stated in 1962. The remarks made in bits and pieces throughout Collier's autobiography were more or less summarized in this longer statement on what he thought education should be.

> The task of education is how to lead the individual into world life, world consciousness, from within his own culture, his native personality, his native loyalties, how to bring the native selves of the thousands of tribal cultures into the world stream, not mutilated, not humiliated or ashamed, but blossoming and glad into the full sunlight of this great world and feeding into the world's endeavors their devotions and powers which are thousands of years old. This is the commanding problem of education, the world-wide problem of education. Let the problem not be solved at all, and incalculable human heritage will be wasted. The personalities of billions of individuals will be thrust into schizophrenia, and devastating social conflicts will be brought about.

In looking at the manner in which this rhetoric was transformed into programs and policy, I found some interesting harbingers of what we have finally come to accept as an almost normal operating base from which Indian education should emerge. It seems to me that Collier, through Willard Beatty, was concerned primarily with the question of how to develop an awareness of the American Indian and his community as part of a larger world. Now, I would also agree with some of the debates that are beginning to emerge on what is the proper term for Collier's policy. Is it assimilation, or is it acculturation? Assimilation, by definition, would have to end in the total vanquishment, the total integration, of the Indian community into the larger society, with loss of identity. I think the debates will continue as to what pluralism meant or could be attributed to in relation to Collier's perspectives on how the Indian community should maintain and utilize its traditions and yet deal, as he said in his remarks in 1962, with the reality of the larger world.

Collier's approach to education was unique in two respects, as well as in the manner in which these two aspects of educational approach converged. First of all, it was through Willard Beatty that Collier utilized the progressive education movement and its policies. Its philosophy was essentially community based, individualized education that dealt with experiences. The individual student's perception of what was home, what were his society, community, and cultural values, was related to the task of learning basic skills. These skills were applied to maintain one's cultural system and at the same time to cope with the larger world.

Converging with that was Collier's deep interest and formal efforts to integrate anthropology and anthropological perspectives or dimensions into a number of strategies to reform American Indian education. He was the only individual within the federal structure that I am aware of, even to the present day, that began to look at the source of knowledge, whether it is good or bad, accurate or distorted. There was a source of knowledge in research and scholarship, especially in the Bureau of American Ethnology in his day, which he felt should be utilized or made accessible because it was information which existed in no other place. It was through Collier's efforts that a unit called the Applied Anthropological Unit was established as a liaison between the Bureau of American Ethnology, Smithsonian Institution, and the Bureau of Indian Affairs.

It set in motion a whole process in which efforts were made, up to the Second World War, to utilize anthropologists and anthropological knowledge in two or three specific ways. One was in providing education, in-service training if you will, to the existing Bureau of Indian Affairs educational establishment in Washington and also to the teaching staff in the field. That effort had varying successes, all very short, but it did set in motion, in certain provisions of Public Law 95-561, one of the aspects of policy change that we have really not seen realized until recent years. It called for full integration and utilization of cultural materials and information and of the cultural expertise of community teachers. That law was highly modified in its final versions, but an effort was made to provide in-service training, not only to teach the development of a set of new materials or the utilitization of extant materials and research, but also to acculturate and to sensitize the existing teacher corps within the Bureau of Indian Affairs.

It is interesting to note that as many as 950 teachers were enrolled in the in-service and other teacher training programs that Beatty and

Collier instigated between 1935 and 1937. Now those programs unfortunately lasted only two to three years. There was tremendous response to them. One must keep in mind, too, that off-reservation boarding school teachers were asked to attend these programs during their summer vacation periods. Incentives of all types were offered, including the awarding of college credit for many of the courses.

Without dwelling on the details, some of the questions that I ask myself are what did Collier set in motion? What whole new perspective did he open on what must be accomplished in order to begin changing a system which was literally hundreds of years in formation? As Floyd O'Neil and others have noted, this system was greatly influenced by both missionary efforts and general mainstream educational philosophy, against which, in the latter case, people in the progressive movement like John Dewey reacted.

Finally, one must look at history and, in this particular case, at the development of a major era of Indian education, with all of its cultural ramifications. This perspective provides a lesson, not only as a study of the Bureau of Indian Affairs or John Collier, but as a continuing study and lesson in understanding the culture of bureaucracy and institutions. There is no difference in modern efforts to change institutions. There is no difference in the same realization that these institutions act and react to eras of liberal or conservative tendencies. And where are we in this process? I happen to believe that we are in one of the great eras of transition and opportunity.

I also want to mention that the Indian Reorganization Act in its educational terms or characteristics ran into what we might expect— problems for full implementation. I have referred to some of them already: a lack of trained Indian personnel, a lack of time to retrain existing teachers, and an absolute dearth of educational materials to reenforce the summer training programs sponsored by the Bureau of Indian Affairs. The greatest limitations, or the greatest defeat, to this phase of the Indian Reorganization Act was certainly the advent of the Second World War. Furthermore, we should realize that it would have taken literally thirty years, a full generation at least, to implement the first stage of change. Time ran out. But the residue and the legacy still is within us.

Finally, the role that I have had in the Inter-American Indian Institute in recent years has shown me an almost classic case of Collier utopianism finally coming home to roost in a very practical way. Some tribes represented in this room have perhaps benefited directly from the fact that there was an Inter-American Indian Institute in the past year. Without it, we would have had major problems with Mexico and the Indian communities that live along the United States-Mexican border.

ALFONSO ORTIZ

One of the things we need to do is to sketch out what kind of specific world the Indian Reorganization Act came into. Before we can meaningfully make evaluative statements or really dependable statements about what was disrupted, we have to understand clearly what was there before. I was not around during the period of the Meriam Report and the passage of the IRA. In order to talk meaningfully about a period which began a decade before my birth, I asked my relatives and friends who were around in San Juan Pueblo, New Mexico, in the late 1920s and early 1930s to tell me what kind of world the IRA came into. We have all read about the impact of the IRA, but know little of the specific reservation situations which existed then as seen from within by participants in the life of those communities.

What follows is a brief report of my findings. I first asked what impact the Great Depression had on life at San Juan. The reply, to my surprise, was no impact at all. Some of you might think that reservation communities were so depressed that the fall in the stock market and subsequent economic crash would not have any effect on them. Actually, the reason was quite different. San Juan Pueblo was not then caught up in the general cash economy, as it is now, fifty years later. There was really very little need for cash on a day-to-day basis. Sugar and coffee and then, occasionally, cheese and soap were the staples most often paid for with cash. Each family needed only to have one member working seasonally to have enough cash for the whole year. Typically, a family sent an older son, or in the absence of an older son the father went, to herd sheep in the mountains of northern New Mexico or southern Colorado to earn the needed cash. A few young women worked as maids on call twenty-four hours a day for well-to-do whites in Santa

Fe. They earned, as they were eager to tell me, thirty dollars per month and were lucky to get one or two Sunday afternoons off per month to go home. A few other people worked for the BIA or in stores in nearby Espanola.

Those families that did not have wage earners traded corn, strings of red chili, and wheat in the nearby store for things they could not trade for with neighboring Spanish-Americans and other Pueblo Indians or which they did not grow themselves. This barter system was the major subsistence activity for things you did not have or grow yourself or gather or hunt. Otherwise, the people just used the occasions of ceremonies and festivals to exchange useful gifts, to sell surpluses, and to try to take advantage of the occasional tourists, with pretty ears of corn done up in braids or with pottery. The pottery that exchanged hands between Indian people and Hispanics, as well as anything else they made or grew, went in the form of gifts or trade.

Already, however, the influence of the Anglo-Americans' new ways were in evidence in diet and in the relative prestige accorded different kinds of food. Those who could eat canned foods were envied because it was a sign that they could afford to buy their food, rather than grow it or trade for it. In the past half century, this envy of the white man's processed food has diminished because worries about the high incidence of cancer and other relatively new diseases and their suspected link to processed foods have become established in the people's minds.

There was a federal extension agent. He was our version of what former Congressman Benjamin Reifel was at the beginning of his career. We had a Tewa name for this fellow. It was "he who knows how to farm." The extension agent was established in San Juan by the late 1920s, and he was busy growing things like carrots, spinach, radishes, and other foods which the people had not known. And he was trying to coax them to grow these new foods, as well, in their fields.

There were two other externally imposed institutions in the pueblo which were not so benign—the Catholic church and the day school. The church was regarded as disruptive by those who were not really true, completely devout believers. The resident priest regularly told the people that, if they did not stop dancing and praying to the sun, moon, and stars, they would all go to hell. A half a century later, the people there are still singing, dancing, and praying to the sun, moon, and stars, and so far as we know, no one has gone to hell. Everyone knows there are no Indians in hell. It is not a place designed for us.

Indeed if anything has changed at San Juan, it is the church itself. Today, the Mass is often said in Tewa by members of the community, and the bilingual, bicultural personnel have translated the entire Mass and, many prayers, hymns, and proverbs into Tewa. Traditional Tewa embroidery adorns the altar. It also often adorns the priest himself, replacing the priestly vestments of yesteryear.

The teachers at the school used less terrifying language, but they also told their charges that everything they were, heretofore, had to end and that they had to go away to boarding schools and learn to be progressive like whites. The BIA had not yet begun to distribute clothing in the 1920s, but by the 1930s, younger students began to get shoes. The fundamental questions about education which we were later to grapple with, such as what kind of education, for whom, taught by who, to be controlled by whom, were not yet being raised audibly in San Juan in the late 1920s and 1930s.

Oftentimes, an era is best defined by everyday life. The daily life back in the late 1920s and 1930s was very different from anything known there in the last three decades. In the San Juan of that time, people never locked their doors when leaving for the day, as a fear of theft was almost nonexistent. The community was truly a community. Neighbors looked out for one another's welfare and interests. Children could pop into any open door they saw when out playing if they got thirsty or hungry. Anyone who denied a gourd of water or a piece of tortilla to a kid soon got a reputation as being stingy and uncivil. Ed Dozier, the late anthropologist from Santa Clara Pueblo, used to talk wistfully about these times because, when he was growing up, he could just pop into any home and, without asking, get the gourd from the wall and help himself to water and then beg a piece of tortilla if he smelled fresh tortillas on the stove.

Similarly, parents never worried about where their children might be during the day. They knew in a most basic sense that their children would be safe, no matter where they were within or around the village. This little point about parents not worrying about their kids caused teachers no end of frustration. They interpreted this permissiveness, at least the culturally insensitive ones did, as a sign that the parents were not concerned about their kids. It was a sign of just the opposite. The parents cared; they knew in a more basic sense that the children were quite safe no matter where they were.

The community was homogeneous and acted in concert. At night, after the day's chores were done, one could step outside and hear the music of flutes playing in different parts of the village. This was what musically inclined men did after the evening meal, especially in the summer when it was likely to be warm inside. They took their flutes and sat outside by the door on adobe benches and played. They also played for the women to entertain them when the women, in a communal ceremony, ground cornmeal.

There was also enough neighborliness that, when one needed a particular kind of medicine but did not have it, he merely asked a neighbor or a relative. Traditional medical herbs and other remedies were freely given when needed. Ben-Gay, Mentholatum, and aspirin were later added to the list of those things that could be given away to neighbors and relatives. When a midwife was called in to massage an expectant mother, she was paid twenty-five cents or fifty cents or given a shawl. When she attended a childbirth, she was paid in food and given several braids of blue corn. A favorite method of treating illness through the 1930s was by smoking the patient, smoking over the patient with someone else's hair, but not the patient's own hair. This practice gave rise to a very common insult in those times in Tewa. The insult could be translated, "He was smoked with his own hair." This meant he was tricked or cheated. To be smoked with one's own hair was to be duped.

The government of that time was very simple, very unpretentious, and very straightforward. There was a council of mostly religious leaders, elders who worked hard to keep things from changing. They appointed the secular officials. They picked men who would be like them, carry out their bidding, and uphold tradition when questioned. There were no budgets, there was no money, and there were no full time employees. By contrast, the present council consists mostly of former governors. For a brief time in the mid–1970s, the council at San Juan was administering a budget of over a million dollars in mostly federal programs, with dozens of employees and a full time tribal programs administrator. This program administrator was paid for by monies which had their origins in the old Office of Economic Opportunity.

As far as religious life was concerned, this was a bad time for Indian religion. Everyone said that the dance lines were short because people were so desperately poor. They had good costumes for their dances only because they were well made at an earlier time. On the other hand, there were many more customs then for passing on cultural knowledge to the next generation, such as story-telling sessions in the autumn and winter months, traditional games, and pilgrimages to get religious items such as fruit up in the mountains.

I am not trying to paint an idyllic picture of life fifty years ago. There were also problems and hardships. Hauling wood and water were two of the severest hardships mentioned by people, especially in the winter. In order to bathe, people had to build fires outside to heat the water, because fire pits and corner fireplaces were not adequate for heating large quantities of water. The major health problems of the time were tuberculosis, trachoma, and cataracts. No one alive then was unaware of the great flu epidemic of 1918. This epidemic, for a time, killed people off so fast in San Juan that some days the church bell never stopped tolling, day and night.

The most serious recurrent internal problems people recalled were domestic quarrels, charges of witchcraft, and land boundary problems. Domestic quarrels were mediated by an extended family group, and if they could not be settled there, they were referred to the tribal council, a move that the family found acutely embarrassing. They did not want to go public on things like divorces which were regarded as purely internal kinship matters. A favorite taunt of women during quarrels was to accuse one another of being promiscuous. The phrase in Tewa went like this: "At least I am not being rolled over and over in powdered dung." And the return would be: "No one would roll you over anywhere." Witchcraft suspicions were submitted to the consideration of the curing society. The council resolved land problems as they arose.

To conclude on a positive note, the elders remembered fondly that their counterparts of the early to mid-thirties received surplus commodities from the federal government. These commodities consisted of slabs of bacon, beans, cheese, and flour.

The last point I want to make is that the pueblos, with the exception of Jemez, supported the IRA. Only three of the pueblos in New Mexico adopted IRA constitutions; they were Santa Clara, Isleta, and Laguna pueblos. The Hopi in Arizona also initially supported the IRA. But the immediate impact of the IRA was not great, even though the Pueblos supported it. I suspect they did so because they regarded John Collier as a great and true friend because of his prominent leadership and support in the two great battles in which they were involved in the decade prior to the 1930s, the fight over the Bursum Bill and the fight over religious freedom. They knew Collier well and regarded him as a trusted friend.

The last point is this, younger people who have not yet had a chance to study history in any detail may be confused by all of this wrangling about whether Collier was bad or sinister in his motives or whether he was as good as some people might have you believe. He comes across as enigmatic because there is a fundamental contradiction in his thinking and his policies. Collier was content to uphold and celebrate and honor our expressive life, our cultural life, namely, the arts and religion. At the very same time, he was also content to deliver our more fundamental freedoms such as sovereignty and tribal self-government into the hands of the federal government. These two things seemed to work simultaneously in his life, and so both things are true. There also are some sharp regional differences and they need to be respected. The Pueblos could only see the positive side of John Collier. In other areas, where Indians had different kinds of experiences, they saw the danger clearly of the Indian Reorganization Act if it were passed without amendments.

CHAPTER THREE

Felix Cohen and the Adoption of the IRA

Lucy Kramer Cohen, Charlotte Lloyd Walkup,
Benjamin Reifel

I wrote two chapters in the early edition of the Handbook of Federal Indian Law. . . . *Felix Cohen was attracted to Indian law because he had a great feel for the land and the return to the simple life. The Indian way, as he read it as a child, had a tremendous attraction for him. . . . Felix wrote some papers when he was in college about the Indians and that it was likely our notion of democracy came from Benjamin Franklin having been ambassador to the Iroquois Confederacy in 1763.*

Mrs. Lucy Kramer Cohen, director of the
Association on American Indian Affairs

Felix Cohen was not just a giant in Indian law. Cohen was internationally known for his work in international law and legal ethics, and is today (and this is rare for a person of that era) studied in the law schools in jurisprudence, ethics, and courses outside of Indian law. Felix Cohen brought a brilliance and resourcefulness into Indian law. It had been almost one hundred years since the Supreme Court had given much serious attention to Indian law. Cohen went back to the Spanish origins, the British origins, and to the great John Marshall opinions. He restated them and made it clear that Indian tribes do have powers of governments.

Charles F. Wilkinson, professor of law, University of Oregon

LUCY KRAMER COHEN

Nathan Margold, the solicitor of the Interior Department, drew my husband Felix Cohen to the Indians. Margold knew that Felix had a very good record of being a legislative draftsman at Columbia University. In 1933, shortly after the New Deal came into effect, he was asked to come down and work on legislation that became known as the Wheeler-Howard bill. His interest in Indians, like that of most people in the East, was very romantic. He was a good legislative draftsman, and he took the task that was given to him very seriously.

We had been married only about a year when Felix was asked by Nathan Margold and Harold Ickes, both of whom had been with the American Indian Defense Association, to work on the law, aimed largely at the ills that the Meriam Report had detailed, that would give Indians a New Deal. Felix's one year extended to twenty, and he died still working to right those wrongs. He appeared and testified against a termination bill just about a month before his death.

My contribution, when I finally arrived in Washington D.C. during the Spring of 1934, was that of an unpaid volunteer. Since two members of a family could not, during the Depression, receive two government salaries, my job was to keep track of how various Indian tribes were reacting to the specific tentative provisions of the Wheeler-Howard bill. I should tell you that I did not come to this task unprepared. I had studied anthropology with Franz Boas. I had the good fortune to have the service of Miss Jennings, a remarkable young woman, who was able to make the most informative, accurate tabulation of those tribal responses, which was supplied daily to both Edgar Howard's House Committee and Senator Burton K. Wheeler's Senate Committee on Indian Affairs. Those chairmen, therefore, could never claim that they were unaware of Indian tribal reaction. It was a bill that reflected the best tribal counsel that was available at that time.

I attended all of the Senate and House hearings, and I enjoyed watching the Indians sitting around the table discussing the various provisions in sign language, much to the chagrin of the chairman. It was a very good way for the Indians to secretly get a consensus.

The Wheeler-Howard Act was not rammed down the throat of the tribes. It was an effort with many flaws, some of which were inserted by powerful congressional personnel or allowed by supporters in order to make certain that some bill would be passed as requested by the president. No one would claim that this was perfect legislation. But it was a powerful, unbelievable, even noble beginning given the Depression, the gathering threat of war, and opposition both by Indians and by non-Indians who had many ill-gained privileges to lose or who thought that Indians were wards of the government instead of sovereign, dependent nations.

This fifty year evaluation is of monumental importance. I want to salute all those who have gone, having given their minds, hearts, and, in many cases, even their bodies to bring about some modicum of progress in the Indians' quest for social justice. Permit me to quote something that my husband lived by. A famous rabbi once said, "The day is short and the task is great. It is not incumbent upon thee to complete the task, but neither art thou free to neglect it." That was the basis of the work of all the good men who helped with the drafting, the passage, and the implementation of the Indian Reorganization Act. The great task was begun fifty years ago, and it is now incumbent upon all of us, especially the young, to continue it, revise it, better it, and complete it, if such a thing is possible.

I would like to conclude with something that Felix Cohen wrote in his *Handbook of Federal Indian Law*:

> What has made this work possible, in the final analysis, is a set of beliefs that form the intellectual equipment of a generation. The belief that our treatment of the Indian of the past is not something of which a democracy can be proud. The belief that the protection of minority rights and the substitution of reason and agreement for force and dictation represent a contribution to civilization. A belief that it is the duty of the government to aid oppressed groups in the understanding and appreciation of their legal rights. A belief that understanding of the law in the Indian fields as elsewhere, requires more than textual exegesis, it requires an appreciation of history and understanding of economic, political, social, and moral problems. These beliefs represent, I think, the American mind in our generation as it impinges upon one tiny segment of the many problems which modern democracy faces. It is fundamentally to these beliefs and to this mind that an author's acknowledgements, gratitude and loyalty are due.

CHARLOTTE LLOYD WALKUP

I would like to add something about Felix Cohen. Felix had an enormous grasp of ethics and what makes the law really work and what is the basis of jurisprudence. He was a teacher as well as a student of ethics. He wrote extensively on the subject and his publications are still studied in Ph.D. courses. He taught at various colleges, universities, and law schools. In his research he became more and more interested in the Indians as examples of the victims of human oppression. He felt human oppression very keenly. He traced out the development of the principles for dealing with the Indians in the New World, which were formulated in Spain and taken over by the British and the French. I must say that the British were a little better in acting on those principles, perhaps, than the Spanish were, but the principles nevertheless were there. He also brought out that, in spite of all our faults, the federal government really tried to adhere to the principle of purchase of the land, recognizing Indian rights and acquiring them through purchase. Of course, settlers came in and undid the good work, and practice never quite took the same high road as principles did.

Lucy Cohen, in all her modesty, has not reported that she compiled, after Felix's death, a marvelous book of her husband's writing called *The Legal Conscience*. It has three parts. The first part is purely philosophical. The second part is the problems of Indian law looked at from a jurisprudential point of view. The third part raised ethical questions of various kinds, not necessarily related to Indians. Felix Cohen had an enormous breadth of mind, and it was focused, much of the time, on the problems of the Indians.

I came to Washington D.C. in October 1934, having just graduated from Columbia Law School, to work in the New Deal. I was asked by Felix to work on Indian affairs. I continued working in the Solicitor's Office on Indian affairs until World War II came along and really diminished the effort that was being made to implement the Indian Reorganization Act.

We were asked to read the Meriam Report when we came into the Solicitor's Office to work on Indian affairs. It laid out, in cold blood and in a very terrifying way, what the problems were that needed to be solved. I worked on the drafting of tribal constitutions, which some people call "boiler plate" constitutions because of their similarity. They all contained material that needed to be in a constitution so that a tribe had a clear, basic way to operate without confusion.

Surprisingly, everything was done quite fast, and the Indian Reorganization Act passed on June 19, 1934. The provisions of the act that were dropped were a federal court for Indian offenses and a provision that would have allowed tribes to incorporate into municipalities and a provision that seemed to require allotments to be returned to tribal ownershp. Those were the major provisions that created a lot of opposition from both Indians and non-Indians, who concluded that they were too drastic.

The Indian Reorganization Act had four principle purposes. The first and most important part of the act was the prohibition of further allotment and the authorization to the secretary of interior to purchase more land for both tribes and individual Indians to help undo the damage from the Dawes General Allotment Act. A second purpose was to recognize and to build up the authority of the tribal governments, but only if they were willing to do so. Indian tribes had to accept the IRA in a referendum, before any of it applied to them. Then they had to vote on whether they wanted to organize under an IRA constitution. Finally, if they had the resources and reason to do so, they could incorporate for business purposes. And all that was by tribal vote, and I might say it was by a majority of the tribal members, not just a majority of those voting.

Rupert Costo's argument that tribal governments were diminished rather than strengthened by these provisions does not seem valid. You have to remember that before the act was passed tribal governments, although they were recognized as sovereignties, were entirely subject to the whim of Congress, and Congress could take away any of the so-called tribal powers. The beauty of an IRA constitution was that it gave the Indians a definite, firm, recognized authority which they could use even if some of the authority was subject to the approval of the secretary of the interior. IRA constitutions also clarified some of the murky areas as to whether or not a tribe had authority over law and order and whether or not they could assess fees against people on the reservation.

The third part of the IRA enabled tribes to equip themselves for business enterprise. This was relevant only to those tribes who had some assets, and unfortunately, not many tribes had assets. But the assets which existed, such as timber, mineral resources, and cattle enterprises, could be put on a businesslike basis, with an opportunity to borrow funds from the IRA revolving credit fund. Incorporation also gave tribes the usual business authority to sue and be sued, except that no judgment could be against restricted Indian land. And, of course, it provided the usual protection against liability that a corporation has: only the assets of the corporation could be taken, rather than the assets of tribal shareholders. Another advantage was that the tribe could give its members shares of the corporation in exchange for their interest in heirship land.

Finally, there was the provision concerning education. The IRA provided for an annual appropriation of $250,000 for loans to Indians to go to vocational schools, high schools, and colleges. It also, incidentally, gave the Indians a preference in employment in the Indian service. Furthermore, the IRA stated that tribes retained all of their existing powers based upon previous court decisions plus certain other powers, such as the right to employ legal counsel and the right to prevent alienation of tribal land.

It is true that tribal constitutions were modeled on other government constitutions. They were modeled that way because other government constitutions covered the things that are necessary for tribal or government organization. First of all, they defined the territory of reservations and who were the members of the tribe. The constitutions also defined how elections should be held and whether councilmen should be elected at large, represent particular districts within the reservation, or represent particular bands who were parts of the same tribes or of different tribes on the same reservation. Most of the constitutions had provisions for initiative and referendum, removal from office, and election procedure. These so-called "boiler plate" constitutions contained basic provisions that every constitution needs. Insofar as my own experience goes, they were all drafted in consultation with the existing tribal council and reflected what the Indians thought were the best provisions.

I will add a little bit about my own experience in going out on the reservations. The Indian Office assigned Ben Reifel to assist me on the Sioux reservations and Oliver LaFarge on the Hopi Reservation. What would happen was the Indians would have a tribal council meeting. The superintendent and I and Ben, if he was there, and other interested persons who were concerned with the tribal constitution met together, and we went over what was necessary and needed in a constitution to make it work. We also asked the Indians what kind of things they wanted to have in it. These issues were talked about and thrashed over for days. I spent at least a week on the Winnebago reservation. I was nearly lost in a blizzard, but the Indians saved me. On my visits to the Sioux reservations we had not only tribal council meetings but we had meetings open to the whole tribe. I remember a lot of people in the room. We would try to explain the provisions of the IRA. The tribal members would then ask us several questions.

One of the disrupting features of these discussions was the tremendous interest of the Indians in their claims. Repeatedly, people would come up to me and say, "Why doesn't the act say something about Indian claims and how we can get our claims adjusted?" And I would have to say, "Well, that has to take separate legislation." As you all know, that separate legislation did come along twelve years later. The only complaint the Indians had was that the IRA did not cover Indian claims, and they did not say anything about "Oh, you are taking away our tribal sovereignty" or "This is going to be just terrible for the tribe."

BENJAMIN REIFEL

In 1933, I came on the reservation next to our reservation and was assigned to a district where most of the families spoke the Lakota language. The superintendent of the reservation selected me off of the civil service rostrum for that purpose. We had to talk about the Wheeler-Howard bill. They had this big Indian congress in Rapid City. It was the first time I saw John Collier, the commissioner of Indian affairs. Walter V. Woehlke, the editor of *Sunset* magazine in California, was the manager of the meetings, which went on for three or four days.

I was impressed with the opportunities outlined in the Wheeler-Howard bill. I thought, "We are going to stop the sale and the loss of our lands. We are going to get an educational program so kids can go on to colleges and universities and trade schools." The bill also provided an opportunity to get some money to buy land. There was a loan program to improve agricultural industries. All of this sounded extremely exciting to me. I went back to the reservation and started studying the bill. The superintendent was very supportive of my going around and explaining this bill in our own Lakota language.

The Indian Reorganization Act was finally passed in 1934. Most of the thousand people in my little district could not speak English. All of our business was conducted in the Lakota language. We had old school flip charts that were used in the day schools. I went to an old commissary, and I found one of these charts on a stand. I put the provisions of the IRA on each section. For education, I put a kid with a mortarboard and explained in our own Lakota language how much money was available. I had all nineteen provisions in this chart form.

In my district, forty or fifty people were delegates to the general tribal council. About ten of them went up to a meeting and they explained the IRA. It was not long before I got a call from the superintendent saying, "You have got to come up and bring your charts and help these councilmen explain the Indian Reorganization Act to their people." Joe Jennings, who was assigned by the commissioner of Indian affairs in our area, took me around the different reservations in South Dakota and North Dakota.

The IRA is one of the few pieces of legislation applying to anybody in the United States that the people could accept or reject. If that is stuffing something down somebody's throat, I have got the wrong information about what it means to stuff things down people's throats.

In April 1935, I got a telegram to go to Washington. I was asked to be an organization field agent, with headquarters in Pierre, South Dakota. I went around to explain the Indian Reorganization Act, and of course, some tribes adopted it, others turned it down. I served as an organization field agent until I was ordered to active duty in the army.

During this time, I got acquainted with Felix Cohen. One night we were driving to Billings, Montana, from South Dakota. We began to philosophize. I said, "Well, American people, you know, are pretty decent people." Cohen replied, "You know, the American community is made up of wolves and sheep, and the sheep have got to be protected against the wolves." It was one of Felix's feelings that we needed to protect the Indians' land, their rights, and their humanness.

The greatest disappointment I had with the Indian Reorganization Act, and this was not John Collier's fault, was the way the senators and congressmen felt about it. They eliminated important parts of the

IRA. We have law and order codes, but our judges are not paid anything like they should be with the tremendous decisions they have to make. There is no independent judiciary on Indian reservations. The court system is the creature of the tribal council.

As I look back over the fifty years, there is nothing in the Indian Reorganization Act that harms any Indian tribe or any Indian individual who has property. But, as John Collier said, "Even the finest social piece of legislation can be made completely useless by bad administration." We still have the IRA constitutions. It is up to the people to amend these constitutions and make them useful.

CHAPTER FOUR

Implementing the IRA

John Painter, Robert L. Bennett, E. Reeseman Fryer,
Graham Holmes

*Misunderstanding of the purposes of the IRA was a very big obstacle.
Where the Indians already had an established traditional kind of government, they were afraid they might lose that. And then there was factionalism on some reservations between the full-blooded and the half-blooded
Indians—the half-blooded Indians being more progressive and wanting to
get on with the job. There was also outside opposition from many church
groups who thought that this was going back to the blanket and turning the
Indians back to paganism.*

Charlotte Lloyd Walkup, formerly with Solicitor's Office,
worked on drafting and implementation of IRA constitutions.

*John Collier established an applied anthropology unit at the Bureau
of Indian Affairs. It was headed by Scudder Mekeel, a brilliant young
anthropologist trained at Yale. . . . There was a number of people in Congress who thought that the discipline of anthropology had sinister overtones
and should not be used in connection with the Indian Reorganization Act.
. . . The applied anthropology unit lasted only about two years. Scudder
Mekeel provided a rather caustic summary of what had happened to this
unit. Collier replied that anthropologists had failed to quickly provide
background material about the contemporary political situation on reservations so the Indian Bureau could draft constitutions that were not based on
obsolete accounts of earlier tribal political systems.*

Fred Eggan, anthropologist

[79]

John Painter

Federal Indian policy prior to 1933 was very ethnocentric. It was designed to bring about individualism and rapid assimilation of the Indian into the mainstream of American life. There were some modest efforts to improve Indian education and health. After the publication of the Meriam Report, in 1928, considerable strides were made by the Hoover administration to rectify earlier neglect, especially in the areas of education, the quality of BIA personnel, and, to a lesser extent, health care. Even with these efforts, enforced acculturation still was the central theme in Indian policy.

A shift in Indian policy occurred with the appointment of John Collier as commissioner of Indian affairs. Collier accented the positive attributes of Indian culture and Indian self-worth. Basically, Collier's policy was one of Indian self-determination. The Wheeler-Howard bill was drafted to facilitate Indian economic opportunity and Indian self-government. We know that the Indian Reorganization Act was considerably different than the original Wheeler-Howard bill. The changes that were made reflected the prevailing attitude in Congress toward Indians.

It is important to note that neither the economic crisis of the 1930s nor the appointment of Collier brought about a basic change in the congressional attitude toward Indians, nor did it bring about an acceptance of the notion of cultural pluralism. Most members of Congress who were concerned with Indian policy continued to hold ethnocentric cultural views for more than a quarter of a century. In doing so, they represented their constituents' attitudes. Members of Congress also continued to represent the economic interests of their constituents and those economic interests often clashed with Indian interests and rights.

It is also important to remember that congressional committee staff members often had considerable power and influence. Albert A. Grorud, a staunch critic of Collier, served for over twenty-five years on the staff of the Senate committee dealing with Indian affairs. He remained in that position until 1956. Grorud was an advocate of rapid assimilation. As counsel to the special Senate committee, he largely controlled who appeared before that committee. This helps explain the disproportionate amount of time given in the hearings to opponents of Collier and his policy. The infamous 1943 Senate Report 310, which called for the liquidation of the BIA, was authored by Grorud. The senators on this committee called Grorud their "chief." He was considered the committee authority on Indian affairs. Grorud remained in a position of power during the late 1940s and early 1950s, when the termination bills were being drafted.

The breadth of this ethnocentric congressional attitude became apparent in 1947 when the Senate Committee on Post Office and Civil Service forced Assistant Commissioner William Zimmerman to draw up a list of tribes to be released from federal supervision. That breadth is also seen in the reluctance by Congress over the years to appropriate funds to carry out the provisions of the Indian Reorganization Act.

When we talk about the implementation of the IRA, one important fact often is forgotten. The IRA greatly expanded the activities of the Bureau of Indian Affairs, and this was mandated in the legislation. Furthermore, the IRA greatly complicated the administration of Indian policy and required greater expertise, particularly in the economic and legal fields. This is best illustrated in the activities of the Indian Organization Division and especially in the activities of that division's field agents.

During July 1935, the personnel of the newly organized Indian Organization Division began to assist tribal groups in organizing under the IRA. Initially the western part of the United States was divided into four regions with a field agent in each region: George LaVatta in the Northwest, Kenneth Marmon in the Southwest and California, Peru Farver in the Great Lakes region, and Ben Reifel in the Northern Plains region. Within a year, Montana and Wyoming were split off of the Northern Plains region. Soon field agents were added in Oklahoma and Alaska. Very little has been done in the area of looking at the organization of groups in Alaska. These organization field agents were initially assisted by some at large agents, including Henry Roe Cloud, and long time BIA employees such as Oscar Lipps and John Holst.

Collier charged the Indian Organization Division with the primary responsibility of implementing the IRA. The organization field agent provided the link between the BIA central office in Washington and the Indian tribes and agency personnel in the field. Field agents had to be knowledgeable, not only about the philosophy and intent and the provisions of the IRA, but also about all aspects of the Bureau's programs and activities. Their work was largely educational. They explained the New Deal Indian policy to tribal leaders, tribal people, agency personnel, Indian school children, and the general public. These field agents initially served as educational resource persons and technical advisors to the tribes and to the BIA field personnel during the early stages of tribal organization under the IRA.

Once tribes had established governments under IRA constitutions, the field agent assisted tribal leaders in making these units function more smoothly. They also advised tribal leaders in establishing cooperative organizations for various economic enterprises. Throughout this process the field agent often acted as liaison between the tribes and the BIA program and technical personnel. The organization field agents initiated educational programs for BIA personnel related to Indian organization, and they initiated training programs for the new tribal leaders of IRA governments. As front line promoters and advocates of Indian self-determination, these agents had a lasting effect upon the nature and the function of tribal governments, not only during the 1930s and 1940s, but in the following decades. Their work, along with that of the tribal leaders, helped to break down the Bureau's paternalistic approach to Indian affairs and brought about a greater acceptance of self-determination in Indian policy.

Each field agent made a considerable impact upon general Indian policy and the tribes and groups with whom they worked. But the collective ideas of those in the Indian organization unit between 1935 and 1943 had the greatest impact. As members of the Indian organization unit worked together to assist tribal groups, they came to recognize that many tribes were facing similar kinds of problems and that tribal leaders could better resolve these problems if some vehicle for greater communication could be established between tribal leaders. From this recognition, coupled with a very strong belief that a larger role for tribal leaders in Indian affairs was needed, came the realization that a viable national Indian organization should be created. The field agents, as well as other Indian organization personnel, provided the catalytic ideas, inspiration, and leadership for what became the National Congress of American Indians in 1944.

ROBERT L. BENNETT

Commissioner John Collier, in 1934, held meetings throughout Indian country to explain the provisions of the Wheeler-Howard bill. Quite a few people at these large well-attended meetings were not fully acquainted with the legislative process. Soon opposition began to develop to the Wheeler-Howard bill. This enabled the Senate Committee on Indian Affairs to draft alternate legislation, the Indian Reorganization Act. Collier was faced with the decision of either accepting the Indian Reorganization Act as written by the Senate Committee on Indian Affairs or having no bill at all. He chose to accept the Indian Reorganization Act. This placed him in an awkward position with the tribes because there were considerable differences between the Wheeler-Howard bill and the Indian Reorganization Act. His credibility with the tribes was in jeopardy because many things that he had stated would be in the bill were not in the Indian Reorganization Act. The implementation of the IRA was clouded by this one fact.

Indian field agents who worked with the tribes for the purpose of implementing IRA constitutions brought with them model constitutions that had been developed by the Bureau of Indian Affairs. There was a great deal of feeling among the tribes that they were more or less obliged to accept the constitutions which were presented to them. Consequently, most of the IRA constitutions were quite similar.

Collier did not know how effective tribes would be under a constitutional form of government. Therefore, it was decided to insert in the drafts of constitutions provisions for the review of the actions of the tribal government by the secretary of the interior. The secretary could, in this review process, disapprove of legislative actions taken by the tribal governments under their constitutional authority. This was not a requirement of the Indian Reorganization Act or any regulation. It was inserted so the Bureau of Indian Affairs could retain some kind of supervisory powers over the actions taken by IRA tribal governments.

There was also a great deal of misunderstanding because the Indian Reorganization Act did not carefully define the sovereign powers of tribes. What it did do, in section sixteen, was to provide tribes the opportunity to organize governments of their own choosing, but section sixteen did not make clear the authority of these governments. The reason for this was because tribes already had sovereign power on all subject matters except where Congress had legislated. Congress was simply authorizing a process by which tribes could exercise their existing sovereign powers. Under IRA constitutions the tribes' sovereign powers were usually delegated to an elected form of government.

Several tribes would not go along with this kind of delegation. The Oneida tribe to which I belong is an example. The Oneida constitution still provides that all of the sovereign powers rest with the tribal membership. Within the constitution, by a process of amendment, there is a provision by which the tribe can delegate certain powers to the business committee. There is no broad delegation of powers by the Oneida tribe to the tribal government as is the case of most constitutions. There are tribes like mine where the power still resides in the tribal membership. This power can be delegated to the business committee by ordinance of the entire tribal membership. It also can be taken away from the tribal business committee without constitutional amendment, because it is given to them by ordinance. The tribes can repeal these ordinances without going through any constitutional amendment process.

As IRA constitutions were developed, there was not a dramatic shift in terms of the operations at the agency level. Even though tribes ratified constitutions, business went on the same as it always had. When the Bureau of Indian Affairs needed something from a tribal government to sanction a particular action, it presented the tribal government with a resolution in order to get favorable action. This allowed the Bureau to proceed as it had before there was a constitution, bylaws, and a charter. In that early period, there were very few legislative enactments or policy statements enacted by the tribes that were not written by the Bureau of Indian Affairs for the convenience of the federal government.

Many tribes that voted for the IRA never adopted a constitution that delegated powers to their tribal government. Decisions are made by the entire tribe. The Quinault tribe of Washington, for example, does not have a constitution in which the tribal council has delegated powers. They have bylaws which set up procedures for the tribal government. Any authority exercised by this government must be obtained from the tribal membership. When the tribal membership does act in particular areas, its decisions are not subject to review by the secretary of the interior. There is no limitation for these tribes in the exercise of their sovereign powers. Any tribal action that does not affect their trust property goes into effect immediately even though they are under the Indian Reorganization Act.

Collier wanted tribal members to participate in school board elections, city governments, and county governments. He felt that they needed a process by which they could learn the democratic processes of government. That is why he developed the concept of tribal governments operating under a constitution. It was not his intention that tribes would always have governments of their own. His concept was that over a period of years, once the tribal membership had learned the democratic processes, they would no longer need a tribal government. They would eventually participate in all kinds of elections the same as the general public.

Collier also understood that tribes wanted to exist as separate entities and would always have trust property managed by the tribe with the approval of the secretary of the interior. Therefore, he favored the concept of corporate tribal charters. The IRA corporate tribal charters were vehicles under which tribes could permanently manage their property. Collier envisioned a separate board of directors for the corporate charter and a separate elected government for the tribe. This was not politically acceptable to the tribal leadership. Consequently, all of the charters contained provisions that the governing body of the charter corporation is the elected tribal government.

The only tribe that does have two separate organizations is the Seminole tribe of Florida. They have an elected tribal government and an elected board of directors for their chartered corporation. This worked until bingo arrived. The chartered corporation, which runs the bingo operation, has millions of dollars, but the elected tribal government does not have any money. This has caused some political confusion. It is not yet clear whether the chartered corporation will appropriate money to the government or whether the government will tax the corporation.

Educational problems also occurred after the passage of the Indian Reorganization Act. In 1948, there was a Special Senate Committee on Education that held hearings on Indian education. At that time school textbooks were written in both Navajo and English. The chairman of that particular Senate committee stated that the Bureau of Indian Affairs was not in business to keep Indians Indians. They were in business to educate Indians to join mainstream society. The Bureau of Indian Affairs was prohibited from printing any more of these bilingual books. Twenty years later another Senate Special Subcommittee on Education criticized the BIA for not having printed those kinds of books.

E. Reeseman Fryer

I came here to praise John Collier and not to bury him. He held the office of the commissioner of Indian affairs longer than any man in history. In my judgement, no more complicated public man than he has graced this century. He was a brilliant, optimistic visionary who could turn in a single moment to violent pessimism when talking about the world outside. He was a mystic, a philosopher, a poet, a reformer, and a community development specialist. He was a writer and a speaker of beautifully hypnotic prose. John Collier was the tenderest man I have ever met and, at suitable times, the most intellectually ruthless man I have ever known. I was devoted to him.

Collier's complex personality was threaded by a single dominant conviction. He believed that man's salvation lay in the preservation of community. At times he saw in capitalistic society the crass indifference where nothing beyond the individual was perceived and the human group was nothing more than a contract between self-seeking individuals. John Collier was frequently accused of being a Communist, but he was not a Communist. He was a commune-ist, in the sense of community. Sometimes he saw communities, it seemed to me, where communities did not exist.

He discovered Indian communities when he made his first visit to Mabel Dodge Luhan at Taos. There he discovered his Red Atlantis. Few of us will debate the cultural richness and social beauty of the ideal community. John Collier visualized community with synonyms in unity and unanimity. However, decisions made on assumptions of community when only its social fragments exist lead to bitter disappointments. So it was with John Collier. His failure to observe facts led to his greatest IRA setback with the Navajo.

I believe that Collier saw the Indian Reorganization Act as the final kind of community. It was a restraining order on the Congress and a salvation of Indianness. The original Wheeler-Howard bill contained fifty-two pages of print. It was ridiculed by its detractors for that reason. Few congressmen, if they read it at all, realized that it was a successor to several thousand pages of Indian law.

Because of the IRA and John Collier, tribal lands are no longer being lost by the process of allotment. The majority of the tribes are self-governing, and while functioning with varying degrees of friction, each tribe has kept its community intact. These communities were held intact and strengthened as long as John Collier was commissioner. The provision in the IRA for a revolving credit fund and its subsequent implementation was among the important triumphs of the Collier administration. He moved quickly to urge the formation of tribal corporations and cooperatives. It is interesting to remember that the first tribe to organize under the IRA, to get its constitution, and to form a corporation was the Flathead. Their quick victory, thereafter, over the robber barons of Montana Power, who had for years held tribal power sites in fief, was a triumph that brought chuckles to John Collier even in retirement.

He exalted in the post-IRA emergence of the four Apache tribes of Arizona and New Mexico. He had described them before IRA as "people sunken in melancholy," "people living in gray squalor at the expense of the government," and "idle prisoners in concentration camps." Those excerpts presented a distorted description of reality, but they were not far from being wrong. During the 1920s, my wife and I had a ranch located between the San Carlos and Fort Apache Indian reservations. We made frequent trips to both reservations, but we always returned sort of depressed by the squalor and the poverty of those two Apache groups. They lived then in brush wickiups near the agency. We were depressed too by alcoholism. Alcoholism among the Apache may still be a problem, but the resorts, the sawmills, the purebred cattle herds, and other things that we see today on both San Carlos and Fort Apache are examples of Indian enterprise. I think that the comfortable homes we see at San Carlos and Fort Apache also are traceable to John Collier's implementation of the Indian Reorganization Act.

The Mescalero and the Jicarilla of New Mexico made equal strides under the IRA. Collier found most impressive the emergence of the Jicarilla. Most notable among their achievements was the rebirth of community, his kind of community. All of the allotees at Jicarilla but one transferred their allotments to the tribe to consolidate their resources. Equally important but with perhaps greater social impact was the money borrowed from the revolving credit fund to organize a corporation. The Jicarillas bought out a store from a local trader. They were successful in the management of that store. They paid off their government loan in five years.

I will conclude with a discussion of what I think was John Collier's greatest failure. The failure that hurt him most was the loss of the Navajo to IRA. In 1933, I was a young fellow working in the Soil Erosion Service on the Mexican Springs Project. Mexican Springs is just north of Gallup. It represented to Henry Wallace, Harold Ickes, and Collier an ideal kind of total valley watershed situation. They wanted to demonstrate to the Navajo what could be done with good range management by people for themselves to save the land and to develop themselves. Shortly after we got that started, I was transferred to Ganado to set up a demonstration area.

About that same time, John Collier made a great swing throughout the country to rally support for IRA. He held about ten meetings. He finally came to the Navajo Reservation in February of 1934. I attended that meeting as a detached kind of person. I was not in the Indian service; I was in the Soil Erosion Service, and I could look at it, I thought, with a reasonable amount of objectivity. John Collier made great headway discussing the provisions of the Wheeler-Howard bill, through the use of interpreters. Finally, he injected, almost extemporaneously, a statement to the Navajo tribe: "You have to sell a lot more of your sheep and goats." Now this was at a time when the Navajo tribe was so desperate for markets that Collier himself was able to arrange through one or two of the emergency agencies of government to buy productive livestock to help take the load off the range.

I say all of this because John Collier in his writings has attributed the Navajo rejection of the IRA to section fifteen which required the practice of conservation. The Navajo associated stock reduction with conservation. If you were to go to the Navajo today and ask about E. R.

Fryer or ask about John Collier, they will remember both of them in terms of stock reduction. Conservation came automatically not to mean conservation to save your land, which is so much a part of the Navajo's psyche. In all of their ceremonies, they refer to Mother Earth. John Collier did himself and the whole conservation movement a great injustice by deciding that the Navajo were lost because of the conservation portion in the IRA.

Conservation was not the most important issue. It was introduced by Jake Morgan and some of Collier's enemies. The real issue on IRA was assimilation. Morgan and other Navajos argued that the IRA was detrimental to Christianity. They concluded that it put the Navajos back in a zoo. The missionaries and the traders and all of the forces who had entrenched interests on the Navajo reservation were able to defeat IRA on the basis of the issue of assimilation. I wanted to say that, because everything I have read by John Collier—and some of his writings have such spiritual qualities that its very difficult to follow the reality in them—always comes back to this: the issue of conservation lost IRA to the Navajo tribe.

I am glad it did. I think that the Navajos are infinitely better off without the IRA. The Navajos have been able to assert, all of these years, their treaty. They have none of the constraints of the IRA. The Navajos have grown from their own culture to a point where their development would probably have been curbed by the constitutional provisions of the IRA.

Graham Holmes

To understand the IRA we must look at it in view of the times. If you were to look at the IRA and Indian tribes as of today, very likely you would come up with something much different than its supporters did in 1934. But, in 1934 things were a lot different. Few, if any, Indian tribes had legal representation or sophisticated governments of any kind. Tribal government had been eroding away for many reasons. Many people wanted to see it destroyed immediately. That happened in eastern Oklahoma in the Five Tribes area. Tribal governments, after statehood, were for all practical purposes abolished. There was much more sentiment to completely abolish tribal sovereignty than there was to preserve it. If we look at it from that perspective, we can adopt a much more benevolent attitude toward John Collier.

Before IRA, no general piece of legislation to define the relationship of Indians with their government had ever been enacted. The rights of Indians had been defined by numerous court decisions. As some of you know, court decisions rest on the facts of the individual case. We had to take each individual case and try to fit it to the situations as they came up without any clear definition of Indian rights or the relation of Indians to tribal governments. It was very difficult to get any kind of general legislation enacted then, as it is now. It took someone with the force of Harold Ickes and Collier and the administration that existed at that time to even propose legislation such as the IRA and get it enacted.

The IRA did not spell out the terms of Indian tribal government, but it did fix forever, as far as I can tell, the rights of Indian tribes to have a government of their own. The people at the BIA and the Indian tribal leadership, as they understood things at that time, put together the best tribal governments they could under the circumstances. So, looking at it from that situation, it is difficult for me to find fault with the IRA. The IRA was double-barreled. It had provisions for a tribal government and for a tribally chartered business enterprise.

Problems occurred in implementing the IRA on reservations, and a lot of the trouble today is involved in that same situation. No political organization, so far as I know, has ever been able to run a business. No state has been able to run a business, and the federal government has never been able to operate a business of any kind very successfully. Yet everybody expects a tribal political organization to operate a business. If the IRA charters and tribal governments had been as carefully pursued as they should have been, it would have worked a lot better. I do not think that was Collier's fault or anybody's fault. People at that time were not far enough along in the evolvement of people to bring that about.

Tribal business and tribal government is so mixed that it is almost impossible to separate. A government ordinarily operates and raises capital by levying taxes and by borrowing money and printing money. Business works on income from doing business with some commodity or something of that nature. A government can spend money and adjust its income by raising taxes, by borrowing more money, or by printing more money. The federal government does that all the time, but no tribe does any of these three things. And yet they try to spend money like a government. A lot of the governmental problems on the reservations grow out of that situation. Now, if there was a way to split off the business part and have the tribal government tax to raise its funds in much the same way that the federal government or the states do, reservation government would operate a lot better, and tribes would be able to operate their businesses a lot better.

It is difficult to run the Navajo sawmill, for example, because the tribal political entity operates it. A patronage situation exists that leads to all kinds of difficulties. The Navajo tribe is not an IRA reservation. It does not have a constitution, nor does it have a constitutional government. Actually, the tribe operates under an Australian or an English system. That creates a lot of problems for the Navajo in their relations with the federal government, but the tribe operates very well under that system.

Would that have been possible if we did not have IRA? The tribes that did not adopt IRA rode on the coattails of IRA. Tribes have drafted constitutions, and the interior secretary has approved constitutions, even though they were not under the IRA. If it had not been for IRA, there would not be any tribal government operating with a constitution and now claiming they were better off without IRA. All tribal government is tied to IRA, and the basic authority for tribal government in dealing with the federal government is the IRA.

It is hard for Congress to enact legislation if there is a lot of opposition. All the BIA has to do is defend the IRA, and Congress cannot upset it. Congress is not going to pass a law that terminates a tribe unless the BIA goes along with it. The IRA has never been materially changed, as far as the government is concerned, in fifty years. It may never be changed. When people criticize the IRA, they had better look at the whole situation, because it did stabilize tribal governments and lead to congressional recognition of tribal governments. Once a constitution is made, it is cast in stone. It is there forever, but it can be amended. You will not find me criticizing IRA or criticizing Collier. The IRA has stabilized tribal government and put the Indian people and Indian tribes where they are today.

CHAPTER FIVE

The IRA and Indian Culture, Religion, and Arts

Alfonso Ortiz, Oren Lyons, Dave Warren, Francis McKinley

Collier worked intuitively. He trusted his vision of what Indians should be doing. Collier thought that all Indians were essentially similar. Taos Pueblo was his model for all Indians. This included tribes that had almost disappeared in a cultural sense. Collier wanted to put their societies and ceremonies back together again. He had, in one sense, an anthropological vision but it was not the reality that anthropologists found after they had studied contemporary Indian groups.

Fred Eggan, anthropologist

The principle thing wrong with IRA is that it is based on the theory that the government can make the tribes operate according to Euro-American ethics. These ethics assume that economic development and profit making are the backbone of progress. . . . The government did not take into account that the Indians had a different way of living. All that the older people wanted was a piece of their land to live on the rest of their lives. Instead, they were saddled with Christian work ethics. . . . The IRA destroyed the Indian way of doing things. The manner of handling Indian affairs in the old days worked. . . . Most tribal elections held throughout the country are contested the minute they are over. In the old days, when we selected leaders by consensus, there was not that kind of situation. The Crow are a good example of how consensus works. They have a general council where all the tribal members attend and make their decisions. When they come out with a decision, there is nobody to blame, because everybody had a hand in it.

Elmer Savilla, director,
National Tribal Chairmen's Association

[92]

ALFONSO ORTIZ

There are many, including me, that believe the most enduring contribution that the Collier policies made to Indian life, especially after half a century, was to encourage traditional cultural expression. I would like to read a couple of sentences from an obituary essay that D'Arcy McNickle chose to write about Collier in *The Nation* just after Collier's death in 1968. He quoted Collier on his experience in 1920 after visiting Taos Pueblo. McNickle observed.

> Watching the dancers, he [Collier] realized these were unsentimental men who could neither read nor write, poor men who lived by hard work, men who were told every day in all kinds of unsympathetic ways that all they believed in and cared for had to die and who never answered back, for these men were at one with their gods.

It is from this attitude that you can understand why Collier wanted Indian people to have religious self-expression, why he wanted to have them feel free in the schools to give expression to their Indian languages and their native arts and crafts.

This may be a regional bias, but in the Southwest, from my reading of the evidence, the impact of IRA was delayed and it was most important really in the area of traditional cultural self-expression. What happened with the Collier New Deal policy was basically to give us breathing room, to let the dancers, let the arts, come back. The arts were not in good shape in the late 1920s and early 1930s. But after the Santa Fe Indian School, through the person of Dorothy Dunn, started encouraging the art program, there was a tremendous efflorescence in Indian art. Granted, latter-day critics have termed it part of the old colonialism, because it was Indian cultural self-expression, but it was channeled into what the well-meaning teachers of that time considered to be genuine traditional Indian art. It was not until after 1962 that a new context was provided for a more creative and individualized artistic expression at the Institute of American Indian Arts.

But back in the 1930s there was an outpouring of basically how the world looked to the people who were at the Santa Fe Indian School at that time. This tremendous efflorescence primarily occurred in traditional religion and the expressive arts. The councils were still conservative. They were still religious, and they continued to be, in some cases, to the present time. The approval of the IRA was, if you interpret it in political terms, an effort to get the government off our backs so that we could go on as we had before. Tribal councils did not want to change, except for those three pueblos in New Mexico that adopted the IRA constitutions.

OREN LYONS

The Six Nations of the Iroquois have taken a very strong position with regard to the IRA. We simply have refused to submit to the IRA. We got a lot of contrary discussion going because our positions were pretty fierce, but we have always been advocates of peace and prosperity.

Al Ortiz has talked about the process of government by his governors and the mediation by the families. He has talked about clans, and that is our system at home. We have clans and we have clan chiefs, and we do precisely what he was describing; but it is contemporary. He was talking about fifty years ago; but I am certain that this process continues today for the Pueblos, but it has been subjugated by a stronger authority —the IRA.

From my perspective as a member of the Council of Chiefs at Onondaga, very often we deal very directly with political questions. I think you have to carefully define the difference between law and politics, and this is what I do not hear. The IRA is a method of bringing in another law to Indian territory. It then activates itself, and it becomes the supreme power. So we have not allowed that to happen, and I hope we do not. The Council of Chiefs that sits at Onondaga and the rest of the Iroquois nations are not paid by the government. Acceptance of money from the federal government is an intrusion. The price that you pay for this budget is your freedom. If tribes are willing to bargain their freedom for money, there is a serious problem for Indian people. It is necessary to look into the future. Our council has been mandated by ancient law that every decision we come to must reflect on the seventh generation in the future. If you have this perspective, which I know all Indian nations have, you really are always concerned about the future. This is the primary law. If you want to talk law, then there really is only one law and that is the natural law.

What was it that Collier saw of value in Indian life? What was he trying to preserve? You know what he was trying to preserve: it was a peaceful community. The United States as it stands today has very little community. Indian nations still have community. For them, the most important thing is how people are going to live together. If laws are not in accordance with natural law, they are going to fail. Indian societies contain pockets of information and understanding that must be preserved for your own preservation. If you kill off our culture and our way, you may kill off your last exit. You may have closed off your last way out.

All the people gathered here have a common goal, and that is survival of life. That is one reason I am here—because we are concerned about the welfare of the world, and our Indian people on this continent have been given a lot of instructions and understanding on how to preserve this. And that is what you are going to lose, that is what Collier saw.

DAVE WARREN

I think what we are trying to draw out of the study of John Collier is an understanding of the effort to bring about change and reform in reaction to what the Dawes Act set in motion. But what we are dealing with in the final analysis is a bureaucracy, and this is not only the Bureau of Indian Affairs. One tends to look at a person as a savior or as a devil and expect that the system will follow behind that person. Well, I think that at a certain moment, as it comes into power, any new administration leaves an imprint. But insofar as the kind of radical change that John Collier was talking about is concerned (essentially decentralizing government and making local tribal governments and tribal communities the masters of their own destiny), one has to look at the apparatus that was supposed to dismantle itself and to allow this kind of decentralization to take place. If you look at the overall theme of the New Deal, it was highly centralized government, so there is contradiction in that. You have to study the institution itself as much as personality.

How much do we know of the institutions of bureaucracy that were established by IRA within the tribal governments? What kind of character have they taken on? I have specifically in mind the difficulties that the pueblo of Santa Clara is dealing with in defining what the Indian law is in relation to civil rights legislation. The question of defining what is tribal membership—who is eligible for certain services that the tribal government will allow to be given to the bona fide legitimate members—has caused the document called the constitution to suddenly take on a life of its own; and people are using that as if it were a surrogate or certainly a new kind of living authority.

We need to look at Collier, it seems to me, in terms of cultural perspectives. Was he fully aware of the implications of using tradition and traditional institutions, in other words, the past that lives through to the present, as a basis of coping with the reality of the present? Those constitutions, it seems to me, were to be enabling devices, instruments for the tribal community to begin to see itself as part of or transitioning into a relationship with the greater society; but the very organization or format of traditional institutions was in and of itself alien. I am speaking of a theocratic form of government, in the case of Santa Clara Pueblo, that suddenly had to work with a kind of split between church and state. What we are dealing with here is who has the authority, the religious authorities or the tribal government called the council?

I have even heard it said, in talking to some of the people at Santa Clara, that maybe we need to draw away from the present issues, which are very difficult, and see what started all this conflict. And they are looking at and talking about the constitution to determine whether that constitution should be retained. If it is retained, how must it be modified to take into account existing provisions which allow tribal government and tribal law to become an instrument of all the people. The younger generations, in particular, have come to feel that such provisions create real leverage on their behalf for their equal rights. Now that is an extreme position. There is also the question of how these constitutions deal with communal versus equal rights, democratic representation, and legislative, administrative, and judicial due process. Those kinds of fundamental enabling elements perhaps were not dealt with adequately or dealt with at all in the IRA period.

The other part of the bureaucracy, cultural bureaucracy, has to do with that human element that must change attitudinally in order for reform and innovation to take place. And you find in the case of the Bureau of Indian Affairs, and it is no different than any corporation, that there is a way to do things. Ultimately, there is a job at stake: if you dismantle yourself, you do not have a job. Yet, ironically, you are supposed to be training the very people that you are administering services to, to take over what you do. There is a kind of an ethos of self-preservation in that culture of bureaucracy as well.

I suggest, as one kind of wild-eyed notion, that the Indian community has now gained self-determination in ways that even Collier could not have thought about. This has happened because of the development of certain authorities and the location of certain resources on Indian reservations and because of the role that Indian reservation lands play in the westward development of the United States. They have taken on tremendous importance in the regional and, in some ways, national development of this country. That is not going to last forever. The land development business is not local, state, or regional development; it is international development. International companies are looking at targeting those lands in and around Indian reservations as high-yield investment opportunities. They are corporations with power and money and the ability to influence state and national level governments on their own behalf.

Now the question becomes (Oren Lyons has referred to it, and maybe we are returning to full circle) what is fundamental and what is valuable to the Indian community as a basis of its value system and its identity? We must also realistically look at what has intervened in that system over the years. In IRA we happen to be dealing with what was, in some ways, a critical intervention for positive development. That did not last long enough to be fully implemented, but it opened the doors and set some precedents. It created institutions that we are having to deal with, either to roll back or to reevaluate. But what do we put in its place? What are those fundamental things called language, culture, custom, and law that somehow have to be incorporated in the new Indian society's government and administrative system? Now, those who have been affected by IRA or affected by any number of other outside influences for a long period of time are having to rediscover and reinstate many things that may not be as integral as what Oren Lyons talks about in his own community.

FRANCIS MCKINLEY

I am a member of the Northern Ute tribe, at the Uintah and Ouray Agency in Utah. During the last fifty years under the IRA, there have been, in my opinion, two tracks that my people have lived under, one track being the political bureaucracy, or anything that is connected with self-government. The other track has been the people themselves, how they have adapted and adjusted, and how they have lived their culture; and I think they would live their culture in spite of the IRA or whatever else. This is what Oren Lyons was talking about.

During the last fifty years my people have retained their cultural beliefs, but they also have adopted other kinds of values. There exists a kind of Indianism among them: they have adopted many of the customs of other tribes. As far as my government is concerned, it has adopted the trappings of the federal government to get money, and it has to abide by federal guidelines that are operative. It has developed into an institution that makes its constituents obligated to that government. It is the old question that political theorists talk about: is it the citizen's responsibility to the state or is it the consent of the governed?

It used to be said that a Navajo family consisted of a father, mother, several children, and an anthropologist. You could say the same thing about the Utes. I grew up around anthropologists. In fact, I am a subject of some of their writings, and I do not recognize myself. I used to sit around listening to anthropologists talk shop. Both Margaret Mead and Ruth Benedict were involved, and Ruth Benedict, of course, was involved with Collier. Now, I know that they were influential among the Indians. They were very influential in the culture both in positive and, in some degrees, negative ways. I am interested in examining what influence those people had.

DAVE WARREN

The short answer to Francis's question is that the influence of anthropologists did not really last beyond the Collier administration. They joined the war effort and never came back together again in the Bureau. Both Collier and D'Arcy McNickle were unable to secure adequate research funds for the Bureau. Unless the Bureau had research funds, it really could not engage anthropologists to find new ways of serving the Indian people. So the influence of anthropology has not been that great directly through the Bureau.

Ruth Benedict was very influential because of her book *Patterns of Culture*. You mentioned Margaret Mead; she too has been influential, but indirectly, by writing books for consumption by the American people. For a long time *Patterns of Culture* was the most widely read book by an anthropologist ever written. It has just been discarded as simplistic, and that discrediting has finally trickled down to people who used to judge anthropology by Ruth Benedict's *Patterns of Culture*. But influence like that is much more serious and enduring.

The 1880s through the 1920s was the era of the Vanishing American, and anthropologists busied themselves buying every artifact, sometimes stealing some, to put them in boxes and sacks to ship them off to eastern museums. They also recorded the sayings without any sense of directional organization, without any sense that there were systems of knowledge and belief; and they just recorded them in notebooks and published them willy-nilly. These books from that era read like the yellow pages of a telephone book.

That era was succeeded by another era, which we might term the "shreds and patches view" of culture. The "shreds and patches view" was a term actually used by University of California anthropologist Robert Lowie. This was the view that there was no coherence to the cultures of Indian people; they were too primitive. In the post-World War II era, anthropologists finally began to formulate the notion that these cultures were complex, coherent, highly adaptable systems that enabled Indian people to survive. Anthropologists finally began to begrudgingly acknowledge that we are going to be around for a while and that these cultures, instead of fading away before the advance of the white man, were fighting back tenaciously, and then a whole new kind of series of questions began to be formulated. A new premise, if you will, began to be formulated in anthropology and the other human studies focusing on Indian peoples, namely, that these are complex and coherent systems.

Now the techniques of the 1880s through the 1940s were not going to comprehend that kind of Indian tenacity or serve a new, broader vision. And now, we are in an era where Indian people are formulating a lot of the questions that anthropologists ask instead of just having them formulated in the universities. Francis is absolutely right. In that era they were being formulated only in the universities, and Indians were asked only to respond to the questions that the professors formulated for their graduate students at the universities. Those questions were based upon ongoing arguments that existed only in anthropology.

OREN LYONS

Questions have been raised about the wisdom of putting the IRA and traditional systems together. I mentioned before that there are value systems. The IRA—your ultimate source of authority—is James Watt at this point. He has a lot of authority over what happens on Indian land. That authority was vested in him through the IRA. And whoever it is, whoever it comes to be, one of the reasons why the Onondaga nation rejected the IRA is simply we did not want to vest authority in somebody living some ten states away or in the federal government. We will maintain our own authority.

Our people had a vote on the IRA, and it was rather close. The reason why it was so close was because people did not believe in voting, but one of the chiefs went house to house at the last minute and said, "If you ever vote in your whole life, you better vote this time." They overturned the process, and we have survived, and we are in existence today. We are recognized by the federal government: we are probably the only nation in the country receiving treaty cloth today.

We could not see putting our system, which was both political and spiritual, in one system. The political situation that the IRA would institute is a separate American form of government that would allow the experts to come from Washington. If you get in trouble running an IRA government, you are going to have to go to Washington because that is where its authority comes from. When you have your own authority and your own power, it becomes harder for federal officials to influence what is going on in your council. The values in our system and in the system of the United States government are too diverse for us to put them together in one place.

CHAPTER SIX

The IRA Record and John Collier

Philleo Nash, Wilcomb Washburn, Robert Burnette,
Russell Jim, Earl Old Person, LaDonna Harris, Ted Katcheak

*Collier's vision has been realized more than he or most others would
have dreamed possible in 1934. Indian tribal governments, however arti-
ficial they may have seemed to the Indians who chose them or to the anthropologists who had studied pre-IRA Indian organizations, are now autonomous, functioning political organisms, capable of maintaining themselves
against the power of their white neighbors as well as against the power of
the states and federal government. In what period of the Indians' existence
can the same statement be made . . . ?*

Wilcomb E. Washburn, Smithsonian Institution

*The unique events of two generations, culminating in a crisis of poli-
tical necessity, catapulted this man into a position of historic importance.
He rode to office on the wings of those events. He stood on the shoulders
of many who had gone before and made himself into a figure of national
importance and influence. But John Collier betrayed us. His autocratic
administration and repressive administration damned him before the
Indians, creating that fault line in historic estimates of Collier and his
works which finally cast him from his seat at the side of the white man's
Jesus Christ, where some historians have mistakenly placed him.*

Rupert Costo, Cahuilla, president of the
American Indian Historical Society

[101]

PHILLEO NASH

In 1934, the year of the passage of the Indian Reorganization Act, I was in a student party doing research on Klamath Indian Reservation in southern Oregon. We were told by our teacher and leader, "Do not go near the Indian agency, because, if you do, the Indian people will not talk to you." This excited my curiosity. The following year I came back to see what the Klamath Agency was like.

During the first full year of the IRA, I was doing research around the agency and I attended tribal council sessions. The Klamath Agency at that time was small. Many of the old buildings were still in use. I was anxious to locate the tribal records that went back to the early days of the agency, in the 1870s. I found them in the hayloft of an old barn. I spent all of November and December 1935 sorting through the agency records. The archives of the United States had not yet been created, but I managed to get them into a vault. Wade Crawford was the first Indian superintendent. He was one of the very early Indian superintendents whom John Collier appointed on the principle that the Indian people ought to be looking after their own affairs. Crawford was violently opposed in later years and, I think, even then to the IRA.

I was a young anthropologist. Generally speaking, anthropologists have regarded themselves as friends of the Indians and enemies of the Bureau of Indian Affairs. When I became commissioner, Wade called on me, and he said, "I never thought I would ever see you behind that desk." It was clear that he thought that I had sold-out. I said, "Well, Wade, you know, as we get older, we all learn. I learned that this is a place where you can do some good, and I am very happy."

I also said, "Things were not always that good, Wade, when you were the first Indian superintendent at Klamath." I reminded him of those tribal council meetings where individual members voted on whether or not to relieve the timber company of its obligations under a cutting contract. At that time, there was bitterness and mild corruption on the Klamath Reservation.

Let me switch the scene. The Indian group nearest to my boyhood home was the Wisconsin band of the Winnebago tribe. They had never received a chance, as far as I know, to vote for the IRA. One of the first things that I did when I became commissioner was to see to it that they had an opportunity. It was not too late, even after thirty years. The

Winnebagos were desperately poor. These are the people who went to Nebraska with all sorts of promises in the 1870s, became disillusioned, and drifted back to Wisconsin where they became squatters in their own home territory.

Since 1930, when I first started attending Wisconsin Winnebago powwows, I have followed intimately the organization of the Wisconsin band of the Winnebago tribe. In the 1930s, they were unhappy, disorganized, and poor. Today, they are not too happy and are somewhat disorganized, but they have a tribal government, and it is a real government. They have elections, and they have different parties or groups. I am not going to use the word "factions." Although things are not perfect, the Winnebago have gained a sense of identity and organization. They feel that they have a future which is quite different from the pre-IRA days.

I do not agree with two observations made earlier about John Collier. He did not want to separate religion from economics and government. I knew Collier over a period of years: he was not abrasive; he was a soul of kindness and generosity and had a very forgiving nature. He had to push the IRA through a hostile Congress which was not committed to Indian reform. Abrasiveness is in the eye of the beholder; sometimes it is in the skin of the beholder. If you are scratched it hurts. It seems to me that Joseph Bruner, who liked fascism and joined the German-American Bund, received a rather gentle letter from Collier. I can assure you that when I got that kind of treatment, as commissioner, I was not anywhere near that polite.

Furthermore, the economic development programs had their births in the IRA. The chartered corporations and the $10 million revolving loan program were intended to get the tribes into business for themselves and to alleviate some of the terrible poverty. When I became commissioner in 1961, Congress had appropriated only $3 or $4 million for the IRA revolving credit fund. This is one of the reasons why Indian people have a very legitimate gripe against the way in which the United States government does things. Programs are started, and they do not receive adequate appropriations. This leads to frustration. You can lay it at the hands of an over-organized bureaucracy. All I can say is that it is like the old man who approached death. He said the alternative to getting old is much worse. The tribes were dying in 1932, in my opinion.

WILCOMB WASHBURN

I would like to elaborate on the apparent contradiction between Collier's approach to Indian culture and religion on the one hand and his approach to economics and politics on the other. There is no real contradiction. The alternative to involving tribes in the context of the American political system was not that they would remain independent nation-states. It was that they would be extinguished entirely. I do not think there would be a single Indian tribe in existence today if it had not been for John Collier and the Indian Reorganization Act. People like Rupert Costo and others seem to think that the alternative was some ideal form of independent sovereignty, which simply was not in the cards. John Collier knew this. He was trying to save the "grouphood" of the Indian tribes from extinction. The Indian today would be merely an individual in the body politic of the United States but for John Collier and the Indian Reorganization Act.

Most of the critiques of John Collier have simply overlooked this reality. They judge his work against an ideal standard, on the one hand, or against his character, on the other hand. Philleo Nash has contradicted the assumption that he was nasty to people. But even if he was abrasive, even if he was mean to his sons, and even if he was contemptuous with people who opposed him, that is irrelevant. If you judge what he did in terms of the Indian Reorganization Act, he saved the Indian tribes from extinction. There would not have been this turnabout in Indian affairs without Collier. The American Indians would have disappeared as separate tribal entities.

ROBERT BURNETTE

I remember John Collier coming to the Rosebud Indian Boarding School and exactly what he said there. I felt like we were being fooled. I was not allowed to speak my language at the Indian boarding school. If we did, we got a whipping. But I did learn one thing: it was how to be real feisty and persistent.

In 1946, I came home fresh out of the Marine Corps. The tribal council was not fully operative at that time. There was a credit committee that approved loans for selected individuals, if the superintendent gave his approval. Once in a while, the tribal council would meet and the superintendent would record the proceedings. A big rancher by the name of Tom Arnold stood at the door after each council meeting. He paid off the councilmen. They each received three dollars to facilitate the exchange of tribal land.

In 1951, I became a councilman. Three years later, I was elected chairman of the Rosebud Sioux tribe. The Rosebud Fair was taking place, and we had only five Indian dancers that were costumed to dance, from all of the Sioux nation in that area. I wondered, Why are there only five Indian dancers? What was happening to our culture and our religion?

I went back up to the tribal council hall the next day and looked at our Rosebud Sioux tribal code, which comes from the Indian Reorganization Act. There was a law on the books which prohibited the Lakota Indian religion, and there was another law that prohibited peyote. Members of the tribe received a $360 fine or six months in jail for committing either offense. A short time after I became chairman, we were confronted with termination and Public Law 280. We fought tooth and nail to get rid of it. I realized that this all came from a little brown book. It had all the law on the Indian Reorganization Act, and our charter, constitution, and bylaws. I quickly found out what IRA was all about.

I soon discovered that there was another book called *CFR—Title 25—Indians*. That book really put the harness on us. Not one of the eighteen councilmen—and some of them had been on there since the beginning of it—knew about CFR. That is how well-informed the superintendent kept them.

I also found out there was an Indian affairs manual, and this manual contained the policy of the Bureau of Indian Affairs. It told the employees what they had to do. Being an ex-serviceman, who fought and almost died in World War II, it struck home that I was handcuffed. I could not get a loan from any bank because I was an Indian. It stirred me up something fantastic. So we started a battle that is still going on today.

The Indian people do not have any rights. None of us are able to enter a United States district court and settle our grievances against our own elected leadership. We spent nine years fighting for the Indian

Civil Rights Act. I do not think there is hardly an Indian leader today who realizes that Public Law 280 disappeared because of this act.

The Indian Reorganization Act was a suppressive kind of government. This so-called Self-Determination Act is a deadly weapon against the Indians. It is misleading practically every Indian leader in this country into believing that some day they are going to have an Indian utopia where Indians can make their own decisions. That is not true, my friends. We have endorsed self-determination, not realizing that if we ever attain it there will also be an end to the government's trust responsibility; and that is something we need to think about.

RUSSELL JIM

Today, the tribes are faced with annihilation and extinction—no different than they were in the days of John Collier. The Yakima nation did not believe Collier was the one that saved Indian country. He does not sit at the right hand of God. But the Yakima nation commemorated Collier because of his perceptiveness.

I fully agree about self-determination being one of the ruses brought on by the federal government. Each and every administration has contributed in one form or another toward the genocide of the indigenous people of this land. For instance, the Yakima nation and a few other timber tribes were lured, in 1977, to Billings, Montana. There, federal officials said, "Five million dollars will be divided among you if you will accept Public Law 93638 in its entirety." The Yakima said, "We do not need reforestation, and there are only certain portions of P.L. 93638 which we will accept." Within two weeks, that five million dollars mysteriously disappeared back into the United States treasury.

The Yakima nation had a society that was like a government. We had unwritten rules and regulations. The formulation of Yakima self-government was not easily achieved. Self-government such as the IRA is government proposed by the main stem of society. In our society everything was linked together, and it came from the laws of the Creator. Our unwritten laws are passed from heart-to-heart, generation-to-generation. Whatever the IRA or P.L. 93-638 attempted to do, they were intended to assimilate us into the mainstream of society.

EARL OLD PERSON

I came on board as a Blackfeet tribal leader in 1954, but I have also acted as an interpreter for the Indian people on my reservation. I cannot go along with the idea that someone such as John Collier came along and saved us. We have had very strong, dedicated leaders who were determined to help our people keep and to hang on to their land. These far-sighted leaders also were determined to preserve our beliefs.

I think the Indian Reorganization Act gave a little more power to the government. According to the old-timers, it was brought to the people with a promise of self-government and the right to administer their own affairs. This sounded awful good to some of our people. But the full-blood people fought against the IRA. They were skeptical because of the many things that had taken place in the past.

Many of my people referred to this law as the Wheel-law. And they said, "We are afraid of that wheel." Today they talk about this as a wheel that is rolling the opposite way. Those old leaders often confronted Burton K. Wheeler. They said, "What about this law? We do not see how it is working for us, even though it might be working for a few people." The response often was "I thought that it was going to work for the Indian people, but it has been administered in a wrong way."

The Blackfeet old-timers have often talked about the vote to accept the IRA. They said that it happened when the majority of people were not there because of bad weather. Once it existed on the reservation, they accepted it. They said, "All right, we are going to have to see what it is going to do for us." They were informed that after ten years they could either do away with it or change it. The Blackfeet did make amendments after ten years, but the people were still against it. We may have had tribal self-government, but I do not see where it changed in any significant way the previous governments that we had.

Many of my people have wanted to do away with the IRA. But government officials told them, "You must come up with a program or something that will replace the IRA." They also said that "Other tribes are using it, and we can not do away with it because it is not working right for you."

We can see that we were not really given self-government. Back in the early 1950s, we wanted to sell a small sawmill. We went to our Bureau people, and they said, "You can not do it." The Blackfeet people responded, "No, we are going to go elsewhere for help." And so, we began to make our turn toward meaningful self-determination.

LaDonna Harris

Economic development is not working under IRA because our instruments of government are inappropriate. We could spend lots of money, and it still would not work. We do not have the institutional structure to make it work. In reviewing what happened, I would like to think that John Collier's idea was great, but when it came to being implemented, somebody in the Bureau said, "Okay, what is constitutional government?" And just like they used to do with the old lease agreements, someone pulled out an old constitution and passed it around the country. The Comanche and other tribes adopted it because the Bureau said that is what you should do in order to function. Nobody, including the Bureau, understood how it was actually going to work.

As we became more enlightened and more sophisiticated, we realized that this document was not working. We have become mere extensions of a federal government in order to carry out federal programs. We are not governing ourselves in any sense of the word that governance means. Right now, everybody is in turmoil. Those first IRA instruments of government that we adopted never fit to begin with. They did not fit the uniqueness of each of the cultures, and they did not work. This is my perception of what happened to the Comanche. The Comanche said, "Well, we are going to pass this constitution to get white people off our back. Who needs it? We will not use it anyway."

Ted Katcheak

I am going to explain how we view IRA in Alaska. In the past our village had a traditional council with no written charter. Decisions were made by word of mouth. The people got together in a place called Passigook. In the evening, when it cooled down, they sat around and talked about the events of the year. They also talked with certain people that had made trouble with the village.

My village has a charter and bylaws under the 1936 Alaska Reorganization Act. Because of that, I am here representing my village. I am also the co-chairman of the United Tribes of Alaska, which was formed last May. How I interpret the IRA or Alaska Reorganization Act in my village is different from the people here in the lower forty-eight.

The Alaska Reorganization Act is the only thing that is left in the village that can speak for the people and protect their land. We really do not have a right to our land now, because the Alaska Native Settlement Act extinguished our aboriginal rights and claims. We have some people living in my village who have been past ARA council members. They still want this act to be in the villages. It is the only tool that can work for the people.

Perhaps there should be an alternative to the IRA. In some areas of Alaska, it does not work. It does not do what it is supposed to accomplish. The people have a lot of different problems. If you can find a meaningful alternative to IRA, I could be happy with some other form of self-government.

PART TWO

Termination

Omaha Indians at a temporary road camp near the Winnebago Agency in 1936 or 1937.

The Navajo mounted patrol in the 1930s.

The Indians were descendants of peoples who knew, before the onslaught of a foreign culture, the freedom of the eagle on wing all across the North American continent. Under Crazy Horse they beat the pants off Custer on the Little Big Horn in a final attempt to preserve it. They won the battle but lost the war. They died mercilessly with Chief Big Foot at Wounded Knee because they did not have that freedom.

The 1930s held a ray of hope that they would again see some of the freedom reappear with the passage of the Indian Reorganization Act. The rising tide of expectations for Indians soared into the 1940s. It disappeared in the dark clouds of World War II.

If Hitler, Mussolini, and Hirohito were bent on destroying freedom, Indians would gladly suffer their sons and daughters to join the battle; most of them did not wait to be drafted. The BIA offices were moved from the Capitol to make space for personnel needed there to prosecute the war. Tribal members left home for far away places to help build ships, tanks, and airplanes. At home they endured the effects of leaner budgets—no law and order personnel in some places, health facilities poorly staffed, if at all—and willingly gave up land for bombing ranges. All these and more hardships they cheerfully endured.

The Indians believed that when the dark clouds of war passed from the skies overhead, their rising tide of expectations, though temporarily stalled, would again reappear. Instead, they were threatened by termination. After the devastation in Europe, there was the Marshall Plan; Japan had its course set by MacArthur. For the Indians, on the other hand, there was House Concurrent Resolution 108. Soaring expectations began to plunge. Termination took on the connotation of extermination for many.

Benjamin Reifel, Sioux, former congressman from
South Dakota and commissioner of Indian affairs

Has the relocation of Indian people been successful? The answer remains as complex and varied as the different people who participated in the program. Unquestionably, those people who took part in the process after 1958 (and who generally were better prepared for their urban experience) achieved a higher degree of "success" than did many of the earlier participants. Indeed, a significant number of Indians from throughout the program's history have "made it" in the white man's world, and although many periodically revisit their former reservation communities, they remain permanently settled in their urban surroundings, successfully supporting themselves and their families.

Others have been less fortunate. They have been poorly prepared to cope with life in the city and have continued to eke out a living in the fringe area of the urban environment. Shackled by the realities of city life, many of these people exist in a limbo comprised of poverty, welfare, and frustration. Of course poverty and frustration also existed back on the reservation, but within the tribal communities individuals had the security of membership in an extended circle of family and friends. There were heavy burdens to bear, but on the reservations the load could always be shared. . . .

There seems to be one general consensus about the Indians' urban existence. Separated from old friends and family and set adrift in an urban wasteland, many of the Indian people have gravitated toward new communities emerging in response to the impersonality of city life. Often centered around urban "Indian centers," new Indian communities have arisen in which the shared experiences of city life transcend many of the older ties to tribes and reservations. Almost all urban Indian people still identify themselves as members of tribal groups, but many have much more in common with other urban Indians, regardless of their tribal affiliations, than with their kinsmen back on the reservation.

It is in the cities that the modern pan-Indian movement flourishes. Lumped together as "Indians" by whites, many urban Indian people have come to see themselves more as "Indians" and less as members of any particular tribe. It is ironic, therefore, that the BIA and the urban experience have done more to foster the pan-Indian movement than all the great chiefs of the past.

R. David Edmunds, Cherokee, professor of
history, Texas Christian University

CHAPTER ONE
Termination as Federal Policy: An Overview

James E. Officer

Thirty years ago this month, on August 1, 1953, the Eighty-third Congress put its stamp of approval on House Concurrent Resolution 108.* With this action, the lawmakers declared themselves disposed, as a matter of official policy, to dissolve the special relationship that through much of the country's history had bound the federal government to the Native American population. Nowhere in the resolution do we find any mention of the word *termination* that has come to carry such ominous portent in more recent times. Rather, the tone of the document is one of emancipation and equalization: "To end the wardship status of the Indians and to grant them all of the rights and prerogatives pertaining to American citizenship."

Although the "whereas" clauses of the resolution state general policy, the "resolved" section is more specific. Singled out for mention as the first groups to be "freed from Federal supervision and control and from all disabilities and limitations applicable to Indians" are the Flathead tribe of Montana, the Klamath tribe of Oregon, the Menominee tribe of Wisconsin, the Potawatomie tribe of Kansas and Nebraska, the Chippewa of the Turtle Mountain Reservation in North Dakota, and all of the Indian tribes and "individual members thereof" located within the states of California, Florida, New York, and Texas.

---

* The full text of the resolution has been reprinted many times. It and numerous other documents of major importance in the field of Indian administration are to be found in Part II of the book *A Short History of the Indians of the United States* by Edward H. Spicer (Van Norstrand Reinhold Company, 1969).

Some of the groups targeted by Congress in its 1953 action had enjoyed the questionable distinction of being similarly mentioned on previous occasions. In his testimony before the Senate Committee on Civil Service in 1947, Acting Commissioner of Indian Affairs William Zimmerman, Jr. had named the Flathead, Klamath, Menominee, Potawatomi, Six Tribes of New York, certain of the California Indians, and —on a conditional basis—the Turtle Mountain Chippewa as groups that with proper precautions might be released immediately from federal supervision. In the Turtle Mountain case, the condition imposed by Zimmerman was that North Dakota, with federal financial assistance, assume responsibility for the continuing administration of the affairs of all Indians within its jurisdiction, including, of course, the Turtle Mountain Chippewa.[†]

In December 1952, just over five years after Zimmerman's reluctant appearance on Capitol Hill, the Bureau of Indian Affairs provided Congress a new list of tribes that it considered ready for emancipation. That list, too, included the Flathead, Klamath, Menominee, Potawatomi, and Turtle Mountain Chippewa as well as groups in New York and California; but it expanded Zimmerman's list considerably to cover all the Indians of Michigan, Texas, and Louisiana; most of those in western Washington and western Oregon; the Osage of Oklahoma; the Nez Perce and Coeur d'Alene of Idaho; and several small groups in Kansas, Nebraska, and Iowa.[‡] Given the length of the list submitted by the Indian Bureau in its 1952 report, it might be suggested that Congress in Resolution 108 showed considerable restraint in targeting so few groups. While the Seminole of Florida were introduced to the roster as a congressional "add-on," the legislators omitted a number of others, perhaps—I might suggest cynically—because of the reluctance of particular congressmen to have their constituents singled out in this fashion.

Later I shall discuss the actions that took place following the passage of House Concurrent Resolution 108, but before doing so, I should like to emphasize that the resolution, or one quite similar to it, might easily have come ten years earlier. In May 1943, Oklahoman

---

[†] *Investigation of the Bureau of Indian Affairs*, H.R. Rep. 2053, 82nd Cong., 2nd sess. (1952), 161–178.

[‡] *Ibid.*, pp. 28–30.

Elmer Thomas, chairman of the Senate Investigating Subcommittee and an adversary of John Collier from the beginning of that commissioner's administration, prepared a report known as S-310 calling for abolition of the Bureau of Indian Affairs. Signed by such other senators as Burton K. Wheeler, co-author of the Indian Reorganization Act, and New Mexico's Dennis Chavez, Thomas's report stated that Commissioner Collier's policies "promoted segregation, made the Indian a guinea pig for experimentation, tied him to the land in perpetuity, and made him satisfied with all the limitations of primitive life."*

The full Congress—its attention diverted to the war effort—was scarcely in a position to give serious consideration to a dramatic internal move such as abolishing the BIA, but the House committee concerned with Indian affairs did hold hearings on the subject, to which they invited Commissioner Collier.† His appearance provided a public opportunity to point out the many deficiencies, distortions, and inaccuracies of the Senate report. It also supplied an occasion to place before the House subcommittee copies of letters addressed to Senator Thomas and signed by himself and Interior Secretary Harold Ickes. These letters, both undoubtedly drafted by the commissioner, are masterpieces of the Collier writing style.‡

Both begin by expressing a certain amazement that a dedicated friend of the Indians such as the Oklahoma lawmaker could possibly have allowed his name to be associated in any way with such a sneaky attack. They go on to outline the basic recommendations of the report: closure of all day schools on allotted reservations; closure of boarding schools wherever situated; discontinuance of tuition payments to public school districts enrolling Indian youngsters; transfer of hospitals to the Public Health Service for general, as opposed to exclusively Indian, use; transfer of Indian forest management to the Department of Agriculture; immediate liquidation of the Bureau of Indian Affairs; distribution of tribal funds to member Indians on a per capita basis; and

---

* S. Rep. 310, 78th Cong., 1st sess. (1943). Quotes from this report are to be found in *John Collier's Crusade for Indian Reform 1920–1954* by Kenneth R. Philp (University of Arizona Press, 1977), p. 208.

† House Committee on Indian Affairs, *Investigation of the Bureau of Indian Affairs*, 78th Cong. (1944), pp. 28–29.

‡ *Ibid.*, pp. 30–39.

withdrawal of federal protection from all property, both individual and tribal.

Paragraph by paragraph, the Collier/Ickes letters quote from the Senate report, pointing out the glaring errors contained therein. With respect to the expenses of operating day schools, the commissioner and secretary observe that their annual cost is but $408,200, as compared with the $2,000,000 alluded to in S-310. In response to a contention that the Indian Bureau duplicates the functions of the Federal Division of Forestry and Grazing, the Interior Department officials carefully point out that there is no such agency as the Federal Division of Forestry and Grazing. With respect to the charge that Indians are "tax evaders," Collier and Ickes take objection to the notion that the Indian immunity from taxation should be classified as "evasion." On and on, page after page, the letters highlight and attack the statements of the report.

It is of passing interest to mention that in the Ickes letter to Senator Thomas, there is a reference to "terminating historic responsibilities."* This is one of the earliest instances I have encountered where the word "terminate" is used in any of its inflected forms to describe the process of ending the special relationship between Indians and the federal government. Even at the height of its actions to modify or dissolve this relationship, Congress carefully avoided employing the term, although it was used informally by members of that body, as well as by the Indians, the employees of the BIA, and the general public.

Neither the fulminations of Senators Thomas, Wheeler, and Chavez nor the hearings that followed them led to any action such as House Concurrent Resolution 108, but the fuss stirred up over S-310 and the commissioner's angry reaction to it did have some effect on Indian administration in the last years of Collier's term of office. Congressman Jed Johnson of Oklahoma, like his Senate colleague a bitter opponent of Collier, used his influence in the House Appropriations Committee to trim the BIA budget for fiscal year 1945 by $2,000,000— a sum that seems small by today's standards, but which at that time represented a disastrous cut.† Although Collier, when he resigned from his position in January 1945, cited his growing interest in international

---

* *Ibid.*, p. 38.
† Philp, p. 38.

affairs as the principal reason for his decision,‡ it seems not unlikely that he was also influenced by his discouragement over the constant and often losing battles with Congress and over the dogged determination of some of its members to "solve" the Indian problem by doing away with tribes, reservations, and the BIA.

William A. Brophy, Collier's successor, took office in March 1945, having established as one of his goals the passage of legislation creating a tribunal for hearing and deciding Indian claims against the federal government, something Collier had long advocated.* He succeeded in this endeavor in the late summer of 1946, thanks to an improvement in congressional-BIA relations following Collier's departure and, not unimportantly either, to the fact that the policy tide on Capitol Hill was running increasingly in the direction of withdrawing the federal government from so much responsibility in Indian affairs. The record of hearings on the various Indian claims bills considered in the seventy-ninth Congress makes clear that some powerful legislators believed that resolution of Indian claims would remove a major barrier to federal withdrawal and, where awards were made to tribes, would help to launch them on the way to economic self-sufficiency. Certain attorneys who later would become wealthy from fees earned in claims cases did little to discourage this thesis, and some openly espoused it.†

It would be a misrepresentation of the intent of Congress for me to suggest that the sole, or even the principal, reason for creating the Indian Claims Commission was to clear away underbrush that impeded the swift retreat of the federal government from its special responsibilities for Indians and Indian tribes; but it would be equally wrong for me to ignore that, for at least a few key congressmen, this was a primary reason for supporting the legislation. The late Arthur V. Watkins, who entered the United States Senate shortly after passage of the 1946 Act and who today is identified both with the commission that it created

---

‡ *Indians at Work*, Volume 12, No. 5, pp. 2–3. In this issue of the publication he directed during his administration, Collier includes a copy of his letter of resignation directed to President Franklin D. Roosevelt on January 19, 1945.

* *Annual Report of the Secretary of the Interior, 1946*, "Office of Indian Affairs," pp. 377–378.

† H.R. Rep. 1466, 79th Cong. (1945), p. 1351; and *Investigation of the Bureau of Indian Affairs*, p. 16.

and with the so-called termination policy, wrote in an article published in 1958:

> Completely within the historic policy of Congress in working toward the elimination of special controls over Indians is its concept of the role of the Indian Claims Commission. The Commission assures legal settlement of long-standing claims for redress against the federal government, which many Indians believe should be a necessary condition precedent to effective decontrol consideration.‡

In view of the foregoing, I am suggesting that, rather than visualize House Concurrent Resolution 108 as something dropped out of the blue into the congressional hopper at the beginning of the Eighty-third Congress in January 1953, we view it realistically as the culmination of a long and determined effort first manifested formally in the Claims Commission Act. In truth, from 1946 until enactment of the amendments to Public Law 83-280 in 1968, Congress took no formal action that we can clearly interpret as a retreat from the withdrawal policy articulated in House Concurrent Resolution 108. Although the defeat of the proposed heirship bills in 1964 signalled a victory for the Indian lobby, in that same session Congress directed the preparation of a program for withdrawal of all special federal services from the Seneca Indians of New York. Two years later, in 1966, the Senate Committee on Interior and Insular Affairs castigated the Indian Bureau for dragging its feet in planning for termination of the Choctaw and the Seneca; and Colville termination legislation remained under consideration for some time thereafter. Thus, if we are to look at the subject of termination from the congressional perspective, we must expand our time frame to more than just the decade of the 1950s.

Fewer than six months after passage of the Claims Commission Act, the Senate Committee on Civil Service, under the direction of William Langer, zeroed in on the Bureau of Indian Affairs as one of several federal agencies to be questioned about an excess of employees. According to popular belief in Congress then as now, the BIA is an organization bloated with personnel whose salaries and travel expenses drain off the

---

‡ Arthur V. Watkins, "Termination of Federal Supervision: The Removal of Restrictions Over Indian Property and Person," *American Indians and American Life*, Annals of the American Academy of Political and Social Science, Vol. 311 (1957).

vast sums that Congress appropriates for the direct benefit of Indians and Indian tribes.

Commissioner William A. Brophy was called upon to testify before the committee not long after it began its inquiry. Being ill, he was unable to comply, and it fell to Bill Zimmerman, the assistant commissioner, to respond. Upon the advice of Interior Department attorneys, he declined to do so. The Senate countered by placing him under subpoena.

The testimony finally presented by Zimmerman is lengthy and detailed.* He began by taking issue with certain drastic recommendations made by the House committee that three years before had conducted hearings on Senator Thomas's report. He went on to suggest that there could be two approaches to reducing the number of Indian Bureau employees—one being that of cutting back on the number and extent of services offered to Indians; the other, that of diminishing the size of the client population through withdrawing federal services altogether from some tribes. Zimmerman then divided BIA field units into three groups according to the condition of the tribes they comprehended: those from whom Indian Bureau services might be immediately withdrawn if certain criteria were met, those that might be ready for such withdrawal within ten years, and those that would require an indefinite time span of preparation before attaining such readiness.

From comments he made to me during the six months we served together on Secretary Stewart Udall's task force, I know that Bill Zimmerman was bitter over the use later made of his 1947 testimony. He was particularly disturbed that so little attention was paid to the four criteria he had proposed with respect to determining the readiness of a tribe for termination. These were its members' degree of acculturation, their economic condition, their willingness to end their special relationship with the federal government, and the willingness and ability of the states in which they lived to assume responsibility for their welfare.

Based on the events that transpired following Zimmerman's testimony, there seems little doubt that the leadership of the Indian Bureau considered termination to be the basic thrust of federal policy. Not long after he appeared before the Senate committee, the acting commissioner

* *Investigation of the Bureau of Indian Affairs*, pp. 161–178.

sent a directive to the heads of field units instructing them to pull together data from previous surveys of reservation resources in anticipation of major programs of economic and social development.[†] In this directive, he noted that beginning in 1943, many jurisdictions had prepared comprehensive long range development plans. These, said Zimmerman, would serve as the basis of efforts over the next few years. The objective of the programs, remarked the acting commissioner, "should be the eventual discharge of the Federal government's obligation, legal, moral, or otherwise, and the discontinuance of Federal supervision and control at the earliest possible date compatible with the government's trustee responsibility." He announced further that certain reservations had been selected to begin the effort and that these were divided into three categories: those in which the Indians had "progressed in the use of their resources and in adapting themselves to competitive society to such a degree as would warrant the withdrawal of the Indian Service in the near future," those "in an intermediate state," and those "in need of major rehabilitation continued over a period of years."

In October, 1948, four months after the ailing Commissioner Brophy had resigned, the Project Committee on Indian Affairs of the Commission on Organization of the Executive Branch of the Government—better known as the Hoover Commission—issued its long awaited report. Assimilation of the Indian population was highlighted as the major goal of federal policy, and the authors of the report observed that, under the trusteeship of the BIA, Indians had lost the education and experience necessary to manage their own affairs.[‡]

Late in the spring of 1949, John Ralph Nichols, who had served on the Hoover Commission, was named to head the Bureau of Indian Affairs. He remained in the office only eleven months, but in his annual

---

[†] Circular No. 36575, May 28, 1948, National Archives, Record Group 75, Numbered Circular File. Zimmerman refers to this circular in his annual report for 1948, but states that the date of issue was April, rather than May. He also provides additional background concerning reservation economic development planning during the Collier administration. See *Annual Report of the Secretary of the Interior, 1948,* "Bureau of Indian Affairs," pp. 370–371.

[‡] Charles J. Rhoads, John R. Nichols, Gilbert Darlington, and George A. Graham, "Report of the Committee on Indian Affairs to the Commission on Organization of the Executive Branch of the Government," (October 1948), pp. 54–55.

report for 1949, he clearly favored withdrawal of the federal government from its special role in Indian affairs as rapidly as the tribes could
be prepared to take over. He also cited two instances—those of the
Stockbridge-Munsee of Wisconsin and the Saginaw Chippewa of
Michigan—wherein tribes organized under the Indian Reorganization
Act had requested withdrawal of the Interior Department from supervision of certain of their affairs. Although Nichols obviously viewed
these as cases that he would have classified under the heading of "termination," they much more closely resemble what we today describe as
"self-determination."*

Midway through Nichols' abbreviated term, Congress enacted
legislation transferring civil and criminal jurisdiction over the Agua
Caliente reservation at Palm Springs to the state of California.† From
this point on, as an important aspect of preparing tribes for termination, the legislators would give special attention to matters involving
jurisdiction.

Replacing Nichols in May 1950 as commissioner of Indian affairs
was Dillon S. Myer, who, during World War II, had been director of
the War Relocation Authority. Myer and Collier had clashed over the
operation of Japanese relocation centers on Indian reservations some
years before, and the new commissioner had little love for either Collier's
policies or his friends. He undertook a thorough housecleaning of the
Washington office of the BIA, and among those associates of Collier who
departed shortly thereafter was Bill Zimmerman, who for all intents
and purposes had run the agency during the preceding three years.

Much of Myer's attention during his first year in office was devoted
to restructuring the Bureau and making other preparations for a full-
scale effort to get Indian tribes ready for a drastic change in their
relationship with the federal government. He felt that one of the keys
to the success of this endeavor was the creation of a programming unit,
free from the day-to-day operations of the agency, that could work with
the Indians in planning for their ultimate release from federal supervi-

---

* *Annual Report of the Secretary of the Interior, 1949,* "Bureau of Indian
Affairs," p. 337.

† Act of October 5, 1949, P. L. 322, 81st Cong.

sion and control.‡ Shortly after the middle of 1951, he had such a unit in place. Toward the end of the first session of the Eighty-second Congress, the Interior Department secured the introduction of legislation drafted by the program unit and directed toward termination of special federal services to the Indians of California and those of the Grande Ronde-Siletz Reservation in Oregon. Also introduced were bills aimed at the transfer of jurisdiction over Indian reservations to the states of Minnesota, Wisconsin, Nebraska, California, Oregon, and Washington.*

The termination strategy of Dillon Myer included another dimension beyond those of overall withdrawal programs for particular reservations and general transfers of civil and criminal jurisdiction to the states. This strategy involved the systematic dismantling of the service structure of the BIA through transfer of its functions to other federal agencies, to the states, and to the tribes. The latter effort was well advanced before the end of 1951, as Commissioner Myer makes clear in his annual report for fiscal year 1952. In that document, the commissioner discusses activities planned or underway to accelerate the enrollment of Indian youngsters in public schools and to place the responsibility for Indian health with "the appropriate state and local agencies." The latter goal had been made more accessible, he noted, through passage by Congress of Public Law 82-291 that authorized transfer of Indian Service hospitals to other agencies and permitted the admittance of non-Indians as patients in BIA hospitals in those areas where no other facilities were available.† The tone of Myer's 1952 report is more decidedly positive with respect to a major change in the federal-Indian relationship than any of its predecessor documents, and any history of recent termination policy must take account of it as a major research item.

None of the pieces of termination legislation considered by the Eighty-second Congress became law, although the bill to transfer jurisdiction to the state of California made it through the House of Representatives. These items were introduced again at the beginning of the

---

‡ *Annual Report of the Secretary of the Interior, 1951,* "Bureau of Indian Affairs," p. 353.

* *Annual Report of the Secretary of the Interior, 1952,* "Bureau of Indian Affairs," p. 389–390.

† Ibid., p. 390.

Eighty-third Congress early in 1953, and by that time, the Department of the Interior had other bills drafted, or in preparation, for the Klamath of Oregon, the Alabama and Coushatta of Texas, the Chitimacha of Louisiana, and the Prairie Island Band of Minnesota. Acting Commissioner W. Barton Greenwood, in the annual report of 1953, observed that termination planning was also well under way for the Osage of Oklahoma, the Menominee of Wisconsin, the Colville and Spokane of Washington, the Flathead of Montana, and a large number of smaller tribes throughout the western states. Greenwood noted too that one of the Indian Service hospitals had been transferred to a locally organized group, and three others had been closed after arrangements were completed for the care of Indian patients in other facilities. Furthermore, he mentioned the drastic cutback in the variety and extent of BIA services to California Indians as a major move in the direction of complete federal withdrawal from that state.‡

When one takes account of all the developments I have cited to this point, it should be clear that House Concurrent Resolution 108 was in a sense almost anticlimatic. While it may have put the Eighty-third Congress on record in a general way as favoring termination, it was by no means the powerful policy document it has often been represented as being. Long before its passage, the Bureau of Indian Affairs felt it already had a congressional mandate to change its historic relationship with Native Americans, and it was moving more rapidly in that direction than was the Congress. Thus, we must distort the facts somewhat to argue that HCR 108 *produced a* termination policy, just as we must distort them to suggest that its repeal—something still advocated by many Indian spokesmen—would signal permanent abandonment of such a policy.

What really happened in 1953 and 1954 is that an incubation process underway for at least a decade finally hatched some chicks. Two weeks after passing House Concurrent Resolution 108, Congress directed the birth of the first of those chicks—Public Law 83-280. This was the act that provided for transfer of legal jurisdiction over Indian reservations to several named states and authorized others to assume

---

‡ *Annual Report of the Secretary of the Interior, 1953,* "Bureau of Indian Affairs," pp. 24–25.

jurisdiction upon their own initiative. By this time, Glenn Emmons, a banker from New Mexico, had been sworn in as the commissioner of Indian affairs. Himself sympathetic with the policy of federal withdrawal, Emmons inherited the administrative machinery to implement that policy that his predecessor had so carefully put together.

Major withdrawal legislation affecting particular tribes came out of the second session of the Eighty-third Congress in 1954. Among the tribes involved were the comparatively large and wealthy Menominee of Wisconsin and the Klamath of Oregon—both owners of extensive timber resources. Also passed were acts to terminate services to the Indians of western Oregon, small Paiute bands in Utah, and the mixedbloods of the Uintah and Ouray Reservation. Approved, too, was legislation to transfer administrative responsibility for the Alabama and Coushatta Indians to the state of Texas. Finally, the second session of the Eighty-third Congress passed an act providing for transfer of health programs from the BIA to the United States Public Health Service.

Early in the first session of the Eighty-fourth Congress, bills were submitted to withdraw services from Wyandotte, Ottawa, and Peoria tribes of Oklahoma. These were finally enacted early in August 1956, a month after passage of legislation directing the Colville Confederated Tribes of Washington to come up with a termination plan of their own.

During the second administration of President Dwight D. Eisenhower, Congress enacted only three termination bills relating to specific tribes or groups. Affected by this legislation were the Choctaw of Oklahoma, for whom the termination process was never completed, the Catawba of South Carolina, and the Indians of the California rancherias. Other withdrawal bills were considered, but by 1958 when Interior Secretary Fred Seaton stated that the administration would not support legislation to terminate tribes without their consent, much of the momentum generated prior to 1953 had been lost.

In spite of the change in the administration's position enunciated by Secretary Seaton, withdrawal programming continued to capture the time and attention of BIA employees during all the Emmons commissionership. The Bureau placed heavy emphasis on education, resource development, and job training and placement—all services destined to make the reservation populations more self-sufficient. The Indian Health Service concentrated on providing and expanding hospital and clinic facilities and on improving the quality of water supplies and sewage disposal systems in Indian communities. Congressmen who favored the termination thrust, as well as those opposed or indifferent to it, voted increasingly larger appropriations for achieving goals set by Commissioner Emmons and his staff. Thus, it is well to keep in mind that while the decade of the 1950s produced strong emphasis on ways of getting the federal government out of the Indian business, it was also a period during which the quality and quantity of services to reservation populations were substantially increased and improved.

One dilemma of federal administrators at this time stemmed from the fact that Indian leaders were often reluctant to encourage their followers to take advantage of new and enlarged service programs, because they felt that if these programs were successful, the advent of termination for all tribes would be hastened. The so-called relocation program was a particularly good example of this concern. Early in the history of its development, this activity came to be viewed by many as a deliberate effort to depopulate the reservations and, thus, make it easier for the federal government to discontinue its subsidies for maintaining schools, hospitals, and other social service facilities in Indian communities. Rather than encouraging Indians to leave the reservations, these persons argued, the Bureau should stimulate the development of local resources and, in this fashion, create employment opportunities for Indians within an environment familiar to them. The program of off-reservation training and placement did enjoy considerable favor with young Indian men and women, thousands of whom availed themselves of its services, but it remained under attack from tribal leaders until the BIA in 1980 finally shut down its urban employment centers.

The impact of termination programming throughout the decade of the 1950s was clearly revealed to members of Secretary Udall's Task Force on Indian Affairs during the hearings they conducted on Indian reservations early in 1961. Spokesmen for small tribes in the Great Lakes area, the Pacific Northwest, the Great Basin, and the state of California demonstrated particular anxiety about their vulnerbility, feeling themselves too politically impotent to combat the proponents of termination. But even the representatives of the larger tribes expressed concern about what might happen to them. Impressed by the testimony offered by Indians everywhere they went, the task force members in their final report recommended that termination *per se* be abandoned as a goal of federal Indian policy.

From the beginning, officials of the Kennedy administration found themselves confronting termination issues on all sides. The Menominee withdrawal program, legislated in 1954, had dragged on through the Eisenhower years and was scheduled for conclusion in 1961 following Kennedy's inauguration. Certain conditions remained to be satisfied before the Choctaw program, approved by Congress in 1956, could be fully implemented. Withdrawal of services to the California rancherias demanded continuing effort, there were aspects of the Klamath program still pending, and the congressional mandate for preparation of a Colville termination program had not been complied with. In addition, some members of Congress were pushing for termination of the Seneca as part of the price for legislation to compensate those Indians for lands they had lost as a result of dam construction on the Allegheny River. A number of issues related to the transfer of jurisdiction over Indian reservations from the federal to state governments also remained to be addressed. In short, the spectre of termination did not disappear with the change of administrations.

As if further to emphasize the vitality of withdrawal programming as a part of national Indian policy, the comptroller general in March 1961 published a report strongly opposing the necessity of Indian consent prior to passage of termination legislation and exhorting the Interior Department to get busy with drafting bills to terminate those tribes that the Indian Bureau had earlier declared ready to "assume their responsibilities."* Senator Clinton P. Anderson of New Mexico, the powerful chairman of the Committee on Interior and Insular Affairs, was particularly taken with the recommendations of the comptroller and at a private breakfast with Secretary Udall and members of the task force late in the summer of 1961 strongly endorsed them.

Suffice it to say that termination issues were around to be dealt with during all the decade of the 1960s, although the tide began to turn

---

* *Report to the Congress of the United States by the Comptroller General of the United States*, "Review of Certain Aspects of the Program for the Termination of Federal Supervision over Indian Affairs, Bureau of Indian Affairs, Department of the Interior," (March 1961), p. 18.

strongly in the Indians' favor with passage in 1968 of the amendments to Public Law 280 of which we spoke previously. The decade of the 1970s opened with repeal or modication of other bills concerned with termination, and until about 1978, Congress seemed determined to wipe out the record of the 1950s. However, during the past five or six years, some congressmen, responding to constituents in various parts of the country, have submitted new legislative proposals that remind us that withdrawal of the special status enjoyed by Indians is by no means a dead issue.

A former tribal chairman and executive secretary of the National Congress of American Indians has suggested that the so-called "self-determination" policy, if successful, will lead ultimately to severance of the special relationship between the government of the United States and its Indian citizens. Exploring the implications of that hypothesis should be worth some of our time. At the heart of this special relationship is, of course, the trustee responsibility. Treaties have been abrogated or ignored, and congressional acts amended or appealed; yet the Indians survive and tribal identities remain—due in some measure at least to the preservation of a land base through continuation of the trust.

A valid question to ask ourselves is whether trusteeship—which many apparently feel is essential to the social and cultural survival of Indians—is consistent with the concept of self-rule, the primary theme of our discussion. If the self-rule we have in mind is one that emphasizes such notions as "nationhood" and "ultimate sovereignty" in their most exaggerated forms, then I suggest that the concepts are not compatible. On the other hand, if we are willing to settle for the "limited self-rule" concept that John Collier had in mind when he proposed the Indian Reorganization Act, self-rule or "self-determination" may not be inconsistent with retention of a trust relationship with the federal government, although a definition of that relationship in more specific terms than is the present case may be required.

CHAPTER TWO

Federal Indian Policy, 1945-1960

Philleo Nash, Sol Tax, R. David Edmunds,
Gary Orfield, Ada Deer

*The termination policy was one of the most radical social policy
experiments of the twentieth century. It was, ironically, inflicted on defense-
less Indian tribes by very strong conservatives acting under the banner of
such basic conservative principles as "free enterprise" and dismantling of
bureaucracies. The idea was to "liberate" Indians from reservations and
the Bureau of Indian Affairs and to force them to become participants in
what the advocates saw as the superior social and economic arrangements
off the reservations. This is one of the oldest and most frequently recurring
themes in Indian policy. When it had been done before through dividing
Indian lands, through turning reservations over the missionaries, through
taking children from their homes to boarding schools, the results had been
damaging and the policies were eventually reversed. When another round
of conservative reformers took the reins of Indian policy in 1953, in the
first period of GOP control of Congress and the White House since the
1920s, the central policy goal was to "terminate" federal protections and
services for tribes that Congress decided were ready to exist without them.
The experiment had a devastating impact on the tribes selected, and termination became the great issue in Indian policy for a generation.*

Gary Orfield, professor of political science,
University of Chicago

*The NCAI, in its early years, was put in a very difficult position when
Wade Crawford and other Indian claimants, who lived in Washington,
breathed down the necks of the NCAI everyday to hasten termination.
Some of the Menominees also were living in Washington. They pushed for*

termination. The NCAI was caught up in a terrible conflict. Do you fight the government of a tribe that is opposed to the position of your organization?

Helen Peterson, Oglala Sioux,
former executive director, NCAI

PHILLEO NASH

Termination is a bad word, a bad name, and an evil thought. Nevertheless, it was with us. We all tend to think of the Congress and the Washington scene as the primary source of the termination push. We also see the Indian Bureau itself, particularly in that helpless floundering period from 1945 until 1958, as being responsible for the policy of termination. We are talking about a rather long period, in which House Resolution 108 comes up almost as a piece of froth on the surface of a very deep undertow.

What were some of the sources of that undertow? There were amazing combinations of people in that drive for termination. The liberal establishment compared reservations to concentration camps and thought of the Indian Bureau as a manager of prisoners of war. We also must include a segment of the Indian people which saw, in their love/hate relationship with the Bureau, an opportunity to get rid of a very uncomfortable and, at times, menacing overseer. Finally, we must not eliminate greed from the picture, because termination brought with it the concept of freedom of property. Who would have been the owners if the trust status on Indian land had been completely dissolved?

There were some interesting thrusts on the other side. One of the principal beneficiaries of the federal aid programs for Indians over the years had been the state and local governments. They had been relieved of very costly obligations for schools, welfare, and roads in the states that had large Indian populations. Where termination was effectuated, it was not only very damaging to the Indian people but extremely costly to the state and local governments.

The main thrust behind termination was Congress, which had long defined the Indian Bureau as the Indian problem. There is a very deep problem in the American value system. We non-Indians came as conquerors. We were greeted with hospitality and we met hospitality with rebuff and force. We are aware of that and we carry this guilt within us, but we do not intend to give the land back. Consequently, there has to be an enemy. Are we the enemy? That is a very difficult thing to admit. Is the Indian the enemy? God forbid! Well, there must be an enemy. So, we make the Indian commissioner and the Bureau the enemy. We have this love/hate relationship between the Indians and the Bureau.

I served as a member of the Kennedy Task Force on Indian Affairs. The task force decided that the only way to cope with termination as an issue was to come out against it and then say: "Let's not talk about it because it is getting in the way of communication between the federal agencies, the Bureau of Indian Affairs, and the Indian people." This did not win us friends in the Congress of the United States.

I had to be evasive in order to obtain confirmation by the United States Senate as Indian commissioner. If I had said, I think that the Indian people are entitled to federal services in perpetuity the same as any other defined group, such as farmers, labor, and business, you can be certain that I would have gone back to my farm much sooner.

The question was how long would termination last as congressional policy. Termination was the denial of Indian culture, the denial of Indian self-government, and the denial of tribalism. And this goes back to the very earliest days of the republic.

The Constitution of 1789 gives the executive branch of the federal government the exclusive right to regulate commerce with Indian tribes. Indian individuals in that same document were denied a position in the body politic. Indians not taxed were put in the same category with slaves. This tells us something about the basic premises of the interaction between the American people as a whole and the Indian subportion of it. The founding fathers could have created, and they did not, a union of states and tribes. Instead, they waffled, and we have confusion in which special interests of every kind, well intended and evil, have an opportunity to operate.

The Indian Bureau is the unit of government which is charged with buffering this interphase. Its goals have never been clearly stated—the undercurrent of goals is what I am talking about. There is a denial of Indian personhood and a denial of tribal status. Tribal governments are a thorn in the state and federal system. They make the state and the other federal agencies most uncomfortable, especially those in the Interior Department other than the Bureau of Indian Affairs.

The Indian commissioner has to fight a continuous battle with the other bureau chiefs for the Indian people's share of what is appropriated through their agencies. It is a difficult and ambiguous role. It is one which I filled for five trouble-filled, but very happy, years, and I can tell you I did not leave voluntarily and I never would have.

SOL TAX

Termination is part of a basic assumption that all Americans tend to make, and that is that the Indians will disappear. This has been going on for a long time. Sooner or later, if you put a few drops of glue into an ocean of water, the glue disappears. Assimilation was the solution for people who had guilt feelings about our treatment of Indians. There would no longer be any Indians.

The remarkable thing that I learned in the 1930s and 1940s was that not one Indian I ever knew made that assumption, and yet, when the Indians had to go before the Washington authorities, they would not deny it. Indian leaders wanted to get things done for their people. They also were exceedingly courteous and polite. When I began to learn what was going on, the Indians were pleased when I got up before white people and said what was really in their minds.

Indians really do not want to become like us. They prefer to do things in their own way. They are willing, as we are not, to let others live their own life, but they are not going to change their culture to please us.

Nothing is ever as crystal clear as it seems. The Indians had to live too. In order to live, they had a deal with white people. They could not avoid, forever, contact with white culture. But the one thing that they would not accept was the thought of their own demise and disappearance. They had come out of the earth and went to the sky in their own country, and they were not going to be like us. I came to understand this difference after living with Indians.

Before I began to write on this subject, very few people, if any, every voiced publicly and in print the idea that the Indians were going to be with us forever. When the atom bomb shelters were being constructed and nuclear fallout maps were made, they left out most Indian areas. The bombs were not going to drop there first. Instead, New York, Chicago, and other places would be destroyed. I told my white friends, "If you think the Indians are going to disappear, now they think that you are."

Dillon Myer was the father of real termination. He was in charge of Japanese-American relocation. Myer had a lot of anthropologists on his staff. He took many of them from John Collier's original collection of people at the Bureau of Indian Affairs. These anthropologists, and others, tried to tell Myer that he should leave the Japanese in their camps because the outside world was dangerous for them.

Myer did not take their advice. It turned out that the Japanese got along beautifully when they relocated. For example, ten thousand of them went to Chicago and immediately got jobs. It was war time and they had no problems. After that, Myer refused to listen to anybody's advice. Myer was the first man in history to end a federal bureau —the War Relocation Authority. That is why they made him commissioner of Indian affairs.

R. David Edmunds

Conceptions of Indians held by the white public are at the heart of the problem of termination. The vanishing redman concept is part of it. It is untrue, but most whites, especially those who have limited contact with Indian people, certainly subscribe to it. In history, it is not so important really what happened as what people think has happened.

Termination and relocation are logical outgrowths of how the white majority has envisoned Indian people and how their misconceptions have shaped Indian policy. There is an interesting paradox in the history of race relations in this country. The Indian people are the only racial minority that whites have generally tried to assimilate. Whites have taken great pains to segregate blacks, Chicanos, and Asians. The thrust of the black civil rights movement, especially in the 1960s, was for a bigger slice of the American pie. Black people were saying, "You have held us out long enough. We want to be part of it." Whites were saying, especially in the South, "You cannot have it."

In contrast to that, whites have said to Native Americans for years,

"Come on in." Indian people, to their credit, have said, "We do not want in." Indian resistance to assimilation puzzles white people very much. They cannot understand why Indian people refuse to become white. In order to change Indian people whites have designed programs to "educate" Indians. The assumption has been that if Indians were "educated" they would eagerly accept the dominant culture.

The question remains, why did whites try to assimilate Indians? The answer is based upon the image of Indian people held by large parts of the white public. Once white people gained military control over Indian people, they began to have guilt feelings, and they created romanticized images of Indian people. As whites, through superior technology or superior numbers, gained military control, they concluded, "Oh, the Indian people whom we have defeated are very brave." This enhanced the white image of themselves. It took superior persons to defeat such brave people. After the Indians were under military control, they became less of a threat. It was safe to create stereotype images of noble savages.

During the first part of the twentieth century there were several fraternal organizations called the noble lodges of the redmen. There were not any Indians in those groups. But they were based upon the concept of the noble savage.

Throughout the rest of this century, whites have believed that Indian people are a rural minority even though Indian people have moved into the cities in large numbers. From the white urbanite perspective, the Indians are a safe minority because they are living some place in the West. They also think that Indians are vanishing Americans. We know that is not correct.

This position is not shared by white people who live where Indian people are the dominant minority. Obviously, Indian people who are living in South Dakota or parts of Arizona or New Mexico do not think that they are a favored minority, and they certainly are not. In those states the Indian people exert enough influence to threaten the white majority.

The 1950s was a logical time for termination to occur. It was a period of great conformity in the United States. Congress went around investigating "un-American activities."

During this period, federal policy makers and pressure groups championed termination. Many of the individuals that favored termination were well-meaning people. They believed that they were offering Indian people an opportunity to join mainstream society. They were doing this, not to Indians, but for Indians. The real tragedy is that many whites then and now still cannot comprehend that Indian people could want anything other than a white existence. This still may be the greatest obstacle to Indian self-rule. Today, such people in Washington D.C. are a great threat to the Indian future.

GARY ORFIELD

As a political scientist, I see things a little differently from historians, anthropologists, and people who have grand policy perspectives. I keep trying to look at the machinery: what went wrong and what problems led particular tribes to the termination disaster. Why did the federal government adopt such an idiotic policy? It makes no sense to dump impoverished tribes on county and state governments without any planning whatever. There was not a shred of intelligent economic analysis in most of the termination cases.

It seems to me that we must examine the general political climate and social policy at the time these things were adopted. Who was controlling the Congress? What does that show about the nature of the decision-making process? Why did some of the termination proposals go through and some not? The Flathead and Seminole were not terminated . What does that show? Even at the worst times, some tribes were able to protect themselves and others were not. What can we learn from that?

We can also learn from the remarkable part of this story, which is the restoration legislation that reversed termination. How did that happen and why? And what does that show about the probability of termination ever happening to anybody again?

Considered in a broader social policy context, termination was part of a general reaction to the New Deal. It came up in the late 1940s, when there was a strong conservative movement against New Deal legislation, all kinds of emergency programs, and price controls. The Congress elected in 1946 was the first Republican Congress since the

New Deal. It was elected on a campaign theme, "had enough." The first people it chose to diminish the burden of government were the people who were least able to defend their government services: the Indians were targeted.

Termination was enacted during the first Congress of the Eisenhower administration. We had not had conservative control of both the presidency and Congress since 1930, when the Democrats took over Congress. These new political actors were very conservative. Termination was enacted, in part, because decisions about Indians were made by the interior committees in Congress. Those committees were loaded with conservative westerners, and very few politicians off those committees cared about what happened in Indian affairs. The cost of learning enough to do anything about Indian policy was just too much.

Most of the decisions on Indian affairs are made by a few people on subcommittees. Almost nobody wants to serve on those subcommittees, because there is very little political mileage to be made. They are lots of trouble because Indian affairs are so complicated.

Conditions were ripe for a general conservative effort to cut back government. The Eisenhower administration wanted to turn federal aid programs over to the state and local governments. In a situation like that the pressure goes out generally, but succeeds where there is the least resistance. No federal aid programs were turned over to the state and local governments by the Eisenhower administration, because the state and local governments said, we do not want them. They were able only to cut things that had very weak constituencies such as public housing and Indian affairs.

One reason this legislation passed was that nobody seriously tried to block it. When hearings were held on a number of these termination bills, there was no testimony against the termination. The Indians who came testified in favor of the legislation. As far as Congress knew, the tribes had given their consent. Members of Congress do not call up the tribal council and say, "Did you really sincerely, honestly, actively mean to consent to this?"

Where tribes were terminated, the state governments did not oppose termination. The Wisconsin state government and the others did not oppose it until after it was already enacted. In Congress it is much easier to block something than it is to change something after it has been enacted. This legislation was enacted in Congress through unanimous consent procedures. That means any one member of either the House or Senate could have blocked it. If local congressmen, senators, or state governments objected, it did not go through. There was no case in which it was imposed on a state government that was unwilling to accept it.

Another basic problem with termination was an Indian organization vacuum. The national Indian organizations were not effective on this. A number of tribal governments were forced into giving what seemed to be their consent by all kinds of pressure that the subcommittees and the BIA exerted. As far as the other members of Congress knew, the Indians had given their consent.

There was almost no serious attention given, even by members of the Indian affairs subcommittees, to many of these pieces of legislation. At many of the hearings, there were only one or two people present. They were usually conservative ideologues who were dedicated to the idea of liberating Indians from the Bureau of Indian Affairs. They controlled the whole process because nobody else was involved with most of these tribes.

There were no monolithic, massive forces compelling Indian tribes to accept termination. Relatively small forces happened to have strategic control of these particular subcommittees. They faced virtually no opposition, in a number of cases. Where they were faced with opposition, they gave way and did not push that legislation through. They were able, by dissembling, to force tribes into thinking that there was a mass judgement by Congress as an institution to impose this policy on tribes. There was not. If a little multiple choice quiz had been given to Congress, 90 percent of the members would not have known what was in the legislation.

The leadership of Congress would not have brought legislation like this to the floor if there had been active battles against it. They did not have time to consider minor pieces of legislation in full congressional proceedings; only a very few pieces of legislation are fully debated each year. The leaders had to do it through unanimous consent procedure. As soon as tribes actively opposed termination, most of the future bills died.

Another thing that came out very clearly in the termination story is that once a stupid and senseless decision is made it is hard to reverse, until a powerful movement comes along. When Congress acts on something like this, the bureaucracy mobilizes, goes forward. All the different levels of government say, "The Congress has decided. We have got to make this work." The fact that it is unworkable does not make a great deal of difference until a long period of time has passed. In other words, it is very easy to block a congressional decision, but it is very hard once it is made to prevent it from going forward for a long time. It is very difficult to get the members of Congress who are involved with passing a policy and the members of the bureaucracy that helped design it to admit that they did something that was really crazy. After termination was enacted, it developed a life of its own, and it took a remarkable process to turn it around.

The restoration legislation is an example of a rather extraordinary thing. Federal agencies, the Department of the Interior, and the key congressional committees all admitted that they were wrong. By restoring the Menominee tribe to federal status, they admitted that they had spent millions of dollars of federal money in a useless pursuit.

I have spent a lot of time around Capitol Hill. One of the most remarkable lobbying campaigns I have seen was the campaign for Menominee restoration. Nobody was safe from Ada Deer and her supporters. Members of Congress just gave up. The White House supported restoration, in part, because Melvin Laird, who used to be the congressman representing the Menominee, was convinced by people like Ada Deer. He was the counselor to the president as the Watergate mess was collapsing around the Nixon administration. I talked to him, and I said, "How did you ever get the president to support restoration?" And he said to me, "Nixon did not care about that kind of stuff. He was just trying to save his skin, so one day I just typed up a notice that said the administration supports restoration, and I had the secretary send it out."

The restoration of the Menominee and two other tribes is a very substantial achievement. It represents the development of a new level of sophistication and lobbying by Indian groups. At the Menominee restoration hearings, there was an incredible mobilization of resources. There was great unity in the Indian communities. This powerful organization was able to roll through both houses of Congress, and it got both the Interior Department and the Nixon administration to turn around. It was impressive and it made a lasting impact.

Is termination really dead? I do not think there is any chance that the termination of the1950s is going to come back through Congress as long as the tribes are aware when legislation is introduced and explain it to their members. As long as national Indian organizations are reasonably effective legislatively, we will not get more termination bills, unless their is political change beyond any measure.

We now have the most conservative Congress and most conservative president since Calvin Coolidge. No termination legislation has been adopted in this Congress. There have been many other very bad things in Indian affairs, but people should not live in mortal fear that new termination bills will be issued. They should keep a watch on what is going on, but this should not be a central focus.

One of the tragedies of termination is that, for a long period of time, it has made people turn inward and become defensive in relation to the formation of Indian policy in Congress. People have been reluctant to formulate new policies. Termination has created tremendous focus on tribal status and land protection, but it has not produced much attention to issues addressing the majority of Indians, who live off reservations.

People should realize that termination went through Congress because of extraordinary conditions. Tribes, the national Indian organizations, and their supporters completely failed in their jobs during that period. They will not do that again. There are people like Ada Deer who are watching and would kill anything like termination before it began to move through Congress. The same cultural values and the same misunderstandings are certainly present in the white population, but the same weakness and poor preparation is not true of the Indian community today.

Ada Deer

I am going to speak as a member of one of the terminated and restored tribes. I am also going to speak as a human being, a woman, a social worker, and as an Indian. There has been a tendency to forget that all of these policies and programs had an impact on the lives of people. These policies were not drafted in a vacuum somewhere. The moral issue has not been given the attention that it should. We hear a lot about Christianity and the Indians. In my opinion, very little Christianity has been applied in Indian affairs. I feel that all of us are moral human beings. We know the difference between right and wrong, and both Indians and non-Indians need to keep this in mind as we proceed to work and live through this next challenge. It is just astounding to me that so few people did testify about termination and that there was not a sense of the immorality of this action. I believe that this could happen again in other types of legislation and in other types of projects.

The impact on the individual of this termination process has been greatly overlooked. I was a college student trying not to be a dropout when this occurred. I knew that a major event was occurring with my tribe, but there was very little information that was distributed. People were confused. They did not understand what was going on.

Many people, over the years, have said that the Menominee consented to termination. This is not true. For many years the Menominee had carried on a suit against the federal government for mismanagement of the trust. They had won the suit. Melvin Laird, who was a congressman at that time, introduced through his committee a simple appropriations request for a per capita payment. This was changed when it got into the Senate. Senator Arthur Watkins felt that in order for the Menominee to receive the per capita payment they would have to agree to termination. There are many misconceptions about this. I do want to state for the record that there was a lot of misinformation. People did not understand what they were voting on. In one account that I have read, 169 people voted for it, 5 voted against it. Another account said that the vote was 169 to 0. In any case, this was not informed consent.

All of us in 1983 can say how wrong all those people were then. This is 20-20 hindsight. I want to emphasize that it is important to understand these events in the framework of the times. Being a social worker and an Indian, I feel that it is important to undertake full consultation. This was not done during the termination legislation. It is incumbent upon all of us, Indians and non-Indians, that are involved in Indian affairs, to pay attention. We must do our homework and become involved in the process of consulting with Congress when legislation is introduced. We also must become involved with the executive branch when regulations are written.

Many people have said that the Menominee tribe was a wealthy tribe. There was approximately $10 million in the treasury at the time, but the individual Indians were very poor. Termination was a cultural, economic, and political disaster. It is going to take several more generations for the people in my tribe to recover from the damage that was done during termination. The hospital and the roads were closed. Our land became subject to taxation. A whole new county, Wisconsin's poorest county, was created as a result of this. Health conditions became a severe problem. In 1965, there were approximately six hundred positive TB tests in a testing of over two thousand Menominees. The withdrawal of federal education, health, and other services was indeed a severe problem for the Menominee people.

The Menominee Restoration Act was an effort by the Menominee people and their lawyers to secure social justice. We also had the assistance of people such as Philleo Nash and Indians across the country. They gave us their support and active assistance. We achieved an historic reversal of American Indian policy. I want to emphasize, especially to Indians, that they can decide what they want. You do not need the Bureau of Indian Affairs or any other group telling you what to do. You can make a decision and work for it. I want to say to all of you that are involved in projects and activities at the community level that it is possible to bring about social change. If the Menominee could do it with a small group of people, almost any group can achieve significant changes. They must work hard and work within the system.

CHAPTER THREE

Undoing the IRA

Clarence Wesley, Graham Holmes, E. Reeseman Fryer,
Robert Burnette

*One of the problems that we have with the Indian Reorganization Act
is who manages the trust responsibility. We have to keep worrying about
the successive waves of federal officials every four years. If adequate funds
had been awarded under the Indian Claims Commission, the tribes could
have survived without the IRA. Real Indian self-determination would
have occurred. The whole problem on Indian reservations is that we do not
have enough money. Congress refuses to appropriate adequate funds.
Instead, it spends billions for defense and billions for foreign aid to countries in Central America.*

Edward Johnson, former chairman,
Walker River Paiute tribe

*A radical change in Indian policy was possible without serious exami-
nation of the consequences in good measure because so few members of
Congress knew or cared about Indian affairs and some of the Indian tribes
and national organizations were so weak or divided or intimidated by pressure from powerful members of Congress or the BIA that they could not
or would not fight effectively. The key policy resolution, House Concurrent
Resolution 108, was passed by Congress in July 1953 by unanimous consent,
under a procedure that could have been blocked by the objection of a single
member of either the House or the Senate. The resolution sounded, on first
reading, like a kind of unobjectionable Fourth of July speech. In the
Senate it passed without a single word of discussion. In the House there
were only a few prefunctory remarks supporting the principles. No one
noted that the resolution required the Interior Department to begin very*

[142]

rapid preparation of policies for ending all federal protections and services for a wide variety of Indian groups, including some living in great poverty and possessing very few resources.

Gary Orfield, Brookings Institution

CLARENCE WESLEY

The Indian Reorganization Act was fully discussed on the San Carlos Apache Reservation. We had CCC camps all over the reservation. Apache elderly men went around from camp to camp with CCC officials. They explained the contents of the Indian Reorganization Act, what it meant, and how it was going to help the Indians.

After a year, a big meeting was held at the San Carlos Agency. The tribe overwhelmingly voted to adopt the IRA. At first, seven elderly men were elected to the council. Two years later, a younger man was selected to serve. While I was up on the mountain working cattle, I learned that I was elected. I was also asked to be secretary for the council. That was the beginning of my career on the tribal council.

Later on, I became chairman of the tribal council. Ernest McCrea was the superintendent at that time. He told us that he still was in charge of the agency and nobody was going to tell him what to do. So, we discussed among ourselves several issues on the reservation that dealt with the control of funds and hiring. I told McCrea, "This is an Apache reservation. We have some Indians who want to work, and that should be our first concern." Later on, he called me in and said, "You have got a big mouth." We did not get along from the start, so we had cross words from the beginning. I was still on the council when he died across the street. I hate to say this, but that was quite a relief.

We were without a superintendent for a while until Al Stover came from Dulce, New Mexico. He was an entirely different person. He believed in the Indian Reorganization Act. He said, "I am here to help you do what you want, and you can depend on it." We wanted to have a tribal store to create jobs for our people. We asked Superintendent Stover about it, and he said, "Why don't you send a delegation over to the Jicarilla Apache Reservation and see how they got their tribal store started." We went to Dulce, New Mexico, and they gave us a lot of information. We also went to Mescalero, New Mexico. They had a tribal store over there too. About a week after we returned, I called a meeting that was attended by approximately two thousand Indians. I stood up, as chairman, and explained to the people that we were trying to establish a store so some of our people could go to work.

At that time there were six white traders on the reservation. When I got through talking, a very prominent individual stood up and told the audience that this was the best thing he had ever heard in his life. He said our tribal council was on the right track. That was the beginning of our operation. We did not get any money from the bank or from the government. We assessed our cattlemen for one year. We raised enough money to build a building and hire a staff. The tribal store operated until 1964.

The BIA superintendent, his staff, and the tribal council must cooperate to make the Indian Reorganization Act work. We did this right from the beginning. The San Carlos Apache tribe celebrated the anniversary of the birth of IRA every June 18. We had a big barbecue, a baseball game, a rodeo, and dances. We would always invite somebody from the area office to speak to the people. It was quite interesting, and a lot of questions were asked. This went on for a number of years until the Apache people lost interest in celebrating the IRA. Then we decided to abandon the anniversary idea.

After Stover retired, the council adopted a resolution. We requested that Tom Dodge, who was part Navajo, come to San Carlos and be our superintendent. Tom Dodge helped us fight racial discrimination in nearby towns. He told us that the way to correct this situation was to get involved with white people. We began to attend chamber of commerce, Kiwanis, Lion's, Jaycee, and Rotary meetings. I was made a member of the Miami Rotary Club, and we worked with these people to whip discrimination. We also asked if some of our girls and our boys could go to work in various business operations in these towns. We got some people jobs and girls were employed by a bank.

We also created other tribal enterprises. We started a timber operation. Because it was a sustained yield operation, we were short of lumber after fifteen years. So we had to quit, but it gave a lot of employment to our people for fifteen years. There also was copper mining on the east and west side of the reservation. We contacted a geophysical outfit in New York and Toronto, Canada, to do an airborne survey of the reservation for minerals. They found low-grade copper below Mt. Turnbull and did some drilling there; but the copper played out, and that ended our intention to mine copper.

There was land south of our present boundary known as the San Carlos mineral strip. It had been ceded back in 1896 for mineral entry only, but there were twenty-six cattle ranches operating on that ceded land. We went to Congress, with the help of the Bureau of Indian Affairs, and 232,000 acres of that land was restored to tribal ownership in 1969. We have not stocked it yet with any cattle.

In addition to these enterprises, we were interested in the education of our children. We have special scholarships to help the boys and girls who want to go to college. In the last school year there were ninety-nine of our youngsters in college.

When I left, in 1964, another person was elected. He was a Christian who went to church. Instead of having council meetings, he would preach. It was under his administration that the tribe went into bankruptcy. The tribal store that we built was closed. After some years with bankruptcy, we had another election. A young man by the name of Buck was elected. He helped revitalize the tribal store. Then, in another election, we chose an attorney from the University of Arizona. The tribal store once again went into bankruptcy. In addition to being bankrupt, the San Carlos Apache tribe was sued by the Internal Revenue Service for over a million dollars. The tribe had failed to pay its withholding tax. This was not the fault of the Indian Reorganization Act. It was the fault of an individual. We are really in a mess at this moment. I do not know how we are going to pay that million dollars. By the time they are through with us, the government might take over both the reservation and the Indian Reorganization Act.

Graham Holmes

It is necessary to look at the situation that existed at the time before discussing the IRA. Prior to 1934, there had been, for a number of years, a steady drift away from tribal sovereignty. Assimilation was occurring, and tribal lands were lost through benign neglect. John Collier decided that it was necessary to stop this because there would be no tribal governments and perhaps no reservations in the forseeable future.

He set out to get the IRA enacted. Now, to get a bill of this kind through Congress is a sizeable undertaking. It is very difficult to start at one end of the funnel in Congress and have the same thing come out at the other end. You can explain a bill like the IRA to the Indians, but by the time it gets through Congress it may be unrecognizable. The criticism that Collier did not explain it properly, that he lied to the people about it, grows out of that kind of a situation.

Collier did the best he could under the circumstances. He came out with a bill that has stood for fifty years. Without the IRA there would have been a steady drift away from tribal sovereignty, tribal government, and we would not have reached a point where we could even talk about self-determination.

Many tribes did not adopt the IRA. Most of the tribes that did not accept it were involved in local political issues on their reservations that did not directly relate to IRA. Anywhere that IRA was the main concern, it was adopted.

Sometimes Collier's personality was identified with the IRA. He was not the IRA, but some people never realized that. At times, he was a rather abrasive individual, and he could be obnoxious. But it would be remarkable, with two hundred or three hundred Indian tribes, if everybody agreed to the IRA. I would be suspicious of it if everybody agreed. The people who did not agree rode the coattails of IRA. Because of IRA, we have a congressional recognition of tribal governments and tribal sovereignty that has carried everybody along.

Under IRA constitutions nearly everything a tribe does has to be approved by the secretary of the interior or the commissioner of Indian affairs, but because of the trust relationship and the trust responsibility, very few tribal councils have tried to take that provision out. Holding on to Indian land has been one of the main problems throughout the last century. That is why there are a lot of restrictions in the IRA. The trustee can not sell Indian lands under IRA. Since the passage of IRA, even the corps of army engineers can not take Indian land without getting an act of Congress. Laws such as IRA protect the weak more than they protect the strong.

Tribes must develop their economies. Unless you can say no to the federal government once in a while, you have undone the IRA and everything else. Regulations accompany federal money. We do not need to graduate ten thousand Indian lawyers. We need to graduate people who know how to explore for minerals, run plants, and develop reservation economies. That will make Indians self-sufficient. They will not have to come to the federal government for anything.

The IRA was a good thing. But it had its faults, and it needs undoing in a place or two as time goes on. The ability to modify the IRA is growing stronger all the time. Tribes that want to amend their constitutions can do so. It is a cumbersome process, but constitutions are designed to have a stabilizing effect.

Most Indian tribes seek consensus. They do not like to act until everybody agrees. IRA constitutional governments are a different way of governing. The majority proposes, the minority opposes, and they argue it out. Then a vote is taken. The side that gets the most votes wins. Consensus is opposite from that. A lot of the governmental strife under IRA—and it has been the undoing of the IRA at times—has come over the problem of consensus.

Under an IRA constitutional government or any other kind of government, you are not going to reach consensus. This has affected economic development on reservations where time is a problem. Indians will act in their own best interest, but you cannot tell when they are going to do it. Unfortunately, an appropriation from Congress will lapse after one year if you do not use it. The problem of timing also has prevented industries from moving to reservations.

There is no word in the Indian language that translates directly to time. If you ask a Sioux what time it is, you ask him how many times does the thing strike. The real problem is getting everything related to the tick of the clock and the movement of the dominant economy. The problem of time undoes some of the IRA. It forces a democratic majority rule system on Indian tribes that are not prepared to adopt it.

Reservations are in turmoil because the paternalistic colonialism that has existed all these years is being changed to promote self-determination and home rule . If IRA is to succeed, two things have to happen. First, we must have stable tribal government. The IRA gave us the backbone of that. Second, we must have tribal economies that work. If you do not have those two things, you cannot successfully end federal guardianship.

E. Reeseman Fryer

When John Collier tried to introduce IRA on the Navajo Reservation in 1934, I saw the turmoil that existed. The Navajo defeat of IRA was based on the issue of assimilation. It was the battle between the assimilationists of the north—the Jake Morgan crowd—and the conventional Navajo of the south. The charges that IRA would return the Indians to a zoo destroyed its consideration among the Navajos. In retrospect, the Navajo showed a certain amount of prophetic wisdom in turning down this legislation.

After the Navajo had rejected IRA, Felix Cohen came to the reservation. He used his great ability to design a constitution that might be presented to the tribe as an administrative action. As soon as that happened, there was a renewed fight. Basically, it was a battle between those people who had assimilated in the north, allied with the missionaries, and the traditional Navajos of the south.

Putting it in terms of personality, it was J. C. Morgan who defeated IRA. He was a brilliantly able Navajo orator. He was the ablest demagogue I have ever heard. Morgan could sway crowds with his demagoguery. He persuaded the Navajos that IRA had bad qualities. He had on his side both the missionaries and traders. The missionaries believed that IRA threatened fifty years of Christian teaching. The traders saw in the IRA a threat to their permanence and to their financial investment. So, the IRA was destroyed by people who were concerned with assimilation and their own security and property.

John Collier never admitted that IRA was defeated by intertribal conflicts. He always blamed the defeat of IRA on stock reduction. I was at Ganado during this period. I observed that IRA was defeated long before the latter part of 1935, when stock reduction finally became an issue. Today, stock reduction is still considered the issue that led to the undoing of IRA. I suspect that the Navajos will remember stock reduction, with all of its mythology, as long as they will remember the Long Walk.

I had one other experience with IRA. In 1948, I was sent to Nevada as superintendent. There were eighteen or nineteen Indian town colonies, each inside a city, from Reno to Las Vegas to Winnemucca. These Indian colonies had separate identities, and they subscribed to IRA. It is my feeling that, without IRA and its federal protection, these Indian colonies would have disappeared. The greed of real estate developers and the people surrounding the Indians would have completely obliterated these colonies. We would have had something similar to the outlying slums of Rapid City where Indians congregated in the late 1930s and 1940s without land, property, or jobs. IRA saved these little colonies from this fate.

The Nevada Indians were having trouble then, and I suspect that they are having trouble now, not with the concept of IRA as a bit of salvation for Indianness, but with their constitutions. These constitutional problems could have been solved by a task force of experts, who might have worked with the Indians at their request. Lawyers and social scientists could have helped the Indians modify their IRA constitutions in order to protect these tiny colonies against the greed of developers and real estate people.

ROBERT BURNETTE

There is a tremendous shortcoming in the IRA that few people recognize. Collier was so adamant in making sure that the government of the United States fulfilled its trusteeship obligation that he left an important provision out of IRA. There is no way under IRA to redress a grievance should your own tribe refuse to recognize something that is legitimate. There is the problem of tribal government accountability.

That is where the United States is supposed to step in and do its job. The federal government has not met this obligation. We have turmoil in every tribe, all across the country. We would like to go to court and sue tribal officials who are responsible for problems, to make them accountable, but we cannot do that. This is the job of the United States government, and it has totally neglected to fill the void left by IRA.

For years, I have fought to get the Bureau of Indian Affairs and the Department of Interior to wake up and fill this legal void. Elected tribal officials must be held responsible and accountable to the people. Because the people, including council people, are absolutely legally helpless we have many lawsuits that add to the turmoil on reservations.

CHAPTER FOUR

The Indian Claims Commission

Charles F. Wilkinson, W. Roger Buffalohead,
E. Richard Hart, Edward C. Johnson

*We have had enough experience with the Indian Claims Commission
Act to know that it has not benefited most tribes. Approximately $800 mil-
lion was awarded through the Indian Claims Commission. If you divide
the number of acres of land that those particular cases involved, the United
States government ended up paying Indian people fifty cents an acre for
the United States of America. The title was quieted, but in many cases it
is still unsettled.*

*We need to pursue further the question of how did the Indian Claims
Commission Act affect Indian people. We all have some notion that its
impact was not good. It did not settle anything. And it certainly did not
provide Indians with the capital to do anything about their economic situation. In order to have sovereignty and self-government, you also need to
have economic self-determination. We have never been able to achieve
that in this country.*

Roger Buffalohead, Ponca, project director,
MIGIZI Communications

CHARLES F. WILKINSON

The field of Indian law and policy is rife with ambiguities. I do not know of a pocket of Indian policy that is more profoundly ambiguous than the Indian Claims Commission Act. I want to provide an objective statement of some of the events leading up to the act. In the late eighteenth and nineteenth centuries, Indian tribes lost most of their land to western expansion. Payment was never made to the tribes for tens of millions of acres that were lost. In addition, it is clear that when treaty negotiators sat down, tribes still had their aboriginal land ownership. There is nothing as fundamental in the field of Indian law as the idea that Indians had an ownership interest in their aboriginal territory after the white people arrived, right up to the moment that they sat down at the bargaining table. It was not a full title. They had a shared title with the United States. But they did have an aboriginal ownership, a legal title recognized by Congress and by the United States Supreme Court. It was this title that was the subject of the treaty negotiations, from the United States' point of view. Tribes granted away most of their aboriginal land at the treaty table. They kept a small part of it, between 5 percent and 15 percent, as their reservations.

It is now clear, particularly after the Indian Claims Commission proceedings, that tribes often were not compensated adequately for the land that they granted away. Unfair bargains as well as trust funds that the United States had not administered properly created pressure from Indian people for recompence. The recompence could be a financial payment or a return of land. Throughout the early twentieth century, tribe after tribe sought relief for the lands that they had lost.

Tribes had no court to go into, because the United States is a sovereign and you can not sue a sovereign until it waives the right not to be sued. The United States did not allow itself to be sued until the Court of Claims was set up in 1855. But in 1863, there was an express statutory decision that Indian tribes could not sue in the Court of Claims. In the early twentieth century, more and more tribes began to press for a resolution of their claims. Congress responded by passing a series of 133 special acts that gave the Court of Claims jurisdiction to hear individual tribes' cases. Congress did not rule on these cases. It simply waived sovereign immunity and allowed individual tribes to bring suits.

The Meriam Report, in 1928, recommended that Congress create a more efficient and fair device to resolve old Indian claims. A few years later, several tribes urged some sort of claims resolution under the IRA, but that was not done.

The Indian Claims Commission Act passed on August 13, 1946. There were various reasons for its passage. Some legislators wanted to be fair to the Indians and allow their claims to be adjudicated. All the act did was create a court. It did not lead to a specific result. There are indications that other legislators felt that it would be part of the termination process. Their notion was that you had to wipe the slate clean by resolving these old claims before you could really get on with termination. Another more pragmatic factor was a simple desire to get rid of the cumbersome device of having Congress pass special acts before each tribe could bring a claim.

The Indian Claims Commission Act did several things. First, it only dealt with claims that occurred before August 13, 1946. In other words, the Indian Claims Commission heard no claim for a taking of land or mismanagement of money that occurred after 1946. The act provided that claims that arose after 1946 would go to the Court of Claims, if a money damage claim were brought. Secondly, the act required that all claims and complaints be filed within five years, before August 13, 1951. There was a tremendous frenzy in many lawyers' offices to get those claims led. People also flew to Washington to meet that filing date.

The Indian Claims Commission Act was liberal. It was fairer to Indians than the existing law required in a number of respects. First, it allowed money recovery for all takings of land, no matter what was the source of Indian title. Prior to 1946, the courts had found that Indian tribes were not entitled to compensation when their aboriginal title was taken. This act did grant recovery for takings of aboriginal title.

It also granted a right of recovery for taking of executive order reservations. If an executive order reservation was set up and then partially broken up, as many were, you could go to the Indian Claims Commission and get recovery for that. Under the law of the United States before the Indian Claims Commission Act, a tribe could not get recovery for that taking. The idea was that only treaty reservations set up by statute were constitutionally recognized under the Fifth

Amendment; land title that was aboriginal or established by executive order was not protected by the Fifth Amendment. Only lawyers could explain how you get compensated for title recognized by Congress but not title recognized by the president of the United States. But that had been the law, until the Indian Claims Commission Act made that kind of title compensable.

The act also went beyond existing law in that it allowed for recovery for unconscionable consideration. Often treaties were negotiated unfairly and tribes did not receive enough compensation. Under contract law, the tribe would not be entitled to payment for that. Under the Indian Claims Commission Act, they were allowed to seek recovery for unconscionable dealings.

There are a few other respects in which the act went beyond existing law to allow recovery. By and large, it did away with what were referred to as gratuitous offsets. During the era of the special acts, before the Indian Claims Commission Act, a tribe would go in and get a recovery. Then the United States would come in and say, "Okay, their land taking was $2 million, but we provided blankets, beads, wagons, and educational services. They are worth $1 million. Therefore, the tribal recovery has to be offset." These gratuitous offsets were extremely important under the special acts. A total of $49 million was awarded under the special acts. Of that amount, $29 million was lost to gratuitous offsets. Tribal recovery was lowered by about 60 percent. This did not happen under the Indian Claims Commission. Generally, gratuitous offsets were not allowed.

The most fundamental problem with the act, from the tribes' point of view, was that it provided for payment in money and not land. That moral and economic issue was never seriously debated. Perhaps, it should have been. The government could have allowed for money recovery and then transferred to a tribe an equal amount of public domain land near the reservation. But that was not done. It was a straight money payment act. A settlement of $1,800 would buy a nice car in the fifties, but it was not the same as receiving a land payment. Many Indian people would point to that as the essential injustice of the act.

There are over one hundred dockets that have not been completed. These cases were filed between 1946 and 1951, and they still have not been completed after almost forty years. The old Indian Claims Commission that had five judges was abolished in 1978. Its cases were transferred to the Court of Claims. Indian people complain that the long delays in settling their claims are another injustice. There is no other area in the judicial system, even antitrust, where you have delays of that magnitude.

Attorneys' fees are a maximum of 10 percent under the act. Because of the big awards that were given—$10 to 12 million being common—the claims attorneys, by any standard, have done well. Nevertheless, there are some honest ambiguities on this issue: the typical contingent fee recovery after trial—and remember that claims attorneys receive nothing if their clients do not prevail—would be 33 percent. So, the fees under the act are less than the typical attorney-client relationship. But there are lots of reasons why that is a false point.

Tribes have received approximately $800 million under the Indian Claims Commission Act. Tribes have raised complaints because that amount was much smaller than it might have been. When you figure the amount of a claim by the value of the land at the date of taking, let's say 1850, that value might be very small in many cases. The key point then becomes whether you award interest. If you award interest, even at 6 percent you are going to multiply that old award many times over. What the courts found was that if aboriginal or executive order land was taken there would be no interest. For example, in my home state of Oregon the Siletz Reservation had some of the richest timber land and scenic coastland in the world, but it was an executive order reservation. Those tribes on the reservation received a dollar or two an acre without any interest to bring it up to the present.

Today, the Indian Claims Commission Act is cited as a precedent for awarding compensation to Japanese-Americans who were detained during World War II. It also is touted in some foreign countries as a progressive way to approach aboriginal claims. That is ironic because many Indian people despise it for some of the problems I have raised. As a lawyer, I do not like what the act did to my profession. There was a period when all kinds of attorneys spent time on Indian law, but it was all on claims. It was terribly important to have lawyers representing tribes during the termination era of the 1950s and early 1960s. They were not there, because they were working on claims. And remember, attorneys could either file with the Indian Claims Commission or Court of Claims for money, or they could go into court and try and get the Indians' land back. Normally, if Indians receive payment in the Court of Claims or Indian Claims Commission, they can not get the land back later. Lawyers had to advise tribes on whether they ought to go into the Indian Claims Commission with 10 percent attorneys' fees and an attorney willing to take that case, or go off and try to get the land. In the latter option, there was no way to pay the attorney fee for a very uncertain case. We went through a long period of time when those decisions were being made repeatedly. Now tribes are in a legal, political, moral, and economic situation of saying we want our land back. The rejoinder is that you have been paid for it under the Indian Claims Commission.

W. ROGER BUFFALOHEAD

On December 13, 1984, my son will receive the benefits from a tribal claim that our tribe started long before I was born. It finally was won in the mid–1970s. He was about five years old when the claim was won. His amount of money was put in a trust fund with a 3 percent annual interest rate, so he will receive about an eighteen hundred dollar check in December. He will probably join the ranks of thousands of other Indians who have received such claims since the Indian Claim Commission Act was passed in 1946 by buying himself a new car. I suspect that the new car will probably be a wreck in two years. His tribal heritage will have gone down the drain.

I have not done a lot of research in the area of the Indian Claims Commission Act, except as it affected the Minnesota Chippewa tribe, with whom I have had a long association as an historical researcher, and also my own tribe. So I feel uncomfortable when talking about the basic principles of the act and how it affected Indian tribes on a much larger scale, but I do know that the idea of granting claims to Indian tribes was something that Indians began to pursue as long ago as the nineteenth century. Some of the earliest attempts were made through the old United States Court of Claims, which required tribes to get a special act from Congress in order to sue the United States.

The Minnesota Chippewa tribal people were robbed out of a tremendous amount of acreage under the Minnesota equivalent of the

Dawes General Allotment Act. It was called the Nelson Act Agreements of 1889. The Chippewa brought suit, in the 1920s, for the lands that were taken through that agreement. In the mid–1930s, they lost those claims. When the Indian Claims Commission Act was passed in 1946, they were ineligible to refile on those claims. It has been a difficult situation for them. Of course, they could go back and file claims on land lost through earlier treaties, which they did, and they won. But, by and large, claims to the enormous amount of land that passed from their hands into white ownership through the Nelson Act Agreements of 1899 were never settled as far as the Minnesota tribal people were concerned. It is something that is still a problem in many other Indian communities.

E. RICHARD HART

There are a lot of problems inherent in claims. They include problems with attorneys and witnesses. There also is the question of making sure that tribes are fairly represented.

In dealing with tribal history, especially in the Great Basin and the Southwest, where I have done most of my work, one thing is very clear: the tribes wanted to have a day in court. They knew that there had been unconscionable transactions or takings of land. They felt they still owned land that was occupied and used by the United States without their consent. It is important to remember that one thing that led to the Indian Claims Commission Act was the tribes' persistent determination to get their day in court. For example, the Zuni began their claims struggle in the 1880s. Every tribal council, every governor, from that time until the present, was concerned with the Zuni having a day in court and getting some kind of justice.

Another problem is the question of whether the land was taken. That is the question the Western Shoshone are facing today. The Western Shoshone had a treaty that was ratified by Congress in 1863. It seems to say that a lot of what is now federal land is still owned by the Western Shoshone and that it will be owned by the Indians until the federal government provides a reservation large enough for them to make a living in agriculture. That is the way I read the treaty. If that is true, the federal government has been collecting allotment fees and rent on all that land for a hundred years when they should have been paying it to the Shoshone.

There are all kinds of difficulties involved with the way that attorneys have represented tribes. For instance, in the Northern Paiute claim: the attorneys for the Northern Paiute were told by the federal government that they had to represent the Owens Valley Paiute. The attorneys representing the tribes had not taken the time to find out who all the Northern Paiute were, let alone ever talk to them. They represented people whom they had never met. They never discussed the case with them or gave the Paiute any of their legal alternatives. The attorneys made stipulations with the Justice Department without the tribes having any input. They determined times of taking without ever discussing it with tribal leaders, and they stipulated values of land at the time it was taken without ever discussing that with tribal leaders.

The percentage of money awarded was a problem. Most attorneys pressured tribes to make quick settlements. They did not go through extended court battles, which might have raised the value of the Indians' land, because it required expense on the part of the attorneys. Attorneys also had something to do with getting tribes to take per capita payments, instead of lump payments that encouraged employment or economic development.

Witnesses also have faced problems with the Indian Claims Commission. Expert witnesses came under pressures from the attorneys for the plaintiff and pressures from attorneys from other tribes. If two tribes claimed that same area and if it could be proven in court that there was joint use of an area, nobody got paid for it. That was true for fairly large tracts of land. In the Zuni's case, almost all of the land that the Zuni claimed already had been awarded to the Navajo.

Historians and anthropologists have been susceptible to considerable pressure because they hoped to keep their work going with tribes. They have generally testified favorably for the tribes in court. The Indian Claims Commission has had a major impact on Indian historiography. The same thing can be said about anthropology. Anthropologists and historians who are friends of tribes sometimes have felt that it was in the best interest of the case to testify just a little bit differently, so that it would look better in court. For instance, you had to first prove in court that a tribe was a tribe. In the Indian Claims Commission and the

United States Court of Claims, that required a certain level of group organization. If you did not testify that there was an organization and a cultural people beyond the family unit, the Indians were not entitled to seek a claim.

Another thing that should be taken into account, and this has come up in the Zuni case, is that some lands can not be conscionably taken from tribes. It is unconscionable for the United States government or anyone else to take a church away from Mormons or Catholics or to take a synagogue away from Jews. The courts would not allow that under any circumstances, whatever the justification. In the case of many tribes, portions of their lands were and are their churches. This land has great religious value to them. It is my belief that for some of those lands that title could not have been conscionably taken.

In the Zuni's case, there is a place that Zunis go after death. It is a small lake in southern Arizona. They make annual pilgrimages there every six years. This region has extreme religious value. There is no excuse for the government's refusal to protect or validate their title to that property.

EDWARD C. JOHNSON

I can remember many years ago when my great grandmother and grandfather talked about getting their Indian money. They never received it, but some of us did. The Northern Paiute obtained $5,000 a piece for their land. That included the Comstock Lode. In the nineteenth century, they took close to $1 billion in gold and silver out of that mine. Today, with the inflated value of money, it would be worth at least $10 to 20 billion.

And of course, we had anthropologists. The government and the tribe each had their witnesses and attorneys. People were interviewed to determine that the tribe was there and that this was their area. An anthropologist determined that this was our land. We had three sections of land that extended from southern Oregon and southern Idaho through western Nevada and into eastern California. We got $21 million for it. Approximately $18 million came from the area that included the Comstock Lode and $3 million from the other two areas. It was one of the biggest claims case payments. I think we got $1.29 an acre for it.

During this claims case, hearings were held and federal officials came out and talked to us. We had an organization called the United Paiutes, Incorporated. It opposed the claims case and advocated getting the land back. We still have people that advocate getting the land back. Others said that we are a practical people. They concluded that all of that land really did not belong to us. Despite the talk about aboriginal title, our reservation was here. The land out there belonged to someone else. Theoretically, we still own it, but we do not possess it. Since we could not prove that we owned all of the land, we could not get claims payments for it. If we had a treaty, maybe we could have rallied around something and fought for getting the land back.

The two major Northern Paiute reservations are Pyramid Lake and Walker River. They each contain about three thousand acres. In 1906 we lost our lake and part of our reservation because someone thought there was another Comstock Lode there. The government dammed up the river that leads to Pyramid Lake. I guess they wanted the lakes, so they have found ways to get the water.

But we are still here. In fact, we just had a meeting with our claims attorneys over various dockets. The government attorneys and our tribal attorneys have come to an agreement on our fishery for $2.5 million. Of course, the claims lawyers will get 10 percent, which is $250,000. I do not know what we will decide to do with the $2.5 million for the fishery, which we lost.

There are other dockets. We have one for trespass on the reservation and one for mismanagement of our funds. We should have more funds coming in until the dockets run out. We are looking forward to this money, but I do not know what we will do with it. Almost everyone wants a per capita payment. The tribal members want a check to show that they got their Indian money. The tribe might have frittered it away, and the people never would have known that they got their claims money.

We are generally a poor people. Most Northern Paiutes live off the reservation or in small colonies. Our people surely could use more lands, wherever they are located, but it is not in the "Great White Father's" scheme of things to give us more land. We can be thankful that we have already got $21 million in claims and another $2.5 million coming down the pike. The attorney really does not tell us much about what is going on in these cases.

A new court has been created to replace the Indian Claims Commission. This tribunal will not bring real justice to the Northern Paiute or to any other tribes. The Indian Claims Commission was simply a legal way to quiet aboriginal title. The government wanted to pay as little as possible for legally taking over these lands. Once the aboriginal title has been solved, the government will go on to other kinds of things.

CHAPTER FIVE
Relocation

Robert L. Bennett, Philleo Nash, Helen Peterson, Gerald One Feather, LaDonna Harris

Armed with Public Law 280 and House Concurrent Resolution 108, the federal government allowed (and sometimes encouraged) state governments to extend their jurisdiction over the reservations, and withdrew federal services from several tribal communities. As part of the termination policies, federal officials hoped to disperse the remaining reservation communities and to scatter the Indian population into the general mainstream of American life. Since the United States was rapidly becoming urbanized, the BIA encouraged reservation people to move to the cities, where the assimilation process could be accelerated by the anonymity of urban life.

R. David Edmunds, Cherokee, professor of history,
Texas Christian University

We need to remind ourselves that off-reservation employment goes back at least to the Wild West days of Buffalo Bill and Sitting Bull. The BIA had been involved in off-reservation employment in a very meaningful way at least since 1929 when the first field agent was appointed for that purpose. It is also important for us to recognize, as we look at the 1950s, that an important part of the post-war planning that took place in the central office in 1943 focused on how to provide greater employment off the reservations for returning veterans. That was part of John Collier's policy.

John Painter, professor of history, Northern State College

[161]

Robert L. Bennett

The relocation program of the Bureau of Indian Affairs, which later became the employment assistance program, was developed as a sort of panacea for the so-called Indian problem. I was in that program for several years from the time of its inception. It was a two phase program. First of all, it relocated people from the reservation areas where jobs were not available to areas where there were jobs. The other phase of the program was to relocate people from reservation areas to primarily urban areas, where they had the opportunity to take vocational training.

One of the difficulties with this program was it became a panacea for all Indian problems. It also was discriminatory. If an Indian family, or an Indian individual, wanted training in a vocational area, the government would pay their living expenses, tuition, and transportation costs and would provide medical training for a period of two years. However, if an individual of the tribe went to college and applied for a scholarship, all they allowed was *his* tuition and living expenses. His family was not included. If a person wanted to be an automobile mechanic, all expenses for himself and his family were paid for two years. If he wanted to follow the academic route, the government paid only his tuition and expenses.

Other federal agencies had responsibilities for relocation. One of the most important was the Employment Security Commission. It is funded by the United States government to provide services for all people. The Employment Security Commission funds the state employment services. My first relocation effort at the Bureau of Indian Affairs was to get the states of North Dakota, South Dakota, and Nebraska interested in securing employment for people living on reservations. We worked out agreements with these states to provide services to the Indian community as well as to the rest of their citizens.

Finding jobs in the local area for Indian people was advantageous to both sides. Sometimes, I developed employment opportunities for which we had no Indian people available. This information was provided to the local office of the state employment service. They filled these jobs with local people if we did not have any Indian people for these particular jobs.

Indians that were sent to the urban areas encountered many problems. There was a high return rate. This was to be expected. The greatest reason for returning was lonesomeness. People who had lived in an extended family relationship were isolated in a nuclear family. People also returned to their reservations because they were taken advantage of by high pressure salesmen. They fell into the trap of installment buying. It was $5 a week for this and $5 a week for that. Eventually, they were not able to take care of all these payments and installments.

We had this situation happen on a reservation where I was superintendent. It concerned Indian families who could not read English buying encyclopedias. I asked one of them: "Why do you do this?" They said: "Well, this person came to my house. I let him in my house and he was my guest. I could not say no because he was my guest." Indians were taken advantage of in that way on both the reservation and in the cities.

It is important to look at the human aspect of relocation. Before relocation, many people had unsanitary conditions on the reservation. Their houses did not have screens on windows, and they did not take care of garbage. When they came back after relocation, they had a little higher standard of living. People put screens on their windows and elevated their living standard as a result of relocation experience. Statistically, the problem might have been a failure. Yet there were spin-offs from this experience which were to the Indians' benefit.

How a policy is administered often determines whether it will be successful. To illustrate the point, I will tell you a story about a young lady that had two children. She was a single parent. She had arranged for these two children to stay with her mother while she went to Denver to take a clerical course. Of course, she was on Aid to Dependent Children. Because she was a single parent, her relocation had to be approved in Washington. We received a letter back stating that this individual received $200 a month being on ADC with two children. If she went to Denver and learned how to be a secretary, the entrance salary would be only $175 a month. She was supposedly better off staying on the reservation as a single parent with two children on ADC.

A relocation situation on the other side was a young lady who was the oldest of about six or seven children. She trained to be a beautician in Minneapolis. She eventually found a job, married her boss, and demonstrated his line of beauty products throughout the upper Middle West. This is an extreme example of a success story, but relocation was good for that particular individual.

In summary, I would say that the relocation program was excellent for some people. The mistake was trying to make it successful for everybody, which it was not. But we did finally get the state employment services and the Employment Security Commission offices interested in the problem of unemployment on Indian reservations. They also made a stronger effort to locate employment opportunities near the reservations, rather than transport people from South Dakota all the way to Los Angeles and other distant places.

Philleo Nash

Relocation was part of the termination policy followed by the Truman administration. I quarreled vigorously with Dillon S. Myer about the wisdom of relocation. It is customary for commissioners to refer to their predecessors as distinguished and capable individuals. So, I will not say anything about him that I did not say to him over the lunch table. I told Myer that he was an idiot and that he was going to get himself and the president of the United States into enormous difficulties.

Before he became Indian commissioner, Myer had directed the relocation of Japanese-American citizens to concentration camps that were called "relocation centers." John Collier and Dillon Myer had a major disagreement about the way in which the Indian Bureau operated the relocation centers for Japanese-Americans that were under its direction at Parker, Arizona. I had nothing to do with those particular things, except that, when I was on the staff in the Office of War Information, I had to review Myer's speeches and the releases from his office. I found him as intractable as other people found him later when he was Indian commissioner.

So Myer approached Indian affairs as though relocation centers and reservations were the same. He viewed Indians on reservations as temporary detainees. He sought to end this detention as quickly as possible. His policy was a form of expulsion. Myer did not understand the difference between the reservation system and his relocation centers. The War Relocation Authority experience was a most inappropriate model to follow when he became commissioner of Indian affairs.

It was a very bad time in Indian affairs. From Franklin Roosevelt's death to about 1950, we had a non-managed Indian Bureau. One of the things the president of the United States and the secretary of the interior have to do is to see that the Interior Department is well run like any other government agency.

World War II had a devastating effect on reservations and on the Bureau itself. The front office was moved out of Washington to Chicago to make room for important wartime agencies. Large numbers of Indians were in the armed forces, and the Indian agencies were stripped of personnel. Building programs of every kind stopped. At the end of the war, John Collier resigned under the most painful circumstances. He resigned while he was in Reno establishing residence for a divorce on Bureau time. That was a very serious mistake.

Bill Brophy, a marvelous human being, was an excellent choice to succeed Collier, but he had an acute upper respiratory disease. The torrid climate of Washington and the stress of the commissioner's job led to a physical breakdown. A short time later, John Ralph Nichols was made commissioner of Indian affairs. He lasted eleven months. Somebody else had to be found.

By this time, Oscar Chapman was secretary of the interior. He had a great feeling for the vigor with which Dillon Myer had prevented the Japanese-American relocation centers from becoming permanent facilities. None of us understood the Indian situation as well as we should have. I take my share of the blame. We were looking for a tough bureau chief. I was among those who recommended Myer for the job as Indian commissioner.

That gave me a certain claim on Myer's attention. At one of our numerous lunches, he said, "I am going to do three things you are not going to like." I responded, "What are they?" He said, "relocation." I told him, "Do not bother with the other two." The other two topics were area offices and the off-reservation dormitories for the Navajo. I also said, "Dillon, you are heading for disaster. You are going to bring yourself down, you are going to bring the house down, and you are going to bring President Truman down with it. I am a faithful and loyal staff member. I am going to have to tell him that I think he ought to get rid of you." That effort was not successful.

I worked as an assistant in the White House. I begged Harry Truman to fire Myer. I also asked for the job, which was possibly a tactical error. Truman said, "How can I respect your judgement if you are just looking for work?" The president then said, "What is the matter, do you think your job here is done?" And I said, "No." He replied, "I do not think it is either. I need you, so let's put an end to this. I do not have that many good bureau chiefs that I can spare one who is managing what I regard as an unmanageable bureau. But if a lot of bad things are going on and they are bad enough so that you think I ought to do something about it, you have my authority to look into it and come back and report to me." That was as far as I got.

Myer worked from the wrong framework. He attempted to repeat his success in the Japanese-American relocation centers. He thought it was an administrative coup to deal with Indian reservations as though they were detention camps. Everybody knew they were not. This policy was bound to face a certain amount of disaster. In the first place, the programs were underfunded. Myer's relocation program was essentially a one-way bus ticket from rural to urban poverty.

Relocation was an underfunded, ill-conceived program with a negative name. It had an unpopular administrator and one whom I failed to dislodge. I finished out my tour of duty at the White House and went back to other jobs. Eventually, the voters of Wisconsin caught up with me and put me out of office. I came to Washington looking for work, feeling very guilty about my part in Myer's appointment. I wanted to be appointed as Indian commissioner and undo some small part of the damage I had already done.

It took a long time to get confirmed. The National Congress of American Indians and Helen Peterson managed, at a very critical time, to get some telegrams sent from Lewiston, Idaho, to the Senate of the United States. One of my supporters, a senator from Wisconsin, held a sheaf of these telegrams in his hand. He did not say I have here a group of papers indicating that somebody was a communist. Instead, he indicated that these papers said that all the Indian tribes wanted Nash to be Indian commissioner.

After I became commissioner, we set up a task force to set policy guidelines for the Kennedy administration. The shabby program of relocation and expulsion from reservations obviously was no good. On the other hand, it was quite clear that it is not right to base a program for any American group on compulsory residence. If you generate a situation in which there is nothing but dependency and poverty in a rural environment, the fact that it is called a reservation does not justify saying, "Well, I am not going to help you get out." If you tell people they must stay because government programs such as relocation are not good enough, then you have made a decision to keep people in poverty.

On the other hand, if you say, "We do not believe in reservations, we are not going to pour good money after bad, and we are not going to have tribal economic development programs," then you are again making a decision. It says that, if you want to escape poverty, you have got to give up your life on the reservation. It was our carefully considered judgement that a dual program was the only thing that made any kind of sense. We favored economic and personal development programs for residents who lived on or off reservations, depending on their individual choice.

It seemed that while our economic development programs were being established, we needed an escape valve in the form of outmigration. We decided that relocation or employment assistance did not have to be a bad program. We discussed this idea at length and decided that instead of buying an Indian a bus ticket, we ought to spend somewhere around $4,000 for employment assistance. The assistance ought to begin with an indication from a family or individual on the reservation that they wanted to leave, an indication of where they wanted to go, counseling about what things would be like, and some vocational testing.

The selection process was very difficult. You can do a lot for a two person family with $4,000. You can do something for a three or four person family. There are very few government programs that can adequately fund relocation for larger numbers of people. Therefore, it is necessary to consciously acknowledge the fact that you will take younger families and help them make a reasonable judgement about where they want to go and what they want to do. It may very well be that the best thing is for them to stay on the reservation. But that has to be their choice.

There had to be a lot of consultation with the community agencies concerning the destination point. We had no right to pick those destinations, but it was necessary to make sure that there was generous support at the community level when the family arrived. This meant adequate job training, schools, community contacts, counseling, and housing.

In the matter of implementing policy, I felt we were victimized by decisions that had been made by my predecessors—Dillon Myer and Glenn Emmons. We were bound by the great American liberal value of non-segregation. Relocated Indians were scattered throughout the cities so they could not form neighborhood cohorts. This made little sense. Every ethnic group that established itself in America did so by creating cohesive neighborhoods that generated their own support. But the Indian Bureau could not follow this practice. That would be practicing segregation. Stupidity has no end under some circumstances. Once you have started something like that it is pretty hard to withdraw your support.

One of the things that we had to tell our relocation people was "Stop telling Indians that they have failed if they come back to their reservations. Abandon the rule that they only get once chance." I dropped out of high school, college, and graduate school. I finally dropped out of the Indian Bureau. I do not think that makes me a failure in life.

During the 1960s adult vocational training and on-the-job training was lavishly financed. At least the Bureau of the Budget thought it was. College students also were getting more money for scholarships. And the tribes were developing on their own. We moved from a $2 million level to about a $25 million level in the college scholarship program, but that college scholarship program was never provided with support in vocational counseling, school counseling, and community development counseling.

Relocation created a generation of street wise people. The Red Power movement, the confrontations on reservations, and the occupation of the BIA building were direct outgrowths of the intimate contact that had developed between blacks and Indians in the cities. People brought back to their reservations the policies of confrontation. They understood the amount of leverage that would be obtained by being bad instead of being good. I cannot be honest with my own feelings, or with my own perception of reality, unless I conclude that in the long run this was beneficial.

Helen Peterson

I am concerned about the omission of the National Congress of American Indians from discussions of that critical period in history between 1945 and 1960. I first became acquainted with NCAI in 1948, when it held a convention in Denver, Colorado. It had been founded, in 1944, in the same city. There is a picture which appears on most tribal council walls of that founding convention. I became executive director of the NCAI in 1953. D'Arcy McNickle, Ruth Bronson, and Bob Bennett were strong and key figures in the early years of the NCAI.

The NCAI was organized on a shoestring, and it never had much money. I was asked to become its director because there was no one there at the time. People like D'Arcy McNickle, Ruth Bronson, in particular, and Bob Bennett persuaded me to leave a very comfortable and happy job with the city of Denver and begin working for the NCAI. It was a job which I knew nothing about.

I think the connotation of the word "relocation" almost precludes a sane consideration of that program. I have been known as someone who was very much opposed to relocation. That is not true, because we had much more important things to worry about at the NCAI. We never opposed the program. We felt it was necessary and a good program. What upset us was the priority that it had in its relationship to other programs. Our concern was that the government needed to spend more time developing the human and natural resources on reservations and put relocation in its proper place. We should not waste our time arguing about relocation when there are really many more important issues to examine. The plain truth is that Indians are probably the most mobile people in the country. Like all other Americans, they moved around the country during World War II.

We had little understanding of what termination really meant, except that it struck terror into the hearts of people. It was complicated because a man named Wade Crawford from the Klamath Reservation lived in Washington for months at a time. He promoted termination.

The carrot was a big cash settlement for individuals. It was a very powerful argument that effectively put down the Klamath's opposition to termination.

In the NCAI office we did all we could to support, encourage, and back up those people who dared to question termination, but it was pretty much a losing battle. The NCAI was in a tough spot. We were deeply committed to respecting the sovereignty of a tribe. Did the NCAI want to oppose termination even when the people involved wanted it? We never really came to a final answer on that question.

The NCAI mobilized at a convention in Phoenix, Arizona, in December 1953. Before that time, its office had been closed. It was really in no position to act as a national organization. But we managed to raise a little money, and an emergency conference concerning American Indian legislation was held two months later. This conference was the beginning of sobering up some of the congressmen. It launched our effort to slow down and stop further implementation of the termination policy.

There are other ways in which tribes can be terminated though. They can be terminated through appropriations. Also, Indians often hurt themselves. Differences exist between reservation and off-reservation Indians. Some urban Indians have tried to undermine their own tribal governments by insisting that they have the right to vote in tribal elections. It is those tribal governments at home on the reservation who are going to ensure the survival of tribes. The words *genocide* and *survival* are thrown around loosely. They mean many different things. If we are not careful, we can be a part of such a movement without even knowing it.

Besides the failure to cooperate with our tribal governments, we have a proclivity for being irresponsibly critical of the Bureau of Indian Affairs. It is true that the BIA can always be improved. We have made jokes about the Bureau for many years. But the general American public now believes that the issue is Indians versus the Bureau. Many people do not realize that the Bureau is staffed by Indians. Almost all the area directors, superintendents, and division chiefs are Indians. It is time to develop training courses and support for these individuals.

GERALD ONE FEATHER

The relocation program had an impact on our tribal government at Pine Ridge. Many people who could have provided tribal leadership were lost because they had the motivation to go off the reservation to find employment or obtain an education. Relocation drained off a lot of potential leadership.

When some of these people returned, they brought back problems that they inherited from urban communities. For instance, we have established reservation ghettos, which we never had before. Public housing is an urban concept that was integrated into tribal planning.

Once people moved off the reservation to Rapid City and neighboring towns, they established themselves in these communities. They also continued to make demands on the tribal government. In many cases, they demanded tribal services even though they lived in urban areas. This has been a political question that the tribe has had to resolve. Where do you draw the line in offering tribal services?

One important thing did happen. The United Sioux Tribes, in South Dakota, contracted for employment assistance. Each tribe put money into this venture, which allowed them to run employment offices in major cities to help people find jobs and to take care of social problems that arose from city living This is a necessary service, especially in the last few years when unemployment has climbed on the reservations.

The people who moved to urban areas formed their own Indian communities. Indian centers became a focal point for the people that lived in cities. When they became organized, these centers allied closely with their respective reservation communities. Today, that relationship has become more refined. Several weeks ago, a Sun Dance was held in San Jose, California. Some of the elders from Pine Ridge were asked to go down there and conduct the Sun Dance. This is one example of how cultural and religious ceremonies of the tribe have been exported from the reservation to an urban clientele.

Tribal government today is complex. On the one hand, we have to deal with resident members. At the same time, we have an absentee group that is still pretty much a part of the tribal government. So, there is a real urban-reservation connection that has been going through a refining process. I do not know where this will lead to in the future.

The relocation program provided opportunities, but it also presented problems for tribal government. People have asked to be terminated from tribal rolls. In some cases, if you are born off the reservation, you are automatically not included as tribal members. So individual Indians are systematically terminating their membership on the tribal rolls.

LaDonna Harris

Back in Oklahoma, a group of us got together to organize Oklahomans for Indian Opportunity. In the process of doing that, we found out that more than half of the state's Indians were residing in Tulsa, Oklahoma City, Lawton, and smaller towns. We had a consciousness-raising just from the exercise.

President Lyndon B. Johnson appointed me to the National Indian Opportunities Council because I had raised the issue of federally unrecognized tribes and the point that one-half of our Indian population was living in urban areas. We decided to hold hearings around the country to make sure that my statement about the large number of urban Indians was accurate. We held hearings in Dallas, Los Angeles, San Francisco, and Minneapolis. I remember going down to Dallas and they said, "We do not have very many Indians here. We have about 2,500 people." I replied, "Oh, I have more relatives from Oklahoma than that in the Dallas-Fort Worth area."

We found out in those hearings that the Los Angeles area had the largest Indian population outside the Navajo Reservation. More importantly, we discovered that there were sociological impacts that evolved from relocation policy decisions. Individual termination was, in some ways, more devastating than tribal termination, where you had group reinforcement to rely on. People that came straight from an Indian boarding school and reservation situation to Los Angeles, Detroit, or Chicago underwent severe cultural shock. And there was little or no training to help people adapt to their new environment.

Relocation went hand in hand with termination. It was for budgetary reasons that Indian were moved to cities. Relocated individuals were no longer eligible for Indian Bureau services.

Relocation has caused social impacts and repercussions that we are still dealing with today. The occupation of Alcatraz was certainly one of those. In fact, the whole pan-Indian movement came out of the urban Indian situation. People were saying, we are Indians and we want to belong to something.

If you take people who come from a reservation and put them in a detached urban environment, you really have problems. In my opinion, that was what Alcatraz was all about. These people were detached from their roots. People cannot function well when you detach them from tribalism, communal living, and their extended families.

Urban Indians created an environment they could exist in. The pan-Indian movement reflected the need to have group reinforcement and a positive self-image. Indians used their imagination to survive in urban areas such as Los Angeles. There were basketball teams, church groups, peyote groups, and dances.

When the American Indian Movement and the urban unrest started, we were asking people to act rational in an irrational situation. In my opinion, people were simply creating an environment that they could function in. To me, that is exceptional. One of the reasons that Indians have survived is that we have the ability to adapt to those kinds of situations.

Alcatraz was very understandable. It was part of the after effect of the policy of relocation. People needed an identity; they needed a tie.

Relocation violated Indian treaties. Treaties were not made with the land. They were made with the people, and the responsibility of federal services continues to be the people. Today, we are once again being terminated for budgetary reasons. Tribes without federal recognition are being terminated from services that would help them to establish their credentials as an organized community of people, and all of those programs that urban Indians have fought so hard for are being cut away.

CHAPTER SIX

The Legacy of the Termination Era

Larry EchoHawk, Mary Ellen Sloan, Russell Jim,
Joe De La Cruz, Sol Tax

*I disagree with the statement that termination is not a threat any-
more. Our enemies, if I can call them that, all have learned from their
mistakes. They have learned over the last twenty years to be more subtle
about what they want. We are, once again, faced with resolutions from
national powerful organizations such as the American Farm Bureau Federation calling for termination of the reservations. I asked leaders of the
federation, "Why have you adopted this resolution?" And they told me
frankly that the Indians are getting too much land and water back. It is
economic reasoning. The machinery also is in place to reduce health and
other services to Indian people. It is the first move toward present day
termination.*

Elmer Savilla, director,
National Tribal Chairmen's Association

*Termination is here to stay. It is going to hit us in the face almost
every day. We had better be prepared for it. The National Interstate
Congress on Equal Rights and Responsibilities is the main thrust of anti-
Indianism in this country. It grew out of South Dakota into Montana and
has spread into seventeen states. It really shocks me that in America we
can have the kind of racial hatred that this organization espouses and
brags about.*

Robert Burnette, Rosebud Sioux, former director, NCAI

*The reason that the idea of termination, of cutting off special provi-
sions for Indians and forcing assimilation, recurs so frequently is that it*

[174]

reflects a deep belief that different economic and community organization modes are inferior to the American norm. There is the continuing temptation for policy makers to assume that everything possible has been done to help Indians but that it has failed. The only alternative, they say, is to stop these paternalistic efforts and force the Indian to be like the rest of us. It is much easier to reach this conclusion, all too often, than to face the extremely difficult conditions in which Indians have been living and the costs of providing a relatively normal range of opportunities to Indian people. This is what makes the termination history so important. It shows that there is no easy answer and that seemingly easy solutions only make things a great deal worse. It was the triumph of the leaders of the restoration movement to prove this to the Congress and conservative political leaders. It would be a tragedy if this knowledge were lost.

Gary Orfield, Brookings Institution,
professor of political science,
University of Chicago

Larry EchoHawk

I think it is important that we talk about what termination was yesterday, what it is today, and what importance it has for us in the future. To me, termination has three basic aspects. Back in the 1950s, the federal government was trying to escape the responsibility that its relationship with Indian people had imposed. Over the years, it had wanted more control over the lives and resources of Indian people, but there was no justification for that control in the United States Constitution. It merely gave the federal government the power to regulate commerce with Indian tribes. It was through the judicial branch of the federal government that the doctrine of guardian and wardship status was created. Eventually, the federal government got tired of paying the price for being vested with that enormous power. Termination was an effort to do away with the trust responsibility, and we see that happening again today.

A second aspect of termination has to do with assimilation. In the 1950s, the government wanted to make the Indian people become more like mainstream society. By placing Indian people under the wing of state governments, doing away with their tribal governments, making them hold their lands as other citizens of the United States hold theirs, and having their property subject to taxation, federal officials thought that assimilation would occur. That was not a new policy, but it received renewed vigor throughout the termination era.

The third and most important aspect of termination has to do with the attack on self-rule, or the sovereignty of tribal governments. It was not only the termination acts that affected particular tribes. It was also the enactment of Public Law 280, which swept away the authority of Indian tribes in jurisdictional areas. There was almost a complete destruction of tribal government for many Indian nations.

The policy of termination has been repudiated, at least in word, by presidential administrations since 1958, but we still suffer the impact of termination. The tribes that were affected by the termination acts were almost completely decimated economically. I say that because of my experience in working with the Paiute people in southern Utah.

I have spoken with many people who were touched by termination. They have bitter feelings toward the government. These people are angry because they have not been identified in the eyes of the government as Indian, even though everyone would readily recognize what they are.

Overall, the termination policy was an abysmal failure. We have looked at termination as a policy that lasted from approximately the mid–1940s into the 1960s. I submit to you that termination has been around a lot longer than that, and you can expect to see it in the future. Maybe the descriptive word has changed, but the thrust of the policy is there. From the time of Indian removal, through the creation of reservations, through the enactment of the Major Crimes Act in 1885, to the General Allotment Act in 1887, you can see the work of the United States Congress in trying to dismantle tribal government and Indian rights.

The actions of the courts in the United States have not been mentioned, but they run parallel to termination. In *Lone Wolf vs Hitchcock,* the *United States vs Montana,* and many other cases, the rights of Indian people as tribal governments have been eroded. It is disturbing to me to hear that termination is only something of the past. I believe we are being set up. We have to be aware that termination is something that we face today. We have got to be better prepared in the future, because the resources that Indian people had are greatly diminished today.

The Shoshone-Bannock Indian tribe was promised, in 1868, that they would have a permanent homeland of 1.8 million acres. That solemn promise of the United States has been reduced to a mere 500,000 acres, and twenty years from now I wonder what acreage will be left on that particular reservation. And the Shoshone-Bannock are one of the luckier groups of Indian people as far as their ability to maintain tribal rights and resources.

The real challenge falls upon tribal governments. No doubt, they will have to deal with the United States Congress to ward off further termination legislation. But ultimately Indian people will prevail because of their own inner strength. I have to give credit to one of the draftsmen of the Indian Reorganization Act for introducing that thought to the dominant society. In the Indian Reorganization Act, John Collier tried to build upon the strength of the Indian people. Whether you like the IRA or not, it was a significant reversal of federal Indian policy. To that extent, Collier deserves credit. But the Indian people are the ones that will provide the final victory.

MARY ELLEN SLOAN

I am an attorney from Salt Lake City. I would like to talk about my experiences in representing the Paiute, who were a terminated tribe. The Paiute are composed of five bands located in southern Utah. In the early 1950s, when termination was in vogue, Senator Arthur Watkins, one of the primary architects of the termination policy in Congress, looked to tribes in his own state to participate in this federal policy. Consequently, the Utah Paiute were selected for termination.

It is important to examine some of the historical background of termination. William Zimmerman developed four criteria to determine which tribes should be terminated. They were (1) the degree of acculturation, (2) the economic resources upon which the tribes could rely after termination, (3) the consent of the tribal officials, and (4) the consent of state and local governmental officials.

A short time later, the Bureau of Indian Affairs undertook a socioeconomic survey of the Utah Paiute. That information was submitted to Congress during its deliberation on the Paiute termination legislation. The record was very clear that the Paiute did not meet Zimmerman's criteria. The quality of Paiute land was so poor that frequently the BIA was unable to find anyone to lease it for grazing purposes. Furthermore, there was no informed consent. There were some Paiutes that agreed to termination, but informed consent, as we would understand it, did not exist. State and local officials also had very little input. They were not particularly interested in the Paiute.

Nevertheless, the end result was that this particular tribe was terminated. Because of termination the Paiute lost approximately fifteen thousand acres of land through tax sales or sales of land in anticipation of being taxed. In addition, they lost any opportunity for federal services and other federal benefits. It is very clear that the selection of the Paiute for termination was a political decision. It was not based upon rational criteria.

In 1968, the Bureau of Indian Affairs once again did a socioeconomic survey of the Paiute. It confirmed the basic information that previously had been included in the legislative record. Their socioeconomic condition was extremely poor. Housing conditions were bad, low educational levels common, and tribal income minimal.

In 1974, after the passage of the Menominee Restoration Act, the Paiute began to explore the possibility of restoration for their tribe. In 1978, legislation was introduced in the Senate and in the House to restore their status as a federally recognized Indian tribe. The original restoration legislation would have restored federal services and federal recognition. It did not provide for the restoration of land. The bill subsequently was amended in the Senate to include a reservation land program. It was then sent to the House. The House concurred, and legislation was drafted that included a provision for the development of a reservation plan, which the Paiute have been working on.

With respect to the specific impacts of termination, federal services and federal recognition were ended. There was also a misconception that was very destructive. It was that termination somehow changed a person's identity as an Indian. That misconception existed for a long time. One of the significant things about restoration was that it put all of that aside and restored federal services.

Federal recognition of the Paiute was extremely important. Since the restoration legislation, the Paiute have developed a tribal government, adopted a tribal constitution, and participated in federal programs such as 638 contracting. These achievements were possible because the restoration legislation provided for the application of the Indian Reorganization Act.

There were non-Indian influences on the restoration legislation. State jursidiction was an issue. Congress provided that Public Law 280, as amended, would apply. There also was a provision that hunting and fishing rights would not be restored.

There have been several pieces of restoration legislation passed for tribes besides the Paiute, but Congress has not adopted a general bill that would restore all the tribes that had been originally terminated. Congress still requires each tribe to propose its own restoration legislation.

RUSSELL JIM

First of all, I would like to clarify the misconception that I am an "activist." This play on words, in this borrowed tongue that I speak, makes it sound as if I am a rebel. The moral responsibility that comes from my heritage prevents me from being a rebel. I have been influenced by elders who told me to be gracious to all people, including the transients that have come to this continent.

The Yakima nation did not accept termination. We were about ninth on the list but were never terminated. The Yakima nation also did not accept the Indian Reorganization Act. I take exception to the statement that if it were not for John Collier, the tribes today would not exist. We refused to accept the IRA, but we still exist as a culturally distinct people. We speak our own language and practice our own religion. It is actually not a religion but a way of life. Everything is tied together.

Termination has been imposed on just about all tribes to a certain degree. There has been a gradual erosion of treaty rights by a small group of influential people that want to have their own way. The most glaring example today of termination and the erosion of treaty rights is the issue of nuclear waste. The Yakima Reservation and the Hanford Works are only thirteen miles apart as the crow flies. The Yakima nation consisted of 12 million acres prior to the Treaty of 1855. In that treaty, we ceded to the federal government 10.8 million acres and retained 1.3 million acres. It was our understanding that in the ceded

10.8 million acres, we retained the right to travel, gather food and medicine, and fish in all usual and accustomed places. But because of the damage done by radiation to the environment, who in their right mind would travel through that area and gather food and medicine.

Boarding schools are another form of termination. I was sent to a boarding school. We were beaten when we spoke our language. The plan, as I see it, when I look back in history, was to prevent Indian children from learning the day-to-day teachings of their families. Instead, foreign values were imposed.

I would also like to refer to the issue of unemployment. Politicians, whether they are running for mayor or president of the United States, always stress the need for employment. This imposes a different value system upon a food-gathering people. The emphasis on getting a job and earning that almighty dollar contributes to greed. It is called the "Great American Way."

The creation of these so-called jobs imposes on the natural resources of tribes. It leads to a form of self-cannibalism. You can observe self-cannibalism in Indian country if you look at the Crow's coal, the Osage's oil, and the Yakima's timber. In the Yakima case, there was mismangaement of timber resources by the Bureau of Indian Affairs. It wanted to cut the timber at an accelerated rate of speed. Approximately 90 percent of the Yakima income comes from the timber. This revenue keeps our government running. Once the prime timber vanishes, the Yakima will become more dependent upon the grants and contracts of the federal government. When the federal government controls the purse strings, they control your sovereignty.

There has been too much apathy in Indian country and too much misunderstanding by the mainstream of society. Christians must start realizing their moral responsibility. It is a shame what they have done and what they are attempting to do to the indigenous people of this planet. I do not wish to be only remembered in the history books by my children's children. The unique indigenous people on this continent need to keep their identity. To have a versatile world is what the Creator intended. If He wanted a melting pot, He would have made it a long time ago. We would have been all one color and maybe the same size.

The Yakima fought hard against the terminaton of any tribe. We were not out in the forefront verbally. My people always have had a tendency to stay back but to speak powerfully and speak wisely. I take exception to the idea that there were just a few people fighting against termination. There were a lot of us. My family has been involved in politics for a long time. Influential leaders in the Pacific Northwest fought very hard against termination. The thwarting of termination would have been nearly impossible without them. The Affiliated Tribes of Northwest Indians are still a very influential group and a segment of the National Congress of American Indians.

JOE DE LA CRUZ

I have been involved in resisting or fighting some form of termination all my life. Ever since the European people arrived on this continent, we have been in the process of termination. But you do not learn much about it in books that people read.

I often ask people, how did Public Law 280 come about in 1953? Only one person has given a response that I feel very comfortable with. After the Second World War, the United Nations was established, and it emphasized the need to decolonize people. The United States was one of the key sponsors of the United Nations. Someone in the United States government realized that people victimized by colonialism lived in their own country. From 1947 until the early 1950s, there was a drive to terminate the colonial rule of the Bureau of Indian Affairs.

Most of us who are involved in Indian affairs know about the negative impact of termination. Concurrent Resolution 108 is still on the books. We supposedly are in another era, entitled self-determination, but we still have many holdovers within the various federal and state agencies who have the mentality of the termination era. We are battling today over the question of jurisdictional authority. Tribes supposedly retained all the powers they ever had, but we are challenged every time we attempt to do something. Because of Public Law 280, we had conflicts with the states and counties over highways. We also had confrontations over our children and the rights of our children. States used Public Law 280 to impose their educational practices on our children.

The Department of Interior and the Bureau of Indian Affairs still have a colonial mentality. When it comes to a question of who has jurisdiction over Indian territory, that trustee is a very weak sister.

I know that because of Public Law 280. During the termination period, the Quinault people lost over 35,000 acres of their timberland. Some of that land was valued at a million dollars per 80 acre stand.

It took several years and thousands of man hours of work to find out what really happened. Recently, the Supreme Court decided in the Mitchell case that we could sue the United States over the mismanagement of those lands and resources. One of the key examples of mismanagement that we found was that none of our people were properly informed about the disposing of Indian property. When they signed documents, they thought they were just selling their timber, not the land. We found instances where Indian people received only $5,000 for an 80 acre stand of timber.

We have worked on this problem since 1965. We went to the Court of Claims. They said we could not sue the United States. Our attorneys appealed to the Supreme Court, which sent the case back to the Court of Claims after ruling 6 to 3 that we could sue the United States for mismanaging Indian resources. A lot of our people thought that they had won. I told them it was just another hurdle. I warned that we might be dead before the case goes through the federal courts again.

It is easy for a few people in the various government agencies to put barriers in the way when tribes start trying to move forward in a direction of self-determination. The Quinault nation has maintained that it has complete jurisdiction on the reservation. In order to uphold our jurisdictional rights, we had to fight the state, the federal government, and especially the Bureau of Indian Affairs. We were challenged every step of the way.

In the early 1960s, the Quinault hired some people to help zone our reservation. The Washington coast within our reservation was zoned a wilderness area. The rest of the reservation was zoned for forestry. It took about eight years before someone challenged our zoning ordinance. First of all, the Bureau of Indian Affairs refused to recognize it. Then, a real estate development corporation from California challenged the Quinault nation zoning ordinance. We beat them in a district and a circuit court.

The tribe also developed its own building code, sanitation ordinance, and highway act. Again, the Bureau did not recognize these laws. After we took some of these cases to the Ninth Circuit Court, the

Bureau finally has started to work with the tribe and recognize the law of the Quinault nation. They also began to recognize our forestry practices, but in 1984, they attempted to deny our 638 contracts on forestry management because we required the Bureau of Indian Affairs, the United States Forest Service, and the state to get hydraulic permits from the tribe any time they were doing anything around a waterway that supported a salmon habitat.

Because of these problems, I do not think that termination has ended. It will always be with us. Indian people will continue to feel the impact of the termination era until policies are created that guarantee sovereign tribal government.

Sol Tax

I think that it is worthwhile for us to see urban relocation as part of the policy of termination. The relocation program in the early 1950s promoted the dispersal of Indian communities. Instead of developing reservations and continuing tribal identity, the government put Indians in cities far away from their homeland.

When Indians came to Chicago, they received relocation assistance for about six weeks. Indian families came on a train with a one-way ticket. Once they arrived, they had no place to go. They were met by somebody in the Bureau of Indian Affairs who took them to a rental house and found them a job. When Indians returned to the relocation office to say they had a problem, which they all did, they were told we do not have any more jurisdiction over you. We have rented you a home; if you want to move to another one, that is your problem. If you do not like the job, that is also your problem.

Over the course of the next few years, thousands of Indians relocated in Chicago. The American Friends Indian Center was established for them. Without this center, there would have been no facility to treat Indians as human beings and help families in trouble. If Indians went back to the Bureau of Indian Affairs office, they got a scolding because there were no resources for them.

At that time I was involved with the Fort Berthold Reservation. I know what happened there. Many Indians on the reservation could have made it in the city, but they were the ones who already had large farms. The Indians who could not do anything on the reservation were the only ones that were tempted to leave and go to Chicago or some other place. People who had no means of making a living at home were taken to strange cities.

In Chicago, we had a meeting with our senator and with the social agencies. Of course, the social agencies were only interested when someone got into real trouble. We also asked for the names of the people before they came and what train they were coming on, so that we could meet the train and tell them where the Indian Center was located. Relocation officials said that was impossible. It was part of the ethics of the government not to give out individual names. It was a public scandal. There was a critical article in *Harper's Magazine.* All it did was make the Bureau of Indian Affairs angry.

The head man from the Denver relocation service came to Chicago more than once. We had meetings at the Indian Center. We tried to explain what was going on. The relocation people said, "We just want Indians to get jobs." We replied, "Why don't you take care of them?" They said, "This is not in the law. Furthermore, the Indians are being offered opportunities to come to the cities and get better employment than they could get on the reservation." There was a big discrepancy between what was actually going on and the notion of relocation held in Washington D.C.

Many Indians were afraid that the people who relocated would no longer be supportive of the tribal view. This was not the case at all. Indians had not left their tribes. They were in the city to locate a job, just as they had gone off to other jobs in the past. In 1961, a large national Indian conference was held in Chicago. About a thousand Indians attended. They represented most of the tribes of the United States. A few individuals came from Canada and Alaska. Those in attendance worried that the Indians from Chicago would dominate the conference, but this did not happen. Indians from the city supported their tribes-people. That was their point of reference. One of the first things that came out in the conference was that no competition existed between urban Indians and those who had remained at home on their reservations.

I saw an example of this when the Census Bureau planned the 1980 census. I was at the meeting where the Census Bureau asked

Indian leaders in Chicago to help with the 1980 census so their people would not be undercounted. The reason for an accurate head count was that the federal budget for different cities was based on per capita estimates. The Indians turned them down because they did not want to compete with the money that was targeted for their reservations. It was clear that they were associating themselves with their tribes and with the reservations from which they came, rather than the city.

Meanwhile, the Indians adjusted to the city. The Indian Center prospered with help from many people outside of the Indian community but mostly with the help of Indians. This was difficult because the center had to get funds from many different sources. It was responsible for youth recreation, education, and health. The Indians did not like to go to non-Indian places if they could have their own Indian health center.

The Indian Center had its own board of directors that made all the policy. Usually, social agencies have rich people on their boards of directors. They have outside professionals who raise money for them and oversee their management. There were no professionals, at that time, among Indians in Chicago, but they have developed their own professionalism in order to be able to manage themselves. They manage the health center, the employment center, and the business association that teaches people how to do things. They are making a life for themselves, not as city Indians, but as Indians whose loyalty remains with the tribe. Their children go back and forth between the city and the reservations.

More than half of the Indians in the United States now live in urban areas where they can make a living and manage their own affairs. Relocation had terrible consequences while it was going on. Now that the Indians are settled, making their own way, and managing urban Indian institutions themselves, it does not look so bad.

PART THREE

Toward Self-Determination

Navajo tribal delegate Scott Preston explaining the government's stock reduction program to people from the western Tonalea area, 1940.

A 1936 meeting on an Indian Reorganization Act charter at the extreme northwest end of the Cheyenne River Reservation.

188

I am not sure that the War on Poverty weakened the integrity of the Bureau of Indian Affairs by farming out too many programs to other government agencies. The strategy, at that time, was to establish tribal eligibility for programs that were available to state and local governments. This underlined the fact that the Indians' relationship is with the entire government, with the BIA having special responsibilities. These other agencies had a duty to serve the Indian people through a tribal delivery system. Part of that strategy also involved an attempt to make the role of the tribes in these delivery systems so locked-in that a future termination in the 1950s style would be more difficult to accomplish. The hope was that when funds came from other agencies it would enable us to target the Bureau money on particular well-defined problems. We then could use the money from the other federal agencies to deal with more general things. That was the theory that we followed.

Philip S. Deloria, Standing Rock Sioux,
director, American Indian Law Center

The NIYC evolved from the 1961 Chicago Indian Conference sponsored by Sol Tax. A number of Indian college students attended this conference. They were expected to act as pages and carry pencils and papers for established Indian leaders. This made the college students mad and they decided to form their own organization.

The National Indian Youth Council was incorporated in Albuquerque, New Mexico, in 1961, with a constitution, by-laws and articles of incorporation. It was involved in the fishing rights situation in the state of Washington. The NIYC published a newspaper called Americans Before Columbus. *Leaders of the NIYC met on various reservations to assist tribes and to pass resolutions concerning federal Indian policy. Many of these individuals also were involved in the 1968 poor people's campaign in Washington D.C. . . . . That was the first time that there was a sit-in at the Bureau of Indian Affairs building. We temporarily took over the BIA headquarters in 1968, to publicize Indian rights and the needs of poor people in general.*

Edward C. Johnson, Northern Paiute,
director/curator of the Stewart Indian
Museum Association, tribal historian
for the Walker River Paiute tribe

Self-determination was one of the political plans in the Indian platform of President John F. Kennedy, and the concept was given added impetus in the messages on American Indians by President Lyndon B. Johnson and Richard M. Nixon. The policy of self-determination for Indian tribes became the offical policy of the Congress of the United States by the enactment of the Indian Self-Determination Act of January 4, 1975. Once the policy of self-determination had been established by the Congress and the executive department of the federal government, aided and abetted by language of the Supreme Court in certain landmark cases, the implementation of the policy became the responsibility of the Indian tribes.

The act authorized assistance to Indian tribes to prepare them to assume responsibilities such as: (a) technical assistance directly from the Bureau of Indian Affairs or grants to tribes to obtain this assistance, (b) detail of staff from the Bureau of Indian Affairs to tribes, and (c) contracts by which Indian tribes might actually provide program services to eligible recipients. With the authority granted them and with the means provided for implementation of the self-determination policy, Indian tribes moved ahead to achieve self-stated goals based upon perceived priority needs.

At the same time, other federal agencies were already able to provide, or were getting into a position to provide, program responsibilities to Indian tribes, implemented by grants and contracts of resources from those agencies. Prominent among these were various types of Indian housing from the Department of Housing and Urban Development, the Comprehensive Education and Training Program (CETA) from the Department of Labor, and American Native Programs (ANA) from the Department of Health and Human Services. From the basic programs of these agencies flowed a variety of programs intended to meet the human needs of tribal people from the cradle to the grave.

This plethora of programs almost inundated the capability of the Indian tribes to administer them and also tended to affect the priority given to these programs. It soon became apparent that the program priorities would be based upon the financial resources available for the various programs rather than priorities established upon need. Furthermore the emphasis was placed upon grantsmanship rather than administrative management and upon employment rather than achievement of goals or objectives. It soon became apparent that this hectic scrambling for funding shunted aside the basic purposes of some of the programs, affecting the results which might otherwise have been obtained from this outpouring of funds for the variety of programs on reservations.

Robert Lafollette Bennett, Oneida, commissioner of
Indian affairs under Lyndon B. Johnson

We were programed throughout the 1970s to write funding applications for federal grants. Most of the Indian people that had a dream were on their typewriters day and night writing grant applications to agencies that kept changing their name and moving. At some point, people are going to suddenly realize that no one is feeling sorry for them. They are going to have to fight for social justice. Desperate people do desperate things. I see people on their bloody knees begging for things that are rightfully theirs. Eventually, folks are going to get mad and take matters into their own hands.

Ramona Bennett, Puyallup, former tribal
council member, fishing rights advocate

CHAPTER ONE

The Era of Indian Self-Determination: An Overview

Philip S. Deloria

Indian tribes and Indian people indisputably possessed a greater degree of self-determination in 1976 than they did in 1960. But my point here is not to celebrate the progress of the modern era. We cannot define, let alone measure, progress until we begin to understand the essential conflict within this country concerning its perception of Indians: the United States wants to preserve a romantic ideal of the Indian way of life, but at the same time numerous federal and state forces press for a wholesale assimilation of Indians.

It is said that the termination policy of the 1940s and 1950s is dead. Termination was abandoned gradually between about 1958— when it was repudiated by Secretary Fred Seaton on a radio program in Flagstaff, Arizona—and 1960, when John F. Kennedy was elected.* Despite the formal rejection of the policy by both parties, congressional committees kept an active interest in termination until well into the 1960s. Many Indians will recall being told by various BIA functionaries throughout this period that "termination is still the policy of the federal government until HCR 108 is repealed" (a legal conclusion of arguable validity).†

---

* Quoted in Felix Cohen, *Handbook of Federal Indian Law* (1982 ed), p. 182.

† H. R. Con Res. 108, 83d Cong., 1st sess., (1953). This argument assumes that a concurrent resolution expresses continuing federal policy until explicitly repealed or superceded by Congress. In fact, such resolution expresses only the policy of the Congress that passed it and does not bind subsequent Congresses. See, e.g. 1A C. Sands, *Sutherland's Statutory Construction* (1972), pp. 337–38. Legalities aside, the pattern of legislation and appropriations on Indian affairs by the middle 1960s cast strong doubt on the validity of HCR 108 as a guiding statement of federal Indian policy.

For the past two decades, people have avoided styling themselves as terminationsts, at least in polite company, but there are now and always will be those who believe it proper social and legal policy to end the special status of Indian tribes. Termination is out of fashion and dead as an announced policy, but termination with a small "t" is not. For tactical purposes other names might be used, but the long range goal will not change. For that reason it will always be important to set out the sources of Indian tribes' right to exist and possess a special status.

The special status of Indian tribes and individual Indians in this country has three sources in law, policy, and popular attitudes. One source is the cultural distinctness of Indian societies. From that cultural distinctness flows the idea that Indians must be shielded from the competitive system. Their special separate status, by this view, should remain intact until Indians can be either (in words of the nineteenth century) "civilized" or (in the modern euphemism) "prepared" to enter the mainstream on their own terms, combining the best of both cultures. Another source of Indian status is the poverty of Indian people. Special programs, special agencies, and special jurisdictional status are justified because Indians are poor and exhibit the social symptoms of their poverty.

The fundamental constitutional basis of Indian status is outlined in the opinions of John Marshall and brilliantly explained and elaborated in the works of Nathan Margold and Felix Cohen.[‡] Marshall established that Indian tribes have a right to a political and social existence and that this right is not derived from the Constitution of the United States. He traced it to natural law and international law, sources of law that could be mentioned in the same discussion without embarassment in Marshall's day. By acknowledging the existence of this right, Marshall made it a part of the law and policy of this country.

I mention these three sources because they are intertwined in the public understanding of the status of Indians and in the rationales that

---

[‡] See *Worchester v. Georgia*, 31 U.S. (6 Pet.) 515 (1832); *Cherokee Nation v. Georgia*, 30 U.S. (5 Pet.) 1 (1831); *Johnson v. M'Intosh*, 21 U.S. (8 Wheat.) 543 (1823). Nathan Margold hired Felix Cohen to work with him in the Interior Solicitor's Office and influenced his thinking. Their collaboration led to the production, under Cohen's supervision, of the *Handbook of Federal Indian Law* (Government Printing Office, 1942). A bibliography of Cohens' writing is found at 9 *Rutgers L. Rev.* 345 (1954).

keep the present system functioning and funded by Congress. The failure to understand and distinguish the differences among them leads to constant confusion in Indian affairs. The first two—cultural distinctness and poverty—find a broad base of support in the simultaneous humanitarian impulse and sense of cultural superiority that are the peculiar heritage of Anglo-American society. But anyone who wonders whether termination is still alive need only ask whether a separate Indian political and legal existence will be tolerated in this country if Indians are no longer poor or viewed by the majority as being culturally distinct. Clearly that is not going to happen. In that sense, every dollar that Congress and the American people spend on Indians, every program that is authorized for Indians, is premised on the first and second rationales for Indian status.

The third source, the rights of Indian tribes as distinct societies with inherent sovereignty, is constitutionally necessary to enable the society to make a legal distinction between Indian tribes and other cultural groups or other groups of poor people. The political status of Indian tribes and their relationship to the United States is, then, the foundation for the entire structure of policies, programs, and laws. Yet it is the one source of Indian status which, as a practical matter, probably cannot stand alone.

Indian governments are thus subjected to a different status than other governments. There are not constant reviews of the demographic status of all the little countries in Europe that are frequently compared in size and population with Indian tribes. No one asks whether Monaco and Liechtenstein are sufficiently culturally distinct from neighboring countries to justify their continued existence. Unlike that of Indian tribes, their political status is taken for granted.

The transition of recent federal policy from termination to self-determination reflects only a tactical shift in the fundamental commitment of the society to bring Indians into the mainstream, not a movement toward a true recognition of a permanent tribal right to exist. If Indian tribes had a relatively greater degree of self-determination during the period under discussion than they did during the dark days of the termination policy, and they obviously did, one still questions whether the basic issue of tribal self-determination has ever been addressed. Nevertheless, it is worthwhile to trace the beginnings of modern self-determination in Indian country.

As the pressure for immediate termination eased, the early 1960s saw some of the roots of later significant developments toward self-determination. Congress authorized the Public Works Administration to give grants directly to Indian tribes under the Public Works Acceleration Act. At about the same time, the interior solicitor and the general counsel for the Public Housing Administration decided that Indian tribes could create housing authorities to administer federal housing funds. Despite the force of the Indian Reorganization Act* or the "Powers of Indian Tribes" Memorandum,† these were apparently the first examples of both the Congress and the executive branch treating Indian tribes as real governments—eligible for federal assistance on the same basis as other governments and capable of creating subordinate public agencies which could also be recognized. These precedents were greatly expanded in the Great Society.

There were also early attempts by the BIA to contract with the tribes to administer programs. Commissioner Philleo Nash has mentioned that when a congressional committee directed the BIA to cut five hundred positions from the education program he contracted with the tribes and let them hire the people. Commissioner Robert Bennett also implemented a contracting policy. Commissioner Louis Bruce and his staff moved more deeply into contracting, but congressional committees questioned whether existing legislation authorized contracting to the degree and in the way it was being carried out. Agreeing in principle with contracting, they felt that new legislation was needed to bring structure and accountability. After hearings, Congress eventually passed the 1975 Indian Self-Determination and Educational Assistance Act.‡

Tribal resource development policy of the 1960s has not been fully or objectively analyzed as it relates to tribal self-determination. An effort was made to attract private capital to reservations by offering long range development deals for mineral, agricultural, and residential

---

* 25 U.S.C. ss. 461 et seq.
† 55 Interior Decisions 14 (1934).
‡ P.L. 93–638. 25 U.S.C.A. s. 450a et seq.

development. It seems clear that the main impetus for this policy came from the federal government, but it is not clear to what extent the tribes resisted or were enthusiastic about it. Tribes able to sell coal in the 1960s were viewed as putting one over on companies who failed to realize that coal was an obsolete and undesirable energy source. This shortsighted view was widely criticized during the 1970s when coal regained strategic importance, but the conventional wisdom has not yet adjusted to coal's more recent devaluation.

Development policy provides a good example of the tension between tribal self-determination and the federal trust responsibility. There is a need for a more detailed analysis and comparison of the leasing of Indian resources under the management and supervision of the Bureau of Indian Affairs and the U.S. Geological Survey in the Department of the Interior. The record of these agencies in failing to protect Indian resources adequately may be, in fact, comparable to the department's record in managing federal resources. If it is not, we should be able to demonstrate the differences more clearly than has been done to date. But if the incompetence or lack of foresight are evenly spread, then we should be reminded of the law which states, "Never attribute to malevolence that which can adequately be explained by incompetence." This is a good rule to adopt when dealing with the government, and it is more helpful to Indian people than the assumption that all of their problems are due to a conspiracy on the part of the federal government to target Indians for bad treatment or poor management.

The hindsight with which the resource development policies of the 1960s are now viewed reveals an almost theological tendency to find a devil to blame, a tendency that is widespread in the scholarly community's treatment of Indian affairs. This does not help any of us learn from the past, and it may lead to Indians having their remaining resources stolen from them while they and their friends maintain vigilance against people in red suits carrying pitchforks. We must, of course, hold the government to standards of trusteeship and identify instances in which it shirks its responsibility. But if that analytical role slips into one of invariably passing all the blame to the federal government, the economic system, or the society at large, then Indian self-determination becomes a concept of power without responsibility. We lack a clear notion of the threat because we are wedded to a method of historical analysis in which tribes are never responsible for their mistakes and the government never makes an honest mistake.

Reservation resource development issues are more complex than similar issues off-reservation because tribes are governments that must tax and regulate economic activity for the public good. At the same time, they are also major landowners and entrepreneurs who participate directly in—and benefit from—development. For non-Indians, the balance that is struck between economic growth and other public interests is brought about by the miraculous and impersonal workings of "the system." For an Indian tribe the same balance must be achieved within the wise judgment of the tribal council itself.

In its turn, the federal government, even in the best of situations, is caught between trusteeship and self-determination. It can be criticised for promoting development (and affecting Indian culture) or for not promoting development (and perpetuating Indian poverty). These issues are easier to pose than to manage, of course, but we will never manage them better if we remain on a simplistic good guys/bad guys level of analysis.

The 1960s was above all else an Office of Economic Opportunity decade. Building on the PWA and Housing and Urban Development precedents, the Great Society programs were the first major instance in which Indian tribal governments had money and were not beholden for it to the Bureau of Indian Affairs. This created an enormous change in the balance of power on reservations and in Washington.

Tribes could, to some degree, set their own priorities. They could hire, supervise, and fire people on their own. They had telephones and copying machines to spread information throughout Indian country and the money to hold conferences to organize for the common good. They could go to Washington whenever they wanted to and not only when the superintendent or the central office of the BIA told them they could. These things altered the nature of the Bureau of Indian Affairs and the relationship between tribes and the federal government. They changed the face of Indian affairs in a way that will never completely be reversed.

There is a story which has been difficult to substantiate that when the OEO was established the Bureau of Indian Affairs wanted to administer Community Action funds as part of the BIA program. Whatever the truth, the OEO made a policy decision at the outset to fund tribes directly. One of the assumptions of the War on Poverty was that "old established agencies" had failed to deal effectively with the problems of the poor, at least in part because they did not involve the poor in planning and administration of programs for their benefit. In the cities, this meant that efforts were made to bypass city governments and establish parallel delivery systems which rivaled the city government and which in theory were controlled by the poor. The decision to fund tribes directly, bypassing the Bureau, implicity recognized the Bureau's historic role as the de facto municipal government of Indian reservations. It viewed tribal governments as representing the poor people because most of their constituents were poor, and it recognized that, for the most part, the CAP funds were the first discretionary funds that many tribes had had.

There were interesting side effects of the OEO. Previously, tribal delegations that came to Washington would spend their time in the BIA or up on Capitol Hill. But during the peak days of the OEO, they would stop by the Bureau to say hello to the commissioner on their way back to the airport. Remember, this is an agency that is well over a hundred years old and that had always been the center of attention and power for Indians. Certainly the impact of being virtually ignored was psychologically devastating; what is less certain is whether the proper simile is sitting on the bench eager to get in the game or sitting in a rocking chair dreaming of glorious days gone by.

A generation or more of Indian leaders had made a commitment to working for the BIA. They wanted to help their people by fulfilling the intent of John Collier and the IRA to have Indians administer their own affairs. Many of them had spent years of frustration trying to implement the lofty goals of the IRA. Their sense of being bypassed by a major national effort, the Great Society, of being considered part of an "old line established agency" (which the BIA certainly was), created in some of these people feelings of rivalry, bitterness, and resentment. In our sometimes self-righteous zeal to criticize institutions and policies, we should have some compassion for the people who could not or for some reason did not jump from the Bureau to the bandwagon of the OEO to solve the problems of poverty once and for all. The OEO has become a part of history; the BIA is still an old-line established agency.

The Great Society and the OEO, in particular, did not provide all the necessary weapons for winning the War on Poverty. For example, the OEO had a legal prohibition against construction. All it could do was remodel—tear down a wall for a Headstart classroom—but it could not build a bridge, a road, or a house. Roger Jourdain, of Red Lake, secured money for a training program for carpenters, plumbers, and electricians, with a half million dollars budgeted for "training materials." Remarkably the "homework" looked a lot like houses, and both the Red Lake people and the Red Lake sawmill benefited immeasurably. Lacking the power to direct OEO funds to the fundamental causes of reservation poverty, tribes tried to deal with immediate concerns of their people. The OEO was annually flooded with recreation program proposals, which solemnly and torturously explained how a summer recreation program on the reservation was going to solve poverty.

Apart from the money, the most important byproduct of the Great Society—of which the OEO was the doyenne—for tribal self-determination was the notion that Indian tribes are or should be eligible for federal services other than those specially for Indians. The Economic Opportunity Act did not provide for tribal eligibility for Community Action Programs; that was an administrative determination. But out of that flowed not only tribal control of funds but the practice of tribes calling on federal agencies throughout Washington to do their share of dealing with Indian problems.

Tribal governments have not fit neatly into this system. Tribes sometimes had to structure their governments so they could conveniently spend these federal dollars. The Economic Development Administration required tribes to form non-profit development corporations chartered by the states, and HUD made tribes charter housing authorities. Some people complain about that, saying that the agencies were making the tribes jump through a hoop to get money. But tribes in this era were moving away from a BIA-focused governmental structure into one adapted, perhaps awkwardly, to enable them to be treated consistently as governments. Certainly it could be argued that this was a price worth paying.

Considerable effort has been wasted over the years looking for the perfect structure of federal Indian programs. In fact, we must see the range of possibilities as a spectrum. One pole is the concentration of all services to Indians into one agency, meaning that no other federal agency need concern itself with Indians. The other pole is the dispersal of responsibility for Indians to appropriate agencies throughout the government, with none having lead responsibility for dealing with Indians. In reality, the structure of Indian affairs has never been at either pole; instead, it moves back and forth along the continuum as circumstances of tribes, federal agencies, and federal policy dictate.

Between 1960 and the middle 1970s, we went from a near BIA/ IHS monopoly over services to the involvement of many other federal agencies. This caused a confusion as to relative roles and responsibilities of the agencies to assist in the solution of Indian problems, complicated by the strategic uncertainty of the Indian political leadership. The question was, to what degree could tribes safely become a part of the general governmental structure of the nation without risking their special status and their special relationship with the federal government through the Bureau of Indian Affairs?

Many people have criticized the Great Society programs. It is true that the flood of federal money onto reservations drastically changed the nature of tribal government by creating a bureaucracy. This tribal bureaucracy also affected Indian community life as well. Tribal governments became dominant employers on the reservation, dependent on the funding of federal social programs. These programs, by and large, dealt with the symptoms of poverty rather than providing the funding for the infrastructure development that is necessary for the permanent solution of reservation economic problems.

But it is inconsistent to criticize the devastating social and cultural decay caused by federal money on reservations and then complain when the government cuts back on these programs. I have been to meetings that were completely devoted to a discussion of the horrendous destruction to Indian individual psyches, family life, and community life caused by federal, social, and educational programs. Participants at these meetings then proceeded to pass resolutions asking for budget increases.

Nevertheless it was through these Great Society programs that Indian tribes became widely recognized by federal agencies as legitimate governments. This was an historic step in the popular, legal, and governmental conception of Indian tribes. It was a milestone of self-determination. We moved from tribes as an administrative convenience of the Bureau of Indian Affairs, governmental only in Supreme Court esoterica, to the point where Indian tribes can now make a credible claim to federal agencies that they should be funded and treated like state and local governments in the federal delivery system.

No one ever thought that the OEO programs alone could solve the problems of poverty, but they employed a lot of people and created a cash flow on reservations. Tribes acquired experience in administering federal funds, BIA contracts, and tribal income. Many present-day Indian leaders received their training on the job as program administrators. There, they gained valuable administrative experience and learned the art and skill of government.

Tribal program administrators now constitute a managerial class of Indians who, sooner or later, are going to create economic development on the reservations. People who have spent years administering programs for the tribe are going to figure out that they can make more money with a hamburger franchise. There are those who think that capitalist society is terrible for Indians and will no doubt see the prospect of Indians joining the middle class as another deleterious effect of the Great Society programs. But just as it is inconsistent to oppose budget cuts in federal programs that we feel are destroying us, we cannot help but create confusion in American society if we blame the system for Indian poverty and then denounce opportunities for Indians to get themselves out of poverty. If there is a real alternative, the obligation is on us to explain what it is and work toward it.

Ironically, the role of tribes as relatively permanent governments—the rationale least preferred by the society at large—was strengthened by the use of tribal governments as the local delivery system for the programs designed to implement the nations's concern for poverty—the most popular rationale for special Indian status. This tribal role created for the first time, in many cases, a tribal executive branch. It raised tribal government aspirations to take over previously neglected functions of taxing and regulating reservation activities in addition to the service delivery functions which these programs made possible.

This era also brought us the 1968 Indian Civil Rights Act. Initially, the federal courts thought that the Civil Rights Act gave them broad authority to review the actions of tribal governments. This ended with the *Martinez* decision, which held that the Civil Rights Act remedies were limited to habeas corpus, thereby effectively limiting judicial review to tribal court criminal proceedings.* Many people saw the Civil Rights Act as an imposition of Euro-American legal concepts on Indian systems. They complained that it lacked a provision allowing each tribe to consent to it despite Felix Cohen's observation that major federal Indian legislation had continued the form of treaty-making by conditioning the legislation on tribal consent.

The principle of Indian tribes as nations is the legal foundation for tribal political existence within the American system. It is also an article of faith among Indians and among the scholarly community. Whatever their fundamental rights to nationhood, Indian tribes today, with the exception of the Navajo nation, are still small communities with populations ranging between one hundred and ten thousand. Communities of this size cannot always solve problems of government accountability by uncritically adopting national scale constitutional models of separation of powers. Yet present scholarship does not give us a basis for comparing the pre- and post-*Martinez* state of affairs on reservations.

Thanks to the *Martinez* decision, tribes are on their own to develop systems of accountability. But to adopt wholesale a national model of separation of powers means to exaggerate, in the tribal context, some of the transitional problems of developing nations. If solutions are to be found, attention must be focused on tribes as they actually function. The creative energies of tribal people and their friends must be set on devising new methods of administering tribal governments. Preoccupation with unwieldy national models will not help. A blind and defensive adherence to the status quo, in the name of tribal sovereignty, will only postpone a later and more politically dangerous accounting; and emotional attacks on the present system in the name of traditionalism— without addressing the details of a traditional system which might be put in its place and how it would deal with the unavoidable tasks of

---

* *Martinez v. Santa Clara Pueblo*, 436 U.S. 49 (1978).

governing modern reservations—is an equal evasion of reality. In the long run, it does a disservice to the real strengths of Indian culture.

From the point of view of federal policy, the high point of the era of self-determination is seen by many as the Nixon message on Indians of July 1970.[†] Although some complain that it was not fully implemented, it stands as the strongest official policy statement for Indian self-determination. I doubt that all of the presidents since Ulysses S. Grant have given, collectively, eight hours of thought to Indian affairs. I doubt that Richard Nixon had the faintest idea of what his 1970 message contained. Nixon did not retire to his study and devote a long reflective evening to writing his message on one of his famous yellow legal pads.

It is not important to know exactly who wrote the message, although nearly everyone in Indian affairs at the time claims to have had a hand in its drafting, but what might be important is to know how such a strong message made its way through the elaborate process of review and comment. Presidential policy statements are thoroughly reviewed by the Department of the Interior, Justice Department, the OMB, and the White House. A policy statement on Indians that finally reaches the president, if any does, is likely to be very different from an original that might have been drafted in the BIA. For that reason, it is not a good idea to press for an administration policy statement unless once has reason to be confident that the Indian position is supported by someone with enough power in the administration to protect it throughout the review process.

The Nixon message was misleading in that it encouraged the hope of many Indians and their non-Indian friends that the key to the solution of Indian problems is to convince someone high enough in government to become an Indian advocate, thereby causing a miraculous change in Washington behavior. Having friends in high places may be nice, but it can only be one tactic in a much larger strategy. The scholars share the blame for tribal unwillingness or inability to learn how to understand and manipulate the process to the degree that they have promoted the view that Washington is a monolith hostile to tribal interests and that tribal problems stem largely from the willful decisions

---

[†] U.S. President, *Public Papers of the Presidents* (Office of the *Federal Register,* 1953–   ), Richard M. Nixon, 1970, p. 564.

An Overview 203

of a few specific individuals. In fact, most tribal problems are due to the fact that tribal interests are not adequately articulated at key points in a federal process that is largely oblivious to Indians.

Much of what passes for scholarship in Indian affairs is a simplistic good guys versus bad guys analysis resting on fundamental ideological criticisms of American culture and society. These philosophical criticisms no doubt play an important role as scholarly commentary and for a larger social and ideological agenda, but they are of limited use as Indian tribes try to deal with their immediate problems. Whether it is good or bad in some cosmic sense, the federal government is an important part of the Indian environment to which, in the name of survival, Indian cultures must make a realistic adaptation—just as all cultures adapt to their environment—not by sacrificing principle but by having a realistic set of expectations of behavior. To refuse, in the name of cultural purity, to learn the skills of survival in the world as it exists is to perpetuate paternalism. It bases continued tribal existence, not on independence, but on the need for non-Indians to maintain a sterile buffer within which Indian cultures can be shielded from the real world. All the while the non-Indian protectors continue to make the key decisions.

During this period, a few tribes, individuals, and organizations displayed considerable skill in manipulating the federal system and other institutions of society to achieve their goals. But there has been surprisingly little progress in turning these few successes into translatable skills that can be used universally throughout the Indian community.

A resurgence of Indian cultural awareness also captured the nation's imagination during this period. The fishing rights struggle in the Pacific Northwest had an enormous impact on the public consciousness and on tribal and individual self-awareness. The Trail of Broken Treaties, the BIA building episode, the American Indian Movement, and Wounded Knee II put Indians on the world stage. These events had an impact on both the Indian people and American society that we still lack the perspective and detachment to measure. But much of it was a romanticized product of the American media's preoccupation with fads. For example, when my brother Vine Deloria's first book was published— a book that had a tremendous impact—an enthusiastic reviewer said that the American Indian had finally found his voice. Vine did not claim to be saying what had not been said before or aspire to be America's official Indian spokesman. America had simply found its ears—briefly. When a *LIFE* magazine team came to Denver to record the remarkable phenomenon of an Indian author, it left in disappointment. It discovered that he had written his book with an IBM typewriter rather than on a deerskin.

Indians did not discover they were Indians in the early 1970s. We were not reborn; we were simply noticed. Somehow the publicity accorded our characteristic independence and determination fueled an even greater spirit and attracted back to the fold some who had drifted away when the nation did not think it was so great to be an Indian. There is no point in questioning the sincerity of these people, but those who were Indians all along can be forgiven if they feel, now that the nation's attention has moved to other things, that the real issues of Indian cultural survival were not addressed at all. We have returned to the time when the country contemptuously appoints as our spokesmen non-Indians who wish they were Indians.

There were many good things about this surge of energy, but we failed to move beyond sheer exuberant self-affirmation to consolidate the gains made possible by several years of worldwide interest in and support for Indians. America did not end the era with a greater understanding of the complex interplay between Indian culture, Indian poverty, and the practical issues facing Indian tribal governments and federal policy. If anything, when the nation's attention wandered, it carried with it an even more pronounced cultural stereotype of what it wanted its Indians to be. And we Indians ourselves are left manipulating code words of tribal sovereignty rather than undertaking the more disciplined and less romantic tasks of dealing realistically with the issues we face today.

To a great degree, we left this era with totally unrealistic expectations. Self-determination or tribal sovereignty cannot be absolutes for Indian tribes any more than they are for other nations. It is foolish to hope that the federal system can somehow change so that it protects Indian interests from non-Indian interests to the consistent degree that we feel we need. The principled Indian view of the tribal-federal relationship as one between nations is inconsistent with the hope that a structure can be found in which the federal agency dealing with Indian affairs will be immune from the pressures of other federal agencies or in which the official who heads that agency is responsible to the tribes and not the federal government. Self-determination is a difficult goal to reach if it must include unlimited federal funding with no accountability for funds. This is not the stuff of day-to-day tribal rhetoric; tribes are generally realistic and sensible about their relationship to the system. But these ambiguities have been a prominent feature of much of the national level rhetoric and as such represent a failure on the part of national leadership and, to a small degree, a scholarly community that is afraid to hold Indian strategic policy to critical and realistic standards.

Slogans cannot alleviate every frustration in the political life of every Indian in this country; they cannot successfully transfer responsibility to a devil. Indians must first decide what to do with their own lives, or risk being lulled into a self-absorbed torpor of passivity, acceptance, and pessimism. It does not really matter what the Indian Reorganization Act says: at present, we are not using to the limit the powers that we have to determine our own lives.

We are still trying to adjust to the changes of the 1960s and 1970s. We are trying to accommodate within our cultural, social, and political lives our sense of status in American society and American political life. Much of the literature analyzing this era has created myths that do not help us understand reality, because they do not deal with Indians as real human beings. Ironically, it is most unfair to Indians themselves to idealize them. There must have been at one point in history at least one Indian who did not know what he was talking about. There must have been at least one person who worked for the Bureau of Indian Affairs who had a good idea. Why do all old Indians have to be wise? Not all old non-Indians are wise.

But many scholars—who note the romantic view of Indians in earlier stages of Euro-American history—have themselves been blinded by the same romantic tradition today and deny us our political life and our humanity. The modern romantic tradition in Indian scholarship imposes on us a cultural ethic that serves as a condition on the political help we can expect from the scholarly community and other traditional sources of support and, implicitly, on our right to exist. This romanticism does not help us to deal with complex problems. We have made mistakes, and you do us a disservice by almost uniformly shifting the blame elsewhere. We need hard-nosed analysis of those mistakes so that we can avoid making them in the future. And above all we would like to have the confidence that our rights do not depend on our satisfying the emotional needs of a romantic tradition.

I administer the Special Scholarship Program in Law for American Indians. When the program was established, in 1967, there were fewer than twenty-five identifiable Indian lawyers in the country. There are now about five hundred, due almost solely to this program. There has been some discussion about whether we do a disservice in sending Indians to law school because we make them less "Indian." Of course, education changes people—that is why you send them to school.

Our job is to make lawyers, Indian lawyers, out of Indians. It is the job of the Indian community and the Indian family to make Indians out of them before we get them. If they have made Indians out of them—culturally and spiritually—then the changes they go through when they go to law school are not going to be fundamentally cultural and spiritual in nature. We should be aware of the values the educational process inculcates along with the skills, but our anguish over the destruction of Indian culture by education is a sign of a lack of confidence in the vitality of Indian cultures.

Education and history have two purposes in a society, and we do not distinguish them clearly enough. One purpose is to socialize, to teach the young how "our kind of people" see themselves and behave. The other purpose is to teach a set of skills and demonstrate knowledge. (One might note here that Indian knowledge is considered "lore," while Euro-American knowledge is scientific fact.) As to basic values, Indian law students are just going to a trade school if their identities have been well established already. They are learning how to work on a machine —the legal and political system. If prospective lawyers are worried that they will not be Indians any more when they finish law school, I tell them this: your cousin who was sent to automechanic school by the Bureau was not a car when he finished his education.

And that is why we must return to the three sources of federal Indian policy. We exist in a distinct status in this society simply because we have a right to exist. Our rich cultural heritage is our own business and not the business of the federal government or the scholarly community. We do not owe an obligation—other than to ourselves—to preserve or not to preserve Indian culture. But scholars can help us, not by romanticizing contemporary Indians, but by helping us move toward relevant and realistic critical standards for our own behavior.

The period between 1960 and 1976 saw an historic and inspiring growth in the role of Indian tribes as governments. Ironically, this was due, in large part, to the society's unsuccessful commitment to abolish poverty throughout the nation. The country also noticed the degree to which Indian people really maintain their fundamental cultural commitments, and by giving this cultural expression a momentary favorable treatment, they helped to strengthen it. But, as if chained together, the era's expressions of the three rationales for Indian status reacted on each other and as the era drew to a close, many, who were most publicly proclaiming their cultural commitments, blamed tribal governments for Indian poverty and for the weakening of Indian culture.

I have characterized the larger developments. But many events and trends have been left out in this short account. We still need a more complete history of the period and a scholarly analysis to help our own efforts to understand, or the next time the cycle of interest in and opportunity for Indians comes back we are not going to benefit more than we did the last time. We must know more and more about how that machine operates. We can no longer abide the insult that to know more is a threat to our culture and identity.

CHAPTER TWO

Federal Indian Policy, 1960-1976

Robert L. Bennett, Robert Burnette,
Alexander (Sandy) MacNabb, Helen M. Schierbeck

*We were operating under the IRA. The basic economic opportunity
that was provided for in the IRA came through the authorization to create
federally chartered tribal corporations which could make investments,
receive grants of funds, make profits, and take care of the business operations of the tribe. Unfortunately, we lacked funds for IRA corporations.
The only sources of funds, at that time, were congressional appropriations
or trust funds on tribal trust property, which under the IRA could then be
appropriated by the councils. In OEO, I saw a source of funds for community development that otherwise would not be available. I was obligated
as commissioner to do everything that I could to get new resources, new
strengths, and new capabilities onto the reservations. We persuaded Congress to give us considerable amounts of money. We played that game successfully for many years.*

Philleo Nash, commissioner of Indian affairs
under President John F. Kennedy and
former lieutenant governor of Wisconsin

*I am not going to bad mouth the Bureau of Indian Affairs. It has
stood off all comers for one hundred years. That says something, I think,
for the competency of the organization itself. I do not have any doubt that
the BIA will continue. And I will tell you why. The Indians really do not
get unusual benefits from the BIA. All they receive are the ordinary programs that everybody gets from some other place. Anyone who thinks that
another federal agency is going to take over Indian programs had better
think again. Nobody else wants to operate Indian schools, build roads, and
police the reservations, least of all the states.*

Graham Holmes, former assistant commissioner of Indian affairs

ROBERT L. BENNETT

In 1961, Interior Secretary Stewart Udall appointed the Kennedy
Task Force on Indian Affairs. Some of the members who served on the
task force were Francis McKinley, Philleo Nash, James Officer, and
William Zimmerman. After a two year study, this commission recommended the separation of many federal programs from the Bureau of
Indian Affairs. This led to the creation of Indian "desks" throughout
the federal establishment. We eventually had Indian desks in the Office
of Economic Opportunity, the Department of Commerce, Housing and
Urban Development, the Department of Agriculture, the Department
of Labor, and many of the other federal agencies that President Lyndon
Johnson felt had a responsibility to Indian people.

In my opinion, self-determination is a philosophy rather than a
goal. Within the philosophy of self-determination, tribes are able to
work toward established goals with the assistance of all available
resources. Tribes had been doing this for many years, prior to the
passage of the Indian Self-Determination and Educational Assistance
Act of 1975. How far tribes could go was more or less dependent on the
philosophy of the person in charge at the reservation level. Policies
are established in the federal government, but their implementation
depends much on the personal philosophy of the individual who happens to be at the seat of power, whether it is at the agency, area, or
Washington level.

In the 1960s, people at the Bureau of Indian Affairs felt that tribes
were in a position to make more decisions than they previously had
done. In some tribes, decision making now extended down to the
family itself. For example, a tribe in Colorado received a substantial
sum of money in a settlement. Rather than pay it all out on a per capita
basis, they set aside money so that each family had an entitlement based
upon its size. This tribe also established the goal that their children
should attend public schools.

As time went on, tribes gained experience in decision making.
When implementing the concept of self-determination, the government
had to be very careful that tribes established their own priorities. When
you work with tribes in the accomplishment of whatever they have
decided, you may have a feeling that there are much more important

things that the tribes should be involved in; and quite often, these were pointed out to tribes. But they did what they wanted to do.

One illustration of this is a tribe that had a considerable amount of money. They had very serious health problems, and attempts were made to include them in a sanitation district; but their highest priority was to build a racetrack and rodeo grounds. They built a racetrack and rodeo grounds. They now have the opportunity to bet and lose their money like everybody else. When you follow self-determination, the priority of tribal people is not always the same as you might perceive it should be.

The policy of self-determination enabled tribes to go to many federal agencies. It widened their horizons. They began to look at their problems and went to the agencies that could help them achieve the goals that they had set for themselves. One thing that we need to be careful about, in the area of self-determination, is this matter of expectations. We have to be careful that we do not hard sell programs and raise expectations too high. We are dealing with people, and people can be easily misled.

What is happening under self-determination is that the federal government is treating tribes the same way they have treated cities, counties, and states. The federal government has always allowed these entities to employ their own people to carry out federally funded programs. Tribes are now being placed in that situation. They are being given the responsibility of hiring their own people to achieve whatever goals they may set for themselves. Service functions will not be carried out by the Bureau of Indian Affairs. Tribes need to be aware of this. They cannot avoid this shift of responsibility and the accountability that comes with self-determination.

Tribes have always had the luxury of being able to point out the failures of the Indian Bureau and other federal agencies. The reality, now, is that if there are any problems with education, health, and social service programs they will rest with the tribes. Self-determination is going to take a great deal of effort, but I have every confidence that tribes can achieve the goals they set for themselves. People in the federal and state governments must also work responsibly with the tribes as they proceed toward self-determination.

There is a major problem that we face in self-determination. Many Indian young people are torn between preserving their traditions and looking toward the outside world and all that it has to offer. The magnitude of this problem is demonstrated by the fact that one-half of the total tribal population is under seventeen years of age. Traditionally, there has been no place in their society for the so-called adolescent or teenager. Self-determination is a new phenomenon with which they will have to deal, but they do not have any experience that they can rely upon. This was never a part of their life.

ROBERT BURNETTE

Self-determination gained momentum in 1961 when Sol Tax convened the American Indian Chicago Conference. It was a fantastic meeting. The historic Chicago Conference brought together, for the first time, 142 tribes. We decided that we were going in one direction. We sought everything we could get, in so far as power was concerned, for Indian tribes, but tribal sovereignty was not a subject that we discussed.

Out of the Chicago Conference came a message to President John F. Kennedy. After President Kennedy was elected, he immediately took action. The National Housing Act had been in existence since 1937 without any Indian participation. The government believed that the Bureau of Indian Affairs was taking care of Indians, but we were not getting any housing at all. We were living in tents, cars, and log houses. President Kennedy immediately ordered the FHA to permit Indians to participate in national housing programs. In 1956, an heirship bill had passed Congress, but it turned into one of those devils that existed among us. In 1962, tribes used connections they had established in the White House: President Kennedy ordered that legislation killed. Lee Metcalf, who was a senator from Montana, told us what had happened.

Indian tribes became more confident that things were going to change. In 1964, we met in the Mayflower Hotel. It was suggested that we go after a $500 million IRA revolving loan fund. Up until that time, $10 million had been authorized by Congress. We discussed this issue for a long time. It was decided not to go after a $500 million loan fund, because it might upset other things we were trying to do at that time.

During the early 1960s, there were several groups that supported Indian tribes. They included the Indian Rights Association and the Episcopal, Catholic, Congregational, and Presbyterian churches. Alvin Josephy and Betty, his wife, and members of the American Friends Service Committee also worked for better things for Indian people.

We gathered a lot of momentum and before long the Office of Economic Opportunity was established. I had known about it because I had been appointed to President Kennedy's Committee on Poverty. Prominent Americans were involved such as Harry Truman and Professor Walter Heller. At first, I was lost among these people, but when I got to know them, I felt at home. President Kennedy had his own method of doing things. When he was killed, the War on Poverty turned into the OEO.

President Lyndon Johnson had an altogether different outlook. When he introduced the OEO, we were not a part of it. So, the National Council on Indian Affairs called a National Capitol Conference on American Indian Poverty. It met in Washington D.C. between May 9 and 12, 1964. It was the largest Indian gathering since the Chicago Conference. It really made an impression on the political system of this country. We were soon made a part of the OEO, and we all know that money flowed to the tribes.

I believe we will not recognize Indian affairs in another ten years. If we permit Indian policy to proceed as it is going today, it is going to be used as an instrument to destroy Indian tribes. Many Indian tribes and leaders are too hungry for dollars. They have been contracting like mad with the United States government, not realizing what might be the end result. Some of us have dedicated our lives so they can turn the right corner when they come to it, instead of going over the cliff.

Self-determination, as a goal, is great, as long as we do not try to legislate something that is impossible into the souls and minds of all of our Indian people. All of us have aspirations and directions for our own lives and we do not like to have somebody tell us what we can do. Indian people know exactly what they want. They should be given a chance to manage their own affairs and make their own mistakes.

ALEXANDER (SANDY) MACNABB

I would like to examine the administration of Indian Commissioner Louis R. Bruce between 1969 and 1973. I am going to look at it from three different perspectives: (1) the time when there was preparation for change, (2) the period when there was license for change, and (3) the era after change was effected. I will begin with Alvin Josephy's report: *The American Indian and the BIA: A Study With Recommendations.* It laid the foundation for the later Nixon message on Indians. Following that report, Secretary of the Interior Walter Hickel traveled to Albuquerque, in 1969, to speak at the NCAI Convention. His entrance was not popularly received. But at the end of the meeting, he was applauded after receiving some admonitions.

Shortly after that, Louis Bruce came on the scene. Involved in the search for the new BIA team were Helen Schierbeck and Bill King, a former superintendent at Salt River. King was a close friend of Jim Officer. By May 1970, the new administration had achieved some success. A Zuni plan was developed based upon an 1834 piece of legislation. It permitted the tribe to direct local federal employees' activities.

On July 8, 1970, the Nixon message was delivered to the NCAI. Early in the Nixon administration, there were people in the White House who were sympathetic to Indian people. A few individuals were knowledgeable, having read one or two of Alvin Josephy's reports. Leonard Garment, a Democrat from New York and a member of Nixon's law firm, was very supportive. So were John Erlichman, Bradley Patterson, and other White House staff members.

This was the period when the license for change was issued. In October 1971, Walter Hickel traveled to Anchorage, Alaska, and gave a speech to NCAI. He made a number of statements. One of them was that people should have the "courage of their convictions." He told the new BIA leaders, "As long as you aim for better conditions for all Indians, I will back you up."

The next time period in the Bruce administration brought about dramatic changes. There was tremendous frustration, not only among Indian people, but also among the political people in the White House and Interior Department, because new policies were not developing fast enough. Early in November 1971, a confidential memo was written by the assistant secretary for public land management. It directed Commissioner Bruce and his executive staff to immediately prepare certain policies. It was a very short deadline. People were required to work all weekend in the BIA building. These new policies dealt with the reassignment and selection of BIA employees, the redefinition of the role of agency superintendent, and more administrative assistance to help tribes take over programs. There also was an inspection and evaluation program, a redelegation of area office functions to agency offices closer to tribes, and an expansion of BIA contract functions.

After the completion of these policies, we prepared press releases. The Interior Department wanted Hickel to get credit. I refused to do that, and we had them written up so Louis Bruce got credit for the new policies. I was told that if I sent these news releases out I would be fired. This threat made me angry. I went down to the general post office and mailed out all of the press packets.

On November 5, 1971, Hickel met with John Erlichman and Richard Nixon. President Nixon told Hickel, "We do not have mutual confidence in each other." That was how Hickel got fired. From my viewpoint, Hickel was a good person. He worked hard for Indians, and he was willing to take risks. His firing had nothing to do with Indian affairs. I think it had something to do with oil companies.

Rogers Morton became the new secretary of the interior. Soon there was a movement to get some of Commissioner Bruce's executive staff out of circulation. John O. Crow was assigned as deputy commissioner. He had thirty-two years experience in the Bureau and was a fine man. Crow's appointment meant that there were two popes running the BIA.

On November 17, 1971, Commissioner Bruce attended the NCAI convention in Reno, Nevada, and he made statements to strengthen his position. He said, "As many of you know, we have been working for a long time on BIA reorganization, and I have just put the finishing touches on it." Then, he reinstated his old executive staff. He also promised a recommitment to protect Indian water rights and land resources and a new tribal economic development program.

Shortly after that, a number of people came to Washington D.C. before the protest over the Trail of Broken Treaties. They wanted to make a citizens' arrest on John Crow for failing to carry out some of his duties. At the same time, tribal chairmen were meeting with Secretary Morton. There was a great deal of turmoil. The demonstration to arrest John Crow was unfounded, and it did not materialize.

The Trail of Broken Treaties demonstration was the next phenomenon that happened. Among other things, there had been a failure of communication between the government and the Indians. At this time, the license for change was either expiring or being revoked. Because of damage by Indian militants, the BIA was moved to temporary office buildings in northwest Washington.

A short time later, I received a phone call from Secretary of the Interior Morton. He asked me to come to Palo Alto, California, and talk about Indian affairs. He was getting radium treatments for a cancer. I spent three days with him. Morton asked me why Indian policies were not moving forward, and about different people and events. He believed that maximum authority should be provided to the tribes to promote self-determination. Before I left, Morton said, "I want somebody to know this. Nixon will get credit for a lot of changes in Indian affairs, and he should because he permitted them to happen." Morton also indicated that Nixon had only talked to him once about Indians during the Wounded Knee crisis. Nixon had called him up and asked about how much money the Indians got and how much money was going to Pine Ridge. Satisfied with the amount of government appropriations, Nixon said, "Well, what the hell are they making all the trouble for?"

HELEN M. SCHIERBECK

The first area I would like to talk about is my work with the National Congress of American Indians. I was the first NCAI Indian trainee. I called Helen Peterson and said, "I know you do not have much money, but I would like to come to Washington and work for NCAI." I was very curious to know more about why I had seen so much poverty and despair among the reservation Indians. I worked as a secretary. Because the NCAI was a struggling organization, I helped set up its files.

In 1959, I saw tribal leaders who had ultimate faith in Washington D.C. They believed in the Bureau of Indian Affairs and its ability to

solve their problems, even though they were going through the termination era. Mrs. Peterson and other NCAI leaders worked with Indian
people to improve their knowledge about Washington D.C. and the
political process.

Eventually, I decided to get a job on Capitol Hill to see if I could
help Indian people. I went to Senator Sam Ervin, and he arranged
for me to join the Constitutional Rights Subcommittee. I wanted to
respond to what I had heard tribal leaders say about termination and
the problems they faced under Public Law 280.

We talked about this in the subcommittee. Because there was a
strong Indian Affairs Subcommittee in the Senate, we had to figure out
a jurisdictional peg to hang our investigation on. That peg became
constitutional rights. I am not going to say whether Senator Ervin
used Indians against blacks. I do not think it is relevant, because prag-
matically speaking, in politics you do a lot of things. He did give us an
opportunity in that subcommittee to hold hearings for five years at
the local community level. And we heard what Indian people were
experiencing.

I want to illustrate two problems that we encountered. We were
in southern California among the Mission Indians. We asked them to
describe for us some of the problems they were having with law and
order. They graphically illustrated the high crime rate in their community and the lack of support from the state and local police. Even
though California had accepted state civil and criminal jurisdiction,
it did not, at the local level, protect Indian people. In Mission, South
Dakota, we watched one Saturday night what happened to Sioux
Indians who came out of bars. The way they were harrassed was a
real problem.

After the hearings we came out with an Ervin Indian civil rights
bill. I believe that this was necessary for a number of reasons. I had
taken a look at all the IRA constitutions while a member of the subcommittee. In my judgment, the BIA had failed to help tribes use those
constiuttions in a benecial way. The civil rights bill also came about
because Indian people had complained that they could not get their
tribal attorney contracts approved without long delays. Furthermore,
we had seen evidence on the Navajo Reservation of violations of religious freedom against the Native American Church. Finally, tribes had

complained about Public Law 280. So, we put in a recision clause about Public Law 280 in the bill.

I feel that the 1968 Indian Civil Rights Act helped focus the attention of the American Congress on the status of Indian tribes. Our goal was to begin putting in motion an Indian political system that could be understood like the federal, state, and local system. One of the problems in this field is that Indians do not conveniently fit anything. Americans are always trying to create a "box" for them.

Next, I want to look at events that led to Indian participation in the Economic Opportunity Act. Private groups laid the ground work. They included the Association on American Indian Affairs, the NCAI, the Episcopal Church, and the Indian Rights Association. They helped sponsor the 1964 National Capitol Conference on Poverty. I helped staff that conference. We expected four hundred people and nine hundred people showed up. It was the enthusiasm from this conference, more than anything else, that helped get Indians in the Economic Opportunity Act.

I helped implement one of the OEO programs to fight poverty. After the National Capitol Conference on Poverty, I took a congressional fellowship and lived with the Menominee Indians. I worked as a consultant and helped the Menominee establish their first antipoverty program. I went to the old Menominee courthouse and met with the Menominee County government. I said, "We would like to get you funded as one of the first rural community action programs." They replied, "We have so many problems, Helen, we do not have time to worry about this." I said, "Well, let's sit down for a few minutes and talk about this. Tell me some of the things that are most needed on this reservation." We talked for three days. Out of that discussion came their Community Action Programs.

It was an interesting experience. A tribe that had been terminated had a federal agency come in and offer once again to bring federal services to attack poverty on the Menominee Reservation. This particular OEO grant was most helpful to the Menominee as they tried to cope with being Menominee County, which was the poorest county in Wisconsin.

On weekends, I traveled and talked to the other tribes in Wisconsin. I spent two days trying to find a lost band of Chippewa. When

I found the tribal chairman, I said, "What can we do to be helpful to this tribe?" And he told me that he had gone to Washington, without success, to get a community water system that was not poisoned. We were able to get the Association of American Indian Affairs to give us a five thousand dollar grant to help this tribe. Out of that grant, we also pulled together the various tribes in Wisconsin and reactivated the Great Lakes Intertribal Council.

The 1963 civil rights march on Washington, and the entire civil rights movement, was extremely helpful to American Indians. It was in this decade that OEO started Upward Bound programs and Headstart programs for Indian students. An Indian desk also was created in the Department of Education. The strategy was to get the elementary and secondary education programs to target resources a little more effectively through states and local educational agencies to Indian people. Both BIA schools and state schools received much needed resources to teach Indian students.

Title 4 of the Indian Education Act was especially helpful. Credit for this act should be given to Robert Kennedy and the National Indian Education Report, *National Challenge—National Tragedy.* The Title 4 program was helpful in getting Indian students into public school systems and designing Indian curriculum for these schools. The Teacher Corps also brought Indan staff into the classroom and encouraged the use of bilingual aids.

There are several things that scholars need to pay attention to when studying this era. Private organizations, including the churches, really pushed hard for the right of tribal self-government and the right of Indians to speak for themselves. The role of these groups in getting antipoverty funds into Indian communities, through Indian tribal groups, has not been studied carefully. Their effort forced the BIA to begin modernizing its procedures and its relationships with tribes. It led to the emergence of Indians in key policy-making positions. Indian people also began, more than ever, to see the importance of education in determining their own destiny and how to use the American system for their own benefit.

CHAPTER THREE

The War on Poverty

Alfonso Ortiz, LaDonna Harris, Robert L. Bennett,
Robert Burnette

*Indians under my jurisdiction really enjoyed the short but happy life
of the Office of Navajo Economic Opportunity. We did not waste all the
money that came to the reservation but we spilled a little bit here and
there. We began the Rough Rock School with OEO money. We also started
the Navajo Community College, the first Indian community college in the
world, with OEO funds. Today, the government has cut back appropriations, but when you rely on government programs you are going to have
feast and famine.*

Graham Holmes, former BIA superintendent and area director

*One of the tragedies of OEO is that it helped make the people of
Alaska dependent upon the non-native economy. Before OEO, Alaska had
one of the most integrated native economies left in the United States.
I do not want to romanticize that subsistence economy. It was a very hard
life. People lived off the resources that were indigenous to the area. It was
not the kind of life that I could lead. But people got by and they did not
need outside assistance.*

*What happened with OEO was that the government decided that
these "poor" people needed access to the goods and services associated with
the non-native economy. I agree that it is not pleasant having ten people
living in a ten by ten foot foot square log cabin when the temperature is
thirty degrees below zero. OEO made it possible to build new houses for
many native people. Who can argue with that? The only problem is that
you have to have heating oil, plumbing, and electricity. That cost money
but it did not make any difference. OEO officials were determined to provide people with a non-native economy in an area that could not support it.*

[219]

Today, the people in rural Alaska that are hurting the most are the ones that participated in that economy. OEO programs were a false promise because President Ronald Reagan is now trying to cut $5 million worth of BIA general assistance money in Alaska. Over 80 percent of that money was targeted to pay for heating oil bills for individual homes and villages. If there had never been an OEO, those people would still be living in small cabins but they would not be freezing to death.

Don Mitchell, Alaska Federation of Natives

Alfonso Ortiz

Whatever positive virtues there have been in various federal programs for Indians since the Indian Reorganization Act, it is clear that they have not lasted long enough to solve problems. This also happened with the Office of Economic Opportunity. By 1976, because of benign neglect during the administration of President James E. Carter, the OEO programs had come to a grinding halt. How can the federal government and the American people expect one or two administrations to solve problems that have been building up for generations? That is why nothing permanent happened when Indian people received $122 million from the Economic Development Administration.

In 1964, I was at home in San Juan Pueblo. I was appointed chairman of the Community Action Committee to apply for federal funds. We met during the late summer and into the autumn. I went with the executive director of the New Mexico State Commission on Indian Affairs from pueblo to pueblo to explain the opportunities under the OEO. The Santa Ana Council could not believe that they could apply directly to Washington for funds. We offered to help them with the forms, and they finally agreed to start the application process. This was repeated in pueblo after pueblo. They were astounded that they could bypass the Indian agency and the area office and go directly to Washington.

This was the kind of world into which OEO came. Once the money started flowing, Arizona State University, the University of Utah, and the University of South Dakota set up technical assistance centers. They brought tribal leaders to those universities for workshops in proposal writing, report filing, and end-of-year accounting procedures. The OEO took the mystique out of the white man's proposal writing. Indians were taught that they could do it themselves.

The OEO funds provided for tribal program administrators. The relationship with the federal government was becoming so complex that a part time tribal chairman or an unpaid governor could not possibly keep up with the paper work and the accountability procedures that were instituted in order to obtain federal funds from a variety of programs. Many future Indian leaders would gain valuable experience working for the OEO.

For example, two successive Navajo tribal chairmen came directly out of the OEO programs. Peter McDonald, who served as chairman for twelve years, was enticed out of a comfortable middle class existence in Southern California where he worked as an engineer. McDonald went back to Window Rock to run the new Office of Navajo Economic Opportunity. He used that experience as a launching pad for his first bid for the tribal chairmanship. Peterson Zah, the tribal chairman who succeeded him in 1982, started out in the OEO legal services program.

The OEO programs bypassed the chain of command in the Indian Bureau. It was not necessary to worry about people who were defensive about keeping their jobs. The OEO created a new class of Indian leadership that is still around today. These people are not intimidated by bureaucratic procedures. When they go to Washington, they are no longer afraid to wander beyond the friendly atmosphere of the BIA offices to ask other agencies for assistance.

Important cabinet level agencies also began to get into the Indian field. The Department of Commerce ran the Economic Development Administration. By 1972, EDA grants and projects had completely overshadowed the old OEO programs. Other agencies that assisted Indians included Housing and Urban Development and the Department of Agriculture, which had a nutritional program for mothers and children.

The Headstart program was very important. It was not only beneficial for kids who learned basic skills. It was also a good thing for Indian communities. It put the parents in the classrooms as para-professionals, teacher's assistants, and cooks and janitors. Long estranged parents no longer felt that they were giving their children over to another world.

Poor people on the reservations were truly invisible in the mid–1960s. When they had problems with off-reservation police because they owed money on television sets, cars, and trucks, they would not go to lawyers. Instead, they would suffer quietly and have their goods repossessed even though they actually had rights to them. The OEO put idealistic young attorneys right in the midst of those communities. These poor people finally had a recourse for their legal problems.

Another legacy of OEO was vocational training. In the Southwest, there was a vocational training program for silversmiths. About one hundred silversmiths were trained in the eight northern pueblos. These people now derive all or a good portion of their income from making silver jewelry. All of this happened because of the training they got under the OEO programs.

There is also a thriving adobe plant that turns out adobe bricks for homebuilding. It is always behind in orders. The plant employs about fifteen people from the eight northern pueblos. It was started under OEO and helped along by HUD. The pueblo home improvement program is another positive benefit of OEO.

LaDonna Harris

Initially, Oklahoma was not eligible for OEO funds, because the state did not have Indian reservations. But everyone in Oklahoma knew that the tribes were not integrated into the community and that they should belong to the local Community Action Programs, so those of us who had been organizing over the western part of the state immediately decided to meet and talk about the problem of segregation.

A short time later, we raised this issue with Washington and could not get an answer. One of the unique qualities of OEO was that people would not let regulations stop them. We persuaded the University of Utah to write us into their OEO program so we could bring both eastern and western Oklahoma tribes together to talk about their concerns. The outcome of this effort was the creation of Oklahomans for Indian Opportunity. It was the first time in the history of the state that the plains tribes got together with the civilized tribes. We discussed how Indian people in Oklahoma could become eligible under the law to take advantage of the OEO program.

We started with Headstart programs. The Kickapoos outside of Norman developed an excellent Headstart program. The Indian Headstart programs were some of the best in the country. They were very unique. When the whole Headstart program was threatened during the Nixon administration, the influence of Indian communities saved it.

We also started a youth program under OEO. People such as Sargeant Shriver and Bobby Kennedy visited the state and this created a lot of consciousness raising. We developed programs for high school dropouts. This was extremely important because 75 percent of the Indian children, which made up 50 percent of the total population, were dropping out of high school.

Lyndon Johnson was the first president to make a major address on Indian affairs. He also created the National Council on Indian Opportunity. President Johnson appointed me to this council because of my interest in urban Indians. We met with every member of the cabinet other than the secretary of defense and the secretary of state. The vice-president was our chairman. It is hard to imagine today that the eight Indian members of the council met as equals around the table with seven cabinet members from all those different executive departments. Unfortunately, this experiment was short lived.

When Richard Nixon was elected, in 1968, the momentum that had been built up from OEO continued. President Nixon advocated self-determination but he also wanted to dismantle OEO. The curious thing is that he did not dismantle the Indian program. Community services continued to exist after the Indian desk was transferred over to the Department of Health, Education and Welfare.

I will stand up and defend OEO as long as I live. Indian leadership developed out of that program. The only people that you could communicate with in the Carter administration were community organizers that came out of OEO. One of the reasons that all of the advocacy groups collapsed was that President Carter co-opted them and brought them into the administration on the second and third level.

Under the Indian Reorganization Act, tribal governments never really functioned. But when OEO was established, tribal governments had the funds to begin Headstart programs and reservation economic development. Tribal governments also established human services programs to help their people.

OEO taught us to use our imagination and to look at the future as an exciting adventure. It taught us that there are other ways of doing things. Today, we must go forward in the same spirit and try to link up with all those other entities that do business with the federal government, to get money and to insure our survival.

ROBERT L. BENNETT

Economic poverty has been very pervasive in Indian communities for a long time when compared with the rest of the country. Most tribes have accommodated themselves to this situation and learned to live with it. For example, in 1924, the trust period on all the allotments on the Oneida Reservation in Wisconsin were not extended. Most of the land was lost when the allottees could not pay their taxes. Because there were no social services, they had to develop a system to accommodate the disaster that had befallen them. The old people were taken care of by the younger people, and bartering was commonplace. It was not unusual for a family to bake a couple of extra loafs of bread and send them next door. People, more or less, took care of themselves.

Poverty is going to remain with tribes for a long time. We have two kinds of poverty. One is where people do not have anything. The other kind is where people cannot manage what they have. I am especially concerned about the latter situation. Tribes that received per capita claims settlements frequently did not invest these funds. I know from experience that tribes placed these funds in local banks when they should have bought the bank. The amount deposited was more than the assets of the bank. These kinds of opportunities were not taken advantage of, and poverty lingers on.

Poverty also is pervasive because of the dysfunction of the capital market within the Indian community. When a million dollars is invested in most communities, it generates approximately ten million dollars of cash flow. But in Indian communities, one million dollars generates just one million dollars of cash flow. Furthermore, in most Indian societies profit making is not a part of their economic system. Most tribes engage in barter. These are basic problems that are related to poverty. Tribes are going to have to come to grips with them.

Today, the government is cutting back poverty programs. The big question is whether people on reservations can reinstitute a way to take care of each other. IRA tribal constitutions and bylaws need to be rewritten to revitalize the district or community system.

There are some real mitigating circumstances in connection with poverty on reservations. Indians had lived with poverty so long they did not know they were poor until the poverty programs came along. The War on Poverty did a lot of good things. I am not arguing that point. But I am suggesting that reservation communities will have to go back to old ways of dealing with these problems now that federal government is dropping programs.

The lack of funding has created a dangerous situation on some reservations. For instance, one tribe had a $150,000 shortfall in their law and order program because of cutbacks in funds. People went to the tribal council and got an appropriation of tribal money for $150,000. How long will tribal funds last, if tribes have to constantly make up for the shortfall in federal programs? Tribes must look at these programs and develop a system of priorities.

Furthermore, if the Congress finds out that a tribe is spending $150,000 on a program, they are going to say, "We do not have to give them any more money." Tribes will have to project their income over the next several years. They must determine how much of their money will be needed to make up for shortfalls as the cost of these programs increases.

We are now in a period of readjustment. Hopefully the managerial experience that Indians received in operating OEO programs will serve them in good stead. It takes good management to retrench, just as it does to expand. When termination was implemented, the tribes were able to marshal a great deal of support because the public concluded that the government was not carrying out its treaty obligations. But you cannot marshal the same support for additional funds that you can to fight oppression. Tribes are going to be forced, more and more, to rely on their own resources. They will have to use their leadership and managerial skills to make a readjustment.

ROBERT BURNETTE

When John F. Kennedy flew into Sioux Falls, South Dakota, in 1960, I met him at the airport and had the privilege of introducing him to the entire state. He put a war bonnet on his head, and he left it on for a few minutes. This encounter set the stage for the future, and I was asked to attend secret meetings of President Kennedy's committee on pockets of poverty. This committee was the beginning of OEO.

We were able to get OEO enacted on the reservations so quickly because we had a lot of friends, not only in government, but out of government. We had the AFL-CIO, the National Council of Churches, and other groups. We were able to pay the travel expenses for many tribal leaders who came to Washington, setting the stage for a show of power up on Capitol Hill and at the National Cathedral. All of these things were well planned and executed.

An unforeseen problem was that OEO diverted the attention of Indian people from their sacred land. People ran over each other to get jobs at $2.50 an hour. They forgot all of the things that they had learned as Indian people, because they were so eager for employment. Everybody wanted to go to work and move off their land. People forgot their gardens, and they even gave up their range units to participate in OEO programs. But the OEO did do a lot of good in the field of education and in the social service areas. We have many Indian leaders today that are products of OEO.

Hardly any of the OEO funds that went to tribes were audited by the United States government. Audits of this money will make us all look very bad in the management of funds. It will appear that an awful amount of corruption existed on the reservations. It is true that tribal councils sometimes did not handle this money correctly, but it was not an indication of outright criminal acts. It was simply mismanagement. The Bureau of Indian Affairs did not help us. The BIA was ignored by the people who rushed around to get OEO money. This grantsmanship business became a disease. We need to document and justify how this money was spent.

During the OEO era, many of our leaders forgot who they were and why they were elected. They were obsessed with getting federal grants. For example, there was, for a short time, a $5 million fund from which tribes could borrow money to start cattle and farming associations. This was exactly what Indian people needed. Pine Ridge BIA policemen organized and bought $120,000 worth of cattle. But this fund was eliminated one year later, and tribes accepted this action without protest.

I do not remember any tribe, individual, or organization recommending amendments to the OEO act. It faded away and nobody went to battle for it. There were no organizations set up to fight for the improvement of OEO. The same thing happened to the Indian Reorganization Act. There is always room for improvement and we ought to do that with future legislation.

CHAPTER FOUR
Activism and Red Power

Lenada James, Ada Deer, Ramona Bennett,
Gerald Wilkinson, Hank Adams

In 1966, Dick Gregory joined members of the Puyallup-Nisqually tribes in fighting for treaty fishing rights. Until fairly recently, Dick Gregory had one of the highest sentences ever given for an arrest on fishing rights. At the time, there was some question of backlash against black involvement with Indians. When Dick Gregory joined us, I was in the army in Washington D.C. I received a telephone call from the fishermen asking if they should allow Dick Gregory to join them. I told them that a black man could recognize injustice just as much as Marlon Brando, who all Indians had welcomed on the rivers two years earlier.

At that time, a number of Indian people, primarily older Indians past their fifties, joined in the National Poor People's Campaign with Martin Luther King and Ralph Abernathy. Few people realize how much the Indian involvement in the 1964 Civil Rights Act caused Hubert Humphrey to fight within the Lyndon Johnson administration for independent Indian programs under OEO, which the Indian Bureau was trying to defeat.

Hank Adams, Assiniboine leader and writer

In the years after Wounded Knee, AIM stopped supporting purely Indian issues. Instead of adhering to the American concept of democracy, it turned to the extreme left and sided with everything from Eastern Bloc countries. Much of AIM's teaching and philosophy was clearly Marxist. . . .

I did not think that the Sioux should become involved in the political affairs of other countries. So I wrote editorials in The Lakota Times *which brought up this point. I never wrote editorials that insulted the American Indian Movement. I simply tried to examine philosophically and ideolog-*

[228]

*ically the things that AIM was espousing on the television, radio, and in
their own newspaper.*
   *I quickly learned that members of AIM could not tolerate criticism.
Rather than exchange ideas, they reacted in a very violent way. My newspaper became a target for shotguns, Molotov cocktails, and threats in the
middle of the night. It was an experience that lasted for almost a year.*

Tim Giago, editor and publisher of *The Lakota Times*

LENADA JAMES

My father interpreted the Indian Reorganization Act to both the
Bannock and the Shoshone tribal members. He explained the good
things that were supposed to come out of the IRA. He was also a
tribal chairman for a number of years and the Bannock and Shoshone
Reservation was prospering. We had good farmers and they raised a
lot of cattle. But government regulations and incompetent BIA administration pushed the Bannock and Shoshone into poverty.

I helped my father write letters to senators, congressmen, and the
Bureau of Indian affairs, but we could never get any help. The federal
government did not carry out its trust responsibility. There was no
enforcement of the laws. The superintendent continued to lease Indian
lands on the reservation.

Frustrated by these conditions, I participated in the BIA relocation
program and went to San Francisco. There, I met people from other
tribes. We refused to assimilate. Instead, we got together and held
powwows. We also pushed the BIA to help us get a higher education.
We did not want to go to trade schools and become beauticians,
plumbers, or carpenters. Those are good skills, but we hoped to become
professionals.

I was the first Indian student to enroll at the University of California at Berkeley under the Equal Opportunity Program. I helped
recruit other Indian students. I was the chairman of the Indian student
club. About that time, blacks were demanding a black studies department. So, we decided to push for an Indian studies department.

We wrote our own proposal and the university agreed to establish
an Indian studies department so our education would become relevant
to the communities that we were going to go back to someday. I spent
a lot of time working on Indian curriculum with different educational

groups in California. We implemented the first university-level Indian studies department in the nation.

Next, we turned our attention to Alcatraz Island. This abandoned prison site was being turned over to the city of San Francisco. We believed that, under treaties, federal surplus property was supposed to revert to Indians, if they claimed it. The Indian student groups at San Francisco State and Berkeley went out and occupied the island. We really did not know what we were doing. We were mad because we could not sing and dance anywhere we wanted to on the university campus.

Nevertheless, we were working for an important goal. We were trying to get the issue that Indians had the right to retrieve federal surplus property litigated in the courts. I spent a whole year on the island. I commuted back and forth to the university with my two-year-old son. We would hitchhike and then catch a sailboat or a speedboat to the island. I wrote all the public relations proposals that were released from the island. I then turned in some of this material for the work that I was doing in my classes.

The protest movement at Alcatraz had positive results. Many individuals were not ashamed to be Indian anymore. People who had relocated in the cities were reidentifying themselves as Indians. But there was riff raff on the island. Many people were using drugs and getting drunk. That was not the kind of image we wanted to project to the press or to the world. We hoped to project a positive image of Indian people. We wanted to show what the federal government was doing to destroy our people. Throughout the United States, Indian men were being sent to prison, people on reservations were starving, and Indian family units were being destroyed. I call this systematic annihilation.

After I graduated, I went to law school in Washington D.C. At that time, a group of Indians took over the BIA. I was not a part of that. I thought that the BIA had good leadership under the direction of Louis Bruce, Sandy McNabb, and other individuals. The occupation of the BIA put a damper on the progress that they were making.

After I lost my scholarship to law school, I went back home to the reservation and started a legal project to enforce tribal laws. I also served on the tribal council. I think that the Indian Reorganization Act, and everything after it, resembled a big rat maze. The Indians are the rats in this maze experiment. I do not want to deal anymore with this problem. I intend to get my feet back on the ground and start looking at things from another direction.

ADA DEER

I would like to comment on my background. I am the oldest of five children. I grew up on the Menominee Reservation in Wisconsin, except for about five years when I received an elementary education in Milwaukee. My mother was a white woman from the eastern establishment who came from a long line of missionaries. She was a nurse on the Rosebud Reservation before being transferred to the Menominee Reservation, where she met my father. On my father's side, I have a medicine man and various other traditional people. When we were going through many of our difficulties over the years, I always felt strengthened because I was covered from both ends.

I have always had a strong sense of self. I did not receive the damaging experiences that many Indian children were exposed to early in life. This has had a substantial effect on my life and the life of the Menominee. I was very fortunate in winning the tribal scholarship to attend college. From my freshmen year in college, I felt a great debt of gratitude for my tribe, because I did not want to be poor. I was ready to do anything to get an education. I attended and graduated from the University of Wisconsin in Madison with a liberal arts degree. Then, I decided to become a social worker. I received graduate training in social work from Columbia University.

The "missionary gene" in my mother's family was transformed into a "social work gene." From the time I was a teenager, I thought about the life of people on the reservation. I wondered why people were so poor and why there was so much drinking. Then I started reading and learned about the injustices that had been forced on the Indian people. I became very angry. Fortunately, at that time, I had a number of interesting experiences as a teenager and as a college student. I graduated from the Christian Leadership Training Camp in Michigan. It was an American Indian based camp. I also attended the Encampment for Citizenship in New York and the American Friends' Service Committee International Students' Seminar. I have had wonderful experiences with interesting people, who have constantly encouraged and motivated me.

After my education and work in New York was finished, I returned to the Midwest. I spent eight years in Minneapolis and worked in a number of agencies as a social work program supervisor. I also worked in a neighborhood house, at the University of Minnesota, in the Minneapolis public schools, and for three years with the Bureau of Indian Affairs.

I decided to go back to Wisconsin because there were no jobs in Minneapolis that I was interested in taking at the time termination occurred. I tried to understand what the Menominee termination bill meant, and I was always conscious of the great suffering that it had caused on my reservation. I started going to tribal meetings, and it was a very interesting experience. People looked around at me and said, "Who are you?" I replied that I had been away to school for a while, but I was still a member of the tribe. The product of my mother's sense of activism, I sat on the front row and asked lots of questions.

After I learned what was going on, I became very angry. I decided that we were involved in a complex legal situation and needed a lawyer. I found Joseph Preloznick, who was the director of Judicare for an OEO legal services program. He said that other Menominees had talked with him about termination, but they had been pressured to not take action. He also said that he needed more than one client. I promised him two other people. They were my brother and sister.

I want to correct for the record the misinformation that I started the fight against Menominee termination all by myself. There were many people and small committees, over a number of years, that wanted to do something. But they did not quite get it all together to proceed. Once these individuals became better informed, they too could do something to combat termination. I want to emphasize that both Indians and their non-Indian friends have a lot of individual power they can use to correct many of the injustices in the world.

We started to meet with other Menominees that had expressed an interest in opposing termination. Once Menominee land was sold, our strength began to grow. It was an exciting but very hard time. Both Indians and whites that were in power did their best to discourage us. We were called agitators and Communists. In 1973, we published a book that explained our struggle to save the Menominee people and their land.

We started the grass roots movement called Menominee Drums. I had heard of Saul Alinsky but had not studied him. He would have been proud of us because we held strategy sessions. We did not wait to get permission from people to do things. I told our lawyer that if Congress had passed a law terminating us they could pass another law "unterminating" us. We held strong convictions and were compelled to work and fight against social injustice.

I have been accused over the years of being a publicity hound. I knew instinctively that we had to get our message out. I also knew that press reporters were often lazy. They liked catchy titles and slogans. They would not focus on abstractions such as freedom and termination. So, a number of the stories focused around my activities. But our long range goal was to stop the land sales and restore federal recognition of the Menominee tribe.

We held meetings and drafted restoration legislation. Preloznick, our lawyer, was a compassionate, knowledgeable and resourceful person. He was aware of the Native American Rights Fund. He called this group, and they provided us with two excellent lawyers for three years. Then, we started succeeding. We had a tremendous march from our reservation down to the state capitol.

We had a very disciplined kind of activism. There were a number of other things going on across the country, and we were certainly aware of this. It was important to be aware of external events, but it was also important to be single minded and proceed with our restoration struggle. We had a number of problems within our group, but our goals prevailed. We succeeded in getting our legislation drafted and in getting the lobbying process completed.

Indians are involved in a love/hate relationship with the Bureau of Indian Affairs. I decided early in life that I was going to be an optimist. It is much easier on your psyche to be an optimist than to be a pessimist. I feel that everyone is a potential friend that can be influenced. I can also intimidate people and use white guilt feelings to my advantage, and I can manipulate the media just as well as other people.

There are good bureaucrats and there are bad bureaucrats. Ernie Stevens, Sandy MacNabb, and Louis Bruce were some of the very good people in the Bureau of Indian Affairs. They were sympathetic and helped us in our struggle, but not everybody was that way. We encountered entrenched bureaucrats. Everytime I had to meet them, they would always ask, "Who are you?" and "Where are you from?" In social work, we have a phrase "the conscious use of self." So I decided, if you want to play a game, I can play a game. I told them, "I have a B.A., a M.S.W., and I have ten years experience. Now let's get down to brass tacks." Of course, they were not accustomed to Indians marching in like this, looking people straight in the eye, and proceeding with business.

I feel that too many American citizens feel isolated from their government, especially during the Reagan administration. But my point is that you can influence people. I want to tell everybody, you can do it. All you have to do is to carefully examine the problem and do your homework. With the excellent legal help that we had, with the wonderful press that we generated, and with the climate of opinion that was created, we went in a very short period of time through a very complicated piece of legislation.

What do we need today in the area of Indian activism? First of all, we need individuals who are going to decide to do something. Then, you have to do your homework. You have to analyze the situation. You have to look at the political climate and social climate. You have to proceed. You cannot be intimidated. The fact that the Menominee achieved an historic reversal of American Indian policy is a concrete demonstration that we can work within the system.

I want to caution people that we now have a very negative administration, but we can all vote. I hope that some of you will run for office. There are many injustices confronting people all across this country. We need good, strong people working to change the system. We have five hundred Indian lawyers and many other professional people. The challenge is there. Do not agonize: organize!

RAMONA BENNETT

About sixteen or seventeen years ago, I was involved with voluntary programs sponsored by the American Indian Women's Service League in Seattle. I met many Indian people who had moved to Seattle because of the BIA relocation program. They had all come to the city to secure improved educational opportunities and find good jobs.

But I discovered that these families had lots of problems. One time, I went to a powwow and met a pretty little girl. She wore a buckskin dress that was sewn with the sinew from a deer. That little girl had rickets and she could not dance. But the dress revealed that her family had at one time been proud and independent. I started to think about that. I wondered how a race of people had become so impoverished that they could not even feed their children.

A short time later, I attended a Puyallup tribal meeting to find out what was going on with my own tribe. I discovered that my tribe had been unofficially terminated by the failure of the federal government to maintain services. The Bureau of Indian Affairs had set up a land office and had alienated the land. Then, the BIA folded up its carpetbag and moved on down the road. The Puyallup tribe did not have a recognized reservation nor any fishing rights.

I had the opportunity to serve on the tribal council. We inherited a broken typewriter and a broken filing cabinet. There had not been an updated enrollment in forty years. Only about twenty out of a thousand people in the tribe received Indian health services. The tribe was in pretty bad shape.

I worked with Hank Adams, who lived with a family at Frank's Landing. Adams was an idea person. He was a very creative, innovative, and slightly madcap individual. When we would go to tribal general meetings, we would encounter a negative attitude. Previously entrenched tribal representatives would say: "No, we tried that in the 1920s and the 1930s. That idea will not work." We started doing research to combat this state of lethargy. We found out that many Puyallup people had been murdered. Their death certificates stated that they had fallen asleep on railroad tracks. We also discovered that the reservation had been taken, literally, at gunpoint through a whole series of thefts. That was why the Puyallup people were scattered around Tacoma and elsewhere without much organization.

I had an opportunity through the Puyallup tribe to meet people who had occupied Alcatraz Island in San Francisco Bay. I read some of the press releases that came out of Alcatraz. One statement indicated that Alcatraz was perfect for Indian purposes. Like many reservations, it had no schools, roads, jobs, or economic opportunities. During that period of time we closely followed the events at Alcatraz, and all kinds of light bulbs started flashing.

We concluded that it was not an accident that Indian people were living in poverty. The federal government had planned the alienation of Indian land. For over ninety years it had been responsible for preventing Indian fishermen from supporting their families with dignity. Because of my increased awareness of social injustice, I attended a National Indian Youth Workshop that was being held in Washington D.C. At this time, President Richard Nixon's self-determination statement was released. We finally realized that we were going to have to defend Indian fishing rights. It was clear that the federal government would not use troops to save our fishermen from the game wardens hired by the state of Washington.

I went back home and joined an armed camp that was set up to protect our fishermen. We were defending the fishermen on our river under a treaty right. We encountered 550 enforcement agents from all of the state agencies. They threatened and physically attacked us. The federal government had an obligation to protect Indians. Instead, it called us radicals. We were only upholding our tribe's treaty right to be self-supporting. When we tried to protect ourselves, they attacked our group, which consisted of only 60 people.

Indians had come from Canada and all over the country. One young Canadian boy was there because white men had raped and murdered his mother. The people would sit around and tell stories about why they were there. Very few of the people had come for the purpose of opening the river so our tribe could safely fish again. They were simply angry because of something horrible that had happened in their lives.

I was part of the Trail of Broken Treaties caravan. I was in the Bureau of Indian Affairs building when the war drums came out. We literally faced death for many nights in that building. We expected federal forces to kill us because the government did not want to abolish the Bureau of Indian Affairs, institute a national Indian government, or address the other issues that we raised.

The most beautiful pictures were drawn in the BIA building. It was fantastic. For a week, Indian artists from all over the country decorated that building. Brave people were involved in this protest movement. They were prepared to sacrifice themselves so that the next generation of Indians could live a better life. I was blessed and fortunate to associate with those people.

This era of Red Power and activism was a very special time. The people that engaged in protest were misunderstood. Hopefully, the well-established and secure reservation Indians will never know what it felt like to be a Puyallup. We looked death in the eye and were threatened with termination. I feel that as long as there is one acre, one fish, or one Indian child remaining in our care, we are always going to be under attack. If we ever forget this, white people will have us for breakfast. They are out to get us. I do not think that is paranoia. To me, that is a conditioned reflex.

GERALD WILKINSON

Indian activism and Red Power, as movements within the Indian community, have changed. Ten years ago, when there was an issue before Congress that affected the lives of Indian people, everybody would get involved. Indians in Washington would gather around the Xerox machine at the National Congress of American Indians before trooping in to see their congressmen. This kind of activity also happened on many different levels outside of Washington D.C.

Today, one of the basic problems is that Indian organizations have become highly specialized groups. We used to have people who were generally involved in education. Now, we have people involved with the education of handicapped Indians. When an omnibus bill is introduced in Congress that affects Indians, only those people interested in a specific aspect of it are there. Indian people are not to blame for this kind of specialization. The nature and the direction of the country has forced Indian groups to become more specialized.

One of the consequences of specialization is that almost no one thinks holistically about Indian problems anymore. Very few people relate what they are doing to a broader context or develop some kind of vision about where Indian people are going and what should be done. Another consequence of specialization is that the market place of ideas has dried up. We have made tremendous progress in many areas, but in terms of intellectual growth, our people have not advanced much over the last ten years.

It was quite a contrast when I recently attended a meeting of Indian organizations in Mexico. There were Indians from Mexico, Guatemala, Bolivia, and Peru. We sat around and talked about things of a philosophical nature. We discussed ideas such as the relationship of Indians to Christianity and the nation state. We also examined the relationship of peasant Indians in Mexico to tribal Indians in the United States. That level of discourse was much different than the kinds of discussions that Indian people have in the United States.

Contact with Indian people in other countries is absolutely essential if we want to intellectually reinvigorate the Indian community. In order to move again, as we did in the 1960s and 1970s, we must have an Indian intellectual revolution. It is essential that we think about who we are as a people and where we are going as a people.

I want to refer to a political study that we did in the Third Congressional District of New Mexico because it illustrates at least one point that is related to what I have said. On the Navajo Reservation, there is a community called Crown Point. During the tribal council election, we went up to Crown Point to pretest our survey and obtain political information about the people. We assumed that the people at Crown Point, for the most part, were concerned about being exploited by the big energy companies and about combating racism from the white ranchers in the area. We also assumed that they agreed with tribal leaders about the need to expand the medical clinic and refurbish the high school.

In our survey, we discovered that those things were not really on many people's minds. The most important issue at Crown Point was dogs. On the Navajo Reservation, ten thousand people a year are treated by the Public Health Service for dog bites. The people also were concerned about clean water and improved roads.

The point is that, even though you are intimately involved with Indian people, you can lose track of what they are thinking. The biggest task before Indian intellectuals is to relate to the common people. We are entering a new era. The development and implementation of ideas is absolutely essential, if we are going to have another Red Power revolution.

HANK ADAMS

The central promises of the Indian Reorganization Act, as stated by John Collier in 1934, were complete economic independence and self-determination for Indian tribes. A half century later, Indian people remain far removed from either goal. One of the basic reasons is that we have never been talking about self-determination, but about self-administration.

As I look back at John Collier's writing, I find that his intent in the Indian Reorganization Act was to provide a mechanism for indirect administration of federal policies and programs. In the last fifty years, an unbelievable number of different policy proposals and policy objectives have been "self" hyphenated. The goal of termination was self-sufficiency. It sounded similar to John Collier's self-rule. In the last month, one of the members of the Indian Affairs Committee stated that he was going to continue his fight against Indian treaties because they violated his concepts for self-fulfillment. In recent years I have almost come to believe that it does not matter what the particulars or details of a policy are so long as you do not divest the Indian leadership of their capacity for self-congratulations.

How far have we fallen from that day in 1830 when Blackhawk was taken prisoner in chains to Washington D.C. to see President Andrew Jackson? Blackhawk told Jackson, "Even in chains, sir, I am your equal." Indians have fallen very far from that day. If there would be a return to the introspective capacities that Indian people possess in analyzing problems, there also would be a return to some measure of respect. That is really essential to have before you ever achieve self-rule, self-government, and something other than self-administration.

When you realize what the good guys have done to Indian people, then you cannot accept the way things are now and how things are moving toward the future. President Dwight D. Eisenhower has been held accountable for carrying out the termination policy, but termination was well under way before Eisenhower entered office. In 1949, the Interior Department met with its created organ, the National Congress of American Indians, to ask it to take the lead in planning termination. The NCAI, at that time, did not object to this request. The lawyers for the NCAI helped write up some of the termination bills.

The Menominee first wrote a termination bill in 1947. They consented to it at a rapid hearing schedule in 1954, when some two dozen tribes and several states were subject to termination. At that point, lawyers led the Menominee toward termination. They did not object until later when there were slight modifications in that termination bill.

I have read in a number of publications that termination ended in 1958. Termination was going strong in the 1960s under Philleo Nash, James Officer, Stewart Udall, and President John F. Kennedy. Another hated policy is the Relocation-Vocational Training Act. Relocation started in 1948 under President Harry S. Truman. It was expanded into a national program in 1950 and received its first statutory authority in 1956.

When James Officer's task force went around the country and met with Indians, it found out how much this program was hated. So, the task force decided that the name of the program should be changed to Employment Assistance. Today, you can hear Indian leaders condemn the relocation policy of the 1950s under Dwight Eisenhower. But in the 1964 Democratic platform, it was proudly proclaimed that the Kennedy and Johnson administrations had doubled the enrollment in the program. Indian leaders did not object because it was called Employment Assistance. Commissioner Philleo Nash, the champion of many Indians, had the authority to stop Menominee termination when he came into office in 1961. But he did not do that until 1964 when a majority of Menominees submitted a petition against this policy to the government of the United States. In 1962 and 1963, both Philleo Nash and James Officer threatened to administratively terminate tribes in the state of Washington. And the Congress of the United States threatened to terminate every tribe that submitted a claims judgement distribution bill in 1965. It took some behind the scenes maneuvering to stop termination from being reinstituted more aggressively than it had been carried out in the 1950s.

Congressional termination ended in March 1965, when Melvin Laird, a conservative Republican from Wisconsin, and Congresswoman Julie Butler Hansen made strong floor speeches in the House of Representatives. They condemned this policy, not only for the Menominee, but for all Indians. They also worked behind the scenes to prevent the Senate from reinstituting this policy.

In 1966, Interior Secretary Stewart Udall and Commissioner Robert Bennett threatened termination in a confrontation with the NCAI at Santa Fe. It took two more years before Lyndon Johnson issued a presidential message against termination. Beyond that, Indian tribes such as the Colville supported termination.

President Richard M. Nixon proclaimed the policy of self-determination on July 8, 1970. Most of the measures that were proposed in the Nixon message grew out of the work that had already been underway through the National Council on Indian Opportunity and various Indian organizations. The good guys in the BIA created the National Tribal Chairmen's Association. They decided that the NTCA would have ten people on its board of directors. The three members of the executive board were supposed to be the voice of the Indian people. Now that is not self-determination when you are talking about several hundred tribes.

The Nixon administration had already committed itself in favor of the Indian Financing Act and the Self-Determination Act. So, why did they need the NTCA? One reason was that they were trying to consolidate a force against commitment to urban Indians. The Nixon administration also used the NTCA to demand an assault on the eight hundred Indians who had occupied the BIA building.

The NTCA requested a police action to "take those people out" of the BIA building. They meant kill them, because members of the American Indian Movement and other activists were in there. Some of the good guys such as Ernie Stevens, Sandy McNabb, LaDonna Harris, and Louis Bruce were even talking about assaulting the building.

John Collier's philosophy was that all power flows to organization. He had a philosophy that the common people, the unwashed people, should look to the experts and enlist their help and assistance. One of the most scandalous things that the experts have done for Indian people in the twentieth century is the claims policy. At first, the NCAI was organized to make the IRA applicable to all tribes, even those who had rejected it. It also had a second goal: to get behind the passage of an Indian Claims Commission Act that Collier had been pushing. On October 30, 1978, the Indian Claims Commission, in its final report, stated that its problem had been a matter of giving the Indian his due while at the same time severing federal relations.

The discussion of Red Power surfaced in the 1930s when John Collier used it to subjugate Indian people. Red Power as a form of activism, was not something that the National Indian Youth Council originated in the 1960s. Every generation of Indian people has fought valiantly against what has been happening to them.

CHAPTER FIVE

Traditionalism and the Reassertion of Indianness

Oren Lyons, Virginia Beavert, Francis McKinley, Sol Tax

How do we make permanent the understanding that tribes are political entities and a part of the American system? We are more than just unique little cultures. But I do not think that most people or the federal government believe that we are a permanent part of the system. We are tired of the burden of constantly educating the Congress and the government about this basic relationship. We are not like the blacks, Hispanics, or any other ethnic group. We are a permanent part of the political structure of the United States.

LaDonna Harris, Comanche,
Americans for Indian Opportunity

After the termination era the Southern Paiutes revived their culture. They held powwows, and a number of them were involved in a July Sun Dance held at Whiterocks, Utah. To me, that is a sign of cultural togetherness. Before they were terminated, they were fragmented and did not pay too much attention to their culture. After the restoration legislation, they came back together again. Life is an up and down thing. It is recycling from periods of almost nothing to periods of reformation, change, and adaptation. The Southern Paiutes are in such a cycle. After restoration, they have had a renaissance

Francis McKinley, Ute, former tribal chairman
at Uintah-Ouray Reservation

[243]

OREN LYONS

I am not a religious or a spiritual leader. I am a runner for the Six Nations. That enables me to be a spokesman at many gatherings. I am also one of the Onondaga Council members. Our first duty is to oversee ceremonies. Then, we sit in council for the welfare of the people.

It is my perception that scholars often have problems in defining contemporary Native Americans. A leading anthropologist from New York State has attacked the Six Nations directly by saying that we do not exist, because there are no chief systems. I also have been told by anthropologists and other people that the medicine masks located in various museums all over the country belong there. I strongly disagree with this attitude. I still belong to that ceremony. It is my job to see that it continues to function. Our religious society is in a painful situation because those masks are still in museums. I am not afraid to speak up about this, because it is important to the continuation of our culture that we have the respect of the people who now occupy our lands.

We will determine what our culture is. It has been pointed out that culture constantly changes. It is not the same today as it was a hundred years ago. We are still a vital, active Indian society. We are not going to be put in a museum or accept your interpretations of our culture. I hope that what I have said will be taken with the respect with which it was presented.

Sam Deloria said something that is very relevant. He has warned that when we cease to be poor and when we cease to be discernible by our cultural differences, then you are not going to allow us to exist as a separate nation. We have never agreed to this. We have the right to exist as a people and a culture, and how that goes on in the ceremonies is our responsibility.

When people refer to traditionalist Indians all of a sudden everybody says: "Oh, well, there must be some teepees around here. Let's look for the people that have got all the blankets on." That is not a proper way to view traditionalism. Traditionalism is the representation and continuum of a culture that has been here from time immemorial and that demands respect. If you think you can talk us out of existence, you cannot.

You perpetuate your culture, your way of life, by insisting that all of your people speak English and go to English schools. What about our language? It is the soul of the Iroquois nation. Without it, we do not have a nation, because there is knowledge in a language that does not translate into English. The English language is quite restrictive in its definitions. It is not a picture language. It is a technical language.

I have been called again and again an unrealistic fellow because of my contention that our people really believe that they are an independent and separate nation. I sit in a council that has been continuous for hundreds of years. We do not have the Bureau of Indian Affairs in our nation. We do not have a federal agent. We do not have anything but Indians. And, in our unrealistic manner, we do not have federal programs.

Nevertheless, we continue to survive. Our chief council is composed of respectable and dignified men. They are profoundly endowed with the spirit of nationhood, freedom, and self-determination. When we travel about and meet with the elders from the other different nations and peoples, we find our friends.

I cannot speak for anybody but the Six Nations of Iroquois, but I can tell you that we have children who believe that they are Onondagas. We have longhouses that are full of our young people. We have a lacrosse team called the Iroquois Nationals that competes with Canada, the United States, England, and Australia.

It is a fact that a small group of people in the northeast have survived an onslaught for some 490 years. They continue their original manner of government. They also drive cars, have televisions, and ride on planes. We make the bridges that you cross over and build the buildings that you live in.

So, what are we? Are we traditionalists or are we assimilated? If you can get away from your categories and definitions, you will perceive us as a living and continuing society. We believe that the wampum and the ceremonial masks should be at home. We will continue our ceremonies. We have the right to exist and that right does not come from you or your government.

We are a very friendly and peaceful people. But we will stand up for principle even if that entails confrontation. I am proud of my people. I am always humble and honored to sit in our council. It is made up of dignified and simple men that know who they are and where they are going.

VIRGINIA BEAVERT

It is difficult to discuss traditionalism when you are speaking in the English language. The native language is very important in Yakima life because from childhood through adulthood you completely depend on your language.

The rituals and taboos that were performed even before a child was born are still observed today. And when the child is born, there is a certain period that is very important to it. Most Indian people know that the umbilical cord that connects the child to somebody that he respects is preserved. We Yakimas do not flush it down the toilet, and we do not throw it in the incinerator. Instead, we put it in a little piece of buckskin. Then, we sew it into a little heart shape and bead it and put it around the child's neck. Some people carry their umbilical cord to their graves.

Adolescence is the most important part of a child's life. There are different things for boys and girls to learn. My grandmother always told me certain things I could not do. This tradition helped me a lot from adolescence to adulthood. My great-great-grandmother taught me to respect religion and all living things. Sunday was a day I could not pick flowers and berries or kill an animal. I was even afraid to step on the grass because that was the day that every living thing worshipped God. It was very difficult when I joined the army because there were certain foods I could not eat. Pork was considered an unclean food.

All the boys in our family were taught how to hunt in the proper way. It was necessary to perform a ritual after shooting a deer. You could not shoot a deer and skin it without thanking the Creator or the deer for the life that he had given for you.

We were thankful for everything. When I went to the mountains during springtime to dig for food, I found the ground where everything was brand new. We observed our religion in the spring. We had to perform rituals when we dug for food. There were certain words that we said, and songs were sung. We always turned counter clockwise when we picked food out of the ground, and we thanked the Creator for this sustenance. Then we went to a longhouse where the tribe waited for the first food of spring. Nobody could go up in the mountains and dig any food until after they had this communion.

The water, salmon, deer, and grouse were the foods that the men took care of. Unfortunately, some of the roots we dug have disappeared. All of the rituals that we performed taught young people how to respect nature. They learned that you do not go out and desecrate what God has created.

After you matured you were responsible for teaching all the knowledge that you had acquired. It was very important that you learned as much as possible about being an Indian. Then you would be able to teach the young the way you were taught. The training was severe and there are a lot of things that we do not observe anymore.

How did religion ever come into our lives? When I was in Mexico City a few years ago at an anthropology seminar, I met some people who were discussing canoe sites that had been found in a few areas around the world. We have one on our reservation. According to my great-grandmother, the people held ceremonies at certain times when something happened in the sky. Nobody seemed to know what it was. The people danced on their knees for days and days, and they fasted and prayed and sang around a particular area that was supposed to have been an overturned canoe.

Our longhouse religion began when Indian people died and in seven days rose again. There were a few choice people who did this. They did not have to have led a clean life. These people would die and rise again and bring back a message. There were women who rose from the dead, too. These people brought back all of the predictions that have happened up to now.

We were told that we will not be destroyed by water but by fire. Certain things would happen to give us the sign. Those things are happening now. I do not want to mention them because it is a very sensitive area, especially where sexuality is involved.

I would like to stress, once again, that it is important to preserve Indian languages. I have made several trips to Washington, D.C. to get programs on our reservation in bilingual education. I am always met by non-Indians who say that there is not money available for Indian bilingual education. But I have been fortunate enough to acquire some funding through Dr. Dave Warren to complete an Indian language dictionary. I hope that someday we will be able to train Indian teachers to teach the Native American language to our children in both public and Indian schools.

FRANCIS McKINLEY

In my childhood days, I lived in an era when it was very difficult to be overt about being Indian if you wanted to be successful in school. My parents constantly stressed that, first of all, I had to get an education to become equal or even superior to the average white man. Then, I would be able to preserve my identity and the culture of my people.

My father used to say, "You know, we always think that white people are superior because they have more things, can read and write better, and are more aggressive. They seem to have more freedom than we have. So, we think they are better people, but they are not. They are stupid and ignorant like we are sometimes. Do you think a smart man would go and destroy everything he touches? Do you think a smart man would try to accumulate a lot of things that he is not going to use, and that he cannot take with him when he dies? That is stupidity." My father believed that if I received a little education I would be better than 90 percent of the people, including the white people. That was the kind of philosophy that was drilled into me as I was growing up.

Our culture and traditions have remained intact over the last fifty years. We are still very proud of ourselves. And we are talking about planning alternatives for the future.

There are some other topics that I want to discuss. When you look at the population, the average age of Indians is about seventeen years, contrasted to twenty-nine years for the rest of the American people. If you examine the Indians tribe by tribe, you will see a gap between the ages of forty and sixty.

In a few years, we are not going to have very many old people. Why has this happened? The death rate of Indian men is particularly high. The men have died from diabetes, alcoholism, and alcoholic related accidents. I have examined the population statistics of a number of Indian tribes, and this high mortality rate concerns me very much. The handing down of values and traditions of Indian culture has been the responsibility of our elders. What is going to happen when we do not have any elders left? Maybe a forty-year-old person will have to become an elder of the tribe.

When I was a young boy, our leaders did not separate secular and religious life. Religion was holistic and part of everyday life. People were taught to be generous, truthful, and have respect for one another. There was a very profound spiritual life. People recognized their creator. These Indian values permeated our life.

When we became associated with the American way of life, we separated secular and religious matters. The leaders of our government under the Indian Reorganization Act do not get involved very much in traditional or cultural life. They are mainly concerned with dispensing money to pay for tribal expenses.

I am not a social scientist, and that is why it is difficult to address the topic of Indian culture. But the one thing that sustains us is language. When I speak the Ute language there is something that occurs psychologically. Indians do not swear like whites, because they have their own kind of slang. Our native language has something to do with the way we look at the world.

We have a symbol system in our language. When we discuss spiritual matters, we cannot touch and taste the things that we are talking about. Yet, we know that we experience them. When we used to talk about those things, we would say: Well, you know we are a very religious and very spiritual people. We live with nature and we are sensitive to nature. We know that nature, in its own way, is alive and that it is has its own communication. It has its own curative and healing power. It also has its own happiness, sadness, and joyfulness. If we intend to live in this life as the Creator wanted it, then we have to love and respect all living things in nature.

Sol Tax

I would like to report an exciting development that has occurred recently in the city of Chicago. It is the successful beginning of the Native American Educational Services College. This institution is the first four-year degree-granting private college by and for American Indians. The college is headquartered in Chicago but it has three other campuses at Fort Peck, Northern Cheyenne, and Santo Domingo

Pueblo. We hope that the NAESC will gain a new campus every year in the immediate future.

The creation of this college was a remarkable achievement. It is characteristic of what happens to American Indians when you let them invent things. Indian leaders planned the NAESC without anybody telling them what to do.

It was founded eight years ago to deal with a special problem. In Chicago there are representatives of several different tribes. Many of these individuals preferred Indian services to general city services. They demanded and received an elementary school as part of the public school system so their children could go to an Indian school with Indian teachers. A separate Indian health center also was established. Furthermore, an Indian businessman's association was trying to organize.

Innumerable other Indian organizations developed. It was discovered that Indian people required special training to successfully operate these organizations. Out of this need grew the Native American Educational Services College. As soon as the college started to train people for urban services, it became apparent that the same sort of thing was needed on reservations.

The students at the NAESC are all adults. In order to enroll, a student must be at least twenty-five year old. The college is interested in older people who are serious and have had work experience.

The NAESC has a new headquarters building in Chicago, but it still needs additional funding. The college had operated out of a church, but the church needed the space. So, it was necessary to buy a building that is mortgaged.

The college has been accredited since it was founded by Antioch College, which gives the degree. We are also candidates for accreditation by the North Central Association of American Colleges. Their accrediting team has been to the college a number of times and examined its curriculum. We think that by next spring they will be ready to accredit the school.

The NAESC is important because it symbolizes the contemporary reassertion of Indianness. The students who come out of the college are all working with and for Indians. They will never forget that it was Indians who were involved with them in their higher education.

CHAPTER SIX

Contracting Under the Self-Determination Act

Earl Old Person, Russell Jim, Gerald One Feather,
Joe De La Cruz

*PL 638 has had a tremendous impact on our Indian community.
When people have a problem with services they do not have to go to
Muskogee, the service unit at Tahlequah, and the area health unit at
Oklahoma City. They simply come to Okmulgee and straighten it out with
their tribal officials. More people are getting services although our resources
are still limited. But tribal officers are now making the choices about how
to distribute those inequities instead of the Bureau of Indian Affairs. When
it is time to cut a program, tribal officers decide what their priorities are
and make those cuts.*

*We should not confuse PL 638 with the issue of self-determination.
PL 638 is not really a self-determination act. All it does is to allow us to
operate programs that had been run by the federal government. The goal of
PL 638 is not self-sufficiency. It is to increase our management capabilities.*

Robert Trepp, member of the Creek tribe of Oklahoma

*Prior to the establishment of the policy of self-determination, tribes
could externalize their criticism of programs administered for their benefit,
but now having assumed this responsibility themselves, tribes need to
internalize their criticism if programs are not properly administered. The
reason for this is that the basic responsibility for service providers has
shifted from the various federal agencies to the tribes. . . .*

*I believe administrative management is the key to successful imple-
mentation of the self-determination policy. There is no question but that
the leadership and other human resources are available, in most cases,
for tribes to emerge fully capable of implementing the policy of self-
determination. Some are already doing so, and others are getting their act*

[251]

together for that purpose. It must be anticipated that organizational and other changes in administrative methods will need to take place as this great transitional effort moves forward. Planning is, therefore, becoming an essential part of tribal management. . . .

As self-determination takes root in the minds and hearts of Indian tribes, it can be expected that they will become more aggressive in asserting their sovereignty. Strong tribal leadership, buttressed by a sound adminis- trative management system, is capable of achieving goals and objectives not contemplated even when the policy of self-determination was estab- lished by the Congress. Indian tribes will face the challenges of the future, confident in their own capabilities to make the right decisions. Self- determination as a concept, now developed into policy, is here to stay, and the Indian tribes are glad of it and will make the most of it.

Robert Lafollette Bennett, Oneida,
former commissioner of Indian affairs

EARL OLD PERSON

I first became a member of the Blackfeet tribal council in 1954. I have been on the council since then, and I have watched things that have taken place. Prior to that time, I had listened to some of our elderly people. They were very cautious about new federal programs and alerted the council. They said, "You are going to be engaged in wars. But these wars will not be fought with guns, bows, and arrows. You are going to be fighting over documents."

The Blackfeet tribe has been very careful. We have not contracted for very many federal programs. In fact, when we talked about con- tracting for self-determination, we asked whether those programs would continue to be funded once the tribe took over. The federal government refused to guarantee funding in the future to back up the tribe. There is more to tribal self-sufficiency than merely declaring that you are self- sufficient. When self-determination was first talked about back in the early 1970s, I was president of the NCAI. Even at that time, I began to question self-determination, because we were not given the oppor- tunity to actually get into policy making, and we were not given the chance to utilize and develop our own resources on a permanent basis.

We faced threats, time and again, that specific programs would be cut or phased out. We never had the assurance that we could rely on federal funding. I certainly agree that we have the kind of people today that can help take over and contract for programs, but they need sustained support from the government.

Two years ago, we were told that we could take over our child welfare programs. This sounded awfully good to us. We started a tribal child welfare program last fall. Six months later we were told that it would not be refunded, because the tribe supposedly failed to comply with federal requirements. The Blackfeet people are discouraged by these events. I do not think that we differ with many of the programs that have been set up by Congress, but we are concerned about how they are implemented.

Tribal leaders today are trying hard to work with contracting under PL 638, but once they set program priorities, they are told by the government that there is not enough 638 money to go around. It is an awful difficult thing to go back to your people and say, "We are going to have to cut programs." Tribal leaders receive criticism but it is not their fault. The higher-ups are calling the shots.

On my own reservation there are a lot of needy people that are not really being provided with help. I can take you to any reservation and show you that kind of poverty. We need much more support to make 638 contracting work for these backwoods people.

The government offered to give the Blackfeet boarding school back to the tribal council, if we wanted to take it over. We agreed, if they would guarantee funding of the school. They only promised to help us a year at a time, which was not a guarantee. Contracting was used as a way of getting rid of that boarding school. It finally ended up in the public school system before it was phased out. Today, the government has it back. It is used as a place to put children who are without homes. It is no wonder that my people are very skeptical about so-called self-determination.

There are dangers within these kinds of government programs. When Community Action was first introduced to the Blackfeet people, they were skeptical. Some of the people believed that it would lead to termination. You cannot blame them. So, we ended the discussion.

Later, we showed a film of an area where a Community Action Program had already started. The same people that feared termination, after they saw this film, said, "Why cannot we have this program here on our reservation?" When they saw the actual operation of the program, they wanted it.

RUSSELL JIM

I would like to give you a Yakima perspective with regard to self-determination and Public Law 638. We tried to instigate the contracting of our timber management on the Yakima nation a few years ago. We felt that the Bureau of Indian Affairs was mismanaging our timber resources. The BIA had fashioned its management policy after St. Regis, Boise Cascade, Louisiana Pacific, and Weyerhauser. It was only interested in economic efficiency which meant growing trees as fast as possible. There was a major thinning program. Trees were staged 18 feet apart. It was almost like an orchard setting. This policy harmed the animals and the environment. Futhermore, certain natural foods and medicines would not grow properly.

In 1977, the Department of Interior informed us that $5 million would be available for reforestation. Many of the timber tribes of the state of Washington went to Billings, Montana. They were told that the $5 million would be divided among them in proportion to the size of their reservations and timber stands, but they had to utilize this money for reforestation and accept Public Law 638 in its entirety. The Yakima Indian nation said, "We do not want to implement all of PL 638, just the portions we would like to use." A government spokesman said, "We brought an expert with us. What are your questions?" There were many questions that even the expert could not answer.

The Yakima proposed that this money be routed through the Bureau of Indian Affairs for forest management. We did not need reforestation. Our forests were already self-propagating to a point where we needed a thinning program. The government refused to accept our suggestion. A short time later, that money mysteriously disappeared back into the treasury. It was not utilized by anyone. I suspect that it was because we would not accept PL 638 in its entirety.

I tried to bring a lawsuit against the Indian Bureau because of the mismanagement of the Yakima's forest and the outright giving away of our trees. We had caught them red-handed. But the old guard downstairs in the Bureau got hold of the old guard upstairs on the council and warned that "If you sue the Bureau, you are going to lose your trust responsibility and set yourself up for termination." There was also a fear that if we instigated contracting of our timber and pushed away the Bureau we would set ourselves up for termination. I spent the next two years going to the intertribal timber conferences and picking out the highest officials in the audience at a general meeting. I asked them, "Can you contract away your trust responsibility?" The answer was always "No." In order to justify its existence, the Bureau of Indian Affairs was playing little games.

There is another worry among all of us. It is this vicious cycle that is imposed upon us in regard to self-determination and self-sufficiency. In the past, when you were a member of a federally recognized tribe, you were deemed incompetent. You became a ward of the government, which had a trust responsibility. This incompetency prevented IRS from imposing taxes upon your land. Incompetency was a degrading term, but it seemed to protect you.

Today, if you become, in some sense, self-sufficient then you are competent. You do not need wardship anymore, and you set yourself up for termination. Many of our people do not wish termination. They want the trust responsibility and treaty rights to remain intact as long as the sun shall shine.

GERALD ONE FEATHER

I have been involved with approximately seven different tribal administrations on the Pine Ridge Reservation since 1961, and I have seen a lot of changes throughout the years. Beginning in 1968 or 1969, the tribe went through a series of confrontations in the field of education. People felt that they were not getting a quality education. They insisted that Indian culture be included in the school. Rogers Morton was secretary of the interior at the time. The tribe went to the federal court over this issue because the Sioux wanted to have a voice in their own education and affairs at the local level. A new concept was born in the tribal government. It was called local control.

Most IRA tribes now have local units of government just like the states. On Pine Ridge, when the constitution was organized, they allowed communities to have certain authority within the tribal system. The communities were allowed to exercise a concurrent tax authority with the tribal council. They also determined who were the members of their communities, and they could set up an economic enterprise and run it without going back to the tribal council.

We have had a law and order program for many years. The tribe paid part of the budget for law enforcement, and the Indian Bureau financed the rest of it. We had a dual police system. This went on until after Wounded Knee, when the tribe decided to take over all of the police jurisdiction. At the present we have contracted for six functions in police work.

For a long time, the tribe would pass legislation and then turn right around and have the BIA enforce that particular law. Then a case arose at Rosebud where the defendant said, "Where does the Bureau of Indian Affairs get their authority to enforce tribal law? Who gave the authority to allow the BIA police to enforce the tribal code?" There was a lawsuit, and it was discovered that nothing in the tribal records gave the Bureau authority to enforce the tribal code. The defendant won his case. The tribe began to question its dependency on the federal government. When the tribe assumed more control of its police powers, it gained a lot of respect from both the state and federal agencies.

I would like to return to the issue of local units of control on the reservation. The Oglala tribe allowed different boards to act as entities of the tribal government. We have a housing authority, park and health boards, community college board, a law enforcement agency, and a public safety commissioner. All of these entities deal directly with both the federal and state authorities. The tribe has institutionalized the functions of its government. This is very important because it allows more people to make decisions in the tribal system. The tribal council is the legislative body that formulates the laws to govern the administration of these functions.

The public safety commission, which I have been involved in, sets standards for police officers. A sergeant on the police force has to have a two-year college degree. Most of our lieutenants have four-year degrees. We also consult with the people about what goals they want to enforce in their local communities.

The actual operation of the law enforcement system lies with the community. Each community selects a five man board. Local people hire and fire their own policemen. They approve all expenditures that are delegated to them at the local level and they set up enforcement priorities.

In July 1983, the tribe asked the FBI to get approval from the tribal chairman before its agents came onto the reservation. The FBI protested this tribal law and refused to come on the reservation. In the meantime, somebody had to investigate murders and burglaries. So our police officers ended up doing the major crime work in conjunction with the United States Attorney's Office. We now carry on the services that were left vacant by the FBI.

The people at Pine Ridge are really advocates of self-determination. They want to run their own affairs. There are several schools that are locally controlled, and we have jurisdiction over law and order. But we are still dependent on federal funding. This fiscal year it was decided to eliminate $425,000 of law and order money. The Indian Bureau set up this priority without consulting with the tribal police commission. I had to go to Congress and ask them to restore that money. This budget cut would have crippled the entire law and order system on the Pine Ridge Reservation.

Because of the diversity of tribal government, the people running programs have to fight for their own survival, but the tribe always backs them up. So, PL 638 has changed the tribal form of government as we know it on the Pine Ridge Reservation, but it also raises questions for the future. At the present time we have a group of young people that say, "You are not bona fide tribal self-government, because everytime you take an action, the secretary of the interior has a right to veto you." These people want to reaffirm the tribe's treaty authority.

JOE DE LA CRUZ

I would like to provide some background information before ana-lyzing Public Law 638. Direct federal aid to tribal governments to develop programs began under the Office of Economic Opportunity. The OEO programs evolved into economic development programs, HUD programs, and eventually PL 638. Some of these federal administrative programs are now being challenged by the states. Tribes have to go through the states for 701 planning money and other types of money. During this same time period, there was also contracting with the Bureau for Indian health services.

Tribes started to worry about the fragmentation of their relationship with the United States government. It was a horrendous responsibility to contract with the various federal agencies because each of them had their own guidelines for transferring money to tribes. Tribal leaders advocated the Indian Self-Determination Act because of the burdens that some of these programs put on tribes.

The Bureau of Indian Affairs and Indian Health Service set up task forces to develop the guidelines for PL 638. They picked tribal people with administrative knowledge to be on those task forces. Both the national Indian organizations and the tribes tried to pressure the Indian Health Service and the Bureau to develop simple guidelines. A meeting was held in Port Angeles, Washington, with the Indian Health Service and the Bureau to see if it was possible to develop satisfactory guidelines to administer 638 contracting. Regional hearings also were held in every region of the United States.

I was on the Bureau task force. Tribal program and technical people gave their input, but when the final guidelines were drafted, the tribes were under the complete control of the federal bureaucracy. The Bureau and Indian Health Service contracts were the worst to administer because they were cost-reimbursable contracts. Most tribes did not have the necessary cash flow to maintain these contracts, and they did not have adequate administrative systems to implement the terms of their contracts.

Pressure was put on the Bureau and Indian Health Service to develop a process for fund transfers other than cost reimbursement. They finally agreed to letters of credit. Even with letters of credit, many tribes got into trouble. The Reagan Administration eventually drafted guidelines to simplify the 638 process, but they are still sitting on a shelf.

The second year after 638 was in existence, there was quite a bit of money for training people because this was a new law. But the money for training never reached the tribal level where it was needed to develop administrative systems. This was unfortunate because tribes had to go through twenty-six steps in the contracting process.

Since PL 638 passed, tribes have complained to Congress and the Bureau about indirect administrative expenses. It cost tribes 34 percent of their own dollars to contract work from the Bureau, Indian Health Service, or other federal agencies. We wonder where this will lead us.

The Indian Bureau under PL 638 has made tribal governments an extension of the federal bureaucracy, but when Congress decides to cut money or programs, the Bureau is not blamed. Instead, tribal governments are criticized.

After PL 638, tribal leaders and organizations worked on two bills to better the lives of Indian people. Congress responded by passing the Health and Improvement Act and the Child Welfare Act. But there were never any appropriations that came with the Child Welfare Act. Tribal people favored this legislation because various religious institutions had taken Indian children away from their homes and raised them. Because Indian people were determined to take care of themselves, they now have child welfare responsibilities under a 638 contract.

It is amazing that some of the tribes still exist when you look at the burdens and responsibilities they took on under PL 638. They started with inadequate funding and no expertise to properly administer the technical help that they needed. When I carefully looked at the Quinault programs, I discovered that we had eighty contracts. They were all under separate bank accounts and bookkeeping procedures. Our efforts to centralize these accounts only led to further problems.

It is my feeling that tribal governments and the national Indian organizations need to take a strong position on self-determination. They should insist on direct grants in the area of federal services. Only then will the government begin to honor its various trust obligations.

PART FOUR

Indian Self-Rule
In the Past and the Future

The dedication of the Fort Defiance Hospital. In front are Navajo medicine men who have gathered from throughout the reservation to participate in the dedication.

A Fourth of July celebration at Kyle on the Pine Ridge Reservation. The Indian Reorganization Act encouraged traditional activities, such as dances, that often were prohibited before its passage.

The Indian Reorganization Act had two basic purposes: self-determination and complete economic independence. The IRA was supposed to reverse the loss of millions of acres of Indian land that had occurred under the Dawes General Allotment Act. Beginning in 1934, land allotment was ended and Indian land holdings increased to over 53 million acres. This did not include Alaska,, which under the Claims Settlement Act added another 40 million acres of land. Today, approximately 95 million acres are collectively held by the poorest people in the United States.

Since 1934, there has not been a conversion of these resources to the economic benefit of Indians. The dissipation of Indian resources has continued at an alarming rate. One of the clearest examples of the failure of the IRA is on the Pine Ridge Reservation. There, you have 11,500 people on a 225 million acre reservation. Fifty-eight percent of the reservation is Indian owned. In 1976, Indians on that reservation who were one-half degree or more of Indian blood were using only 25,000 acres of leased land, even though there are 900,000 acres of tribal land. And one tribal member has been allowed to lease and manage 95,000 acres. This lease system has accelerated the diversion of land away from Indian people.

Another example is a reservation in Arizona where Ira Hayes, the Marine who raised the flag at Iwo Jima, was born. On this reservation, Indians with their own hands and without financing had constructed irrigation systems. As soon as they got the irrigation in, the bidding and lease system operated against them. They were put off the land that they had developed because they were outbid on leases by very marginal amounts. They eventually lost all their farming equipment.

Hank Adams, Assiniboine, activist and writer

The total sovereignty that a lot of people are espousing these days is out of the question. It really does Indians a great disservice to try to claim complete sovereignty for Indian nations, because they are not able to protect their sovereign rights. It also arms our enemies. And we do have many enemies who would like to destroy Indian tribes. In South Dakota, we can identify these people.

In my estimation, there are only two jurisdictions in the United States. They are state and federal jurisdiction. Indian tribes happen to be under federal jurisdiction, which is superior to state jurisdiction. If people keep claiming tribal jurisdiction to be a fact, they are bound to lose to states' rights because tribes do not have the population or power to maintain their sovereignty.

Robert Burnette, Rosebud Sioux, former director,
National Congress of American Indians

Our natural resources are finite. . . . The United States is like a big octopus. It has tentacles that are sucking up valuable resources so everybody can live a beautiful life. Indians throughout the West have been subjected to that philosophy. Los Angeles is pulling all the water out of the Owens Valley for its development. And the Indians in Nevada are relegated to a few colonies with no water rights and no land.

Edward C. Johnson, Northern Paiute, director/curator
of the Stewart Indian Museum Association

The National Indian Youth Council is deeply involved in the issue of Indian religious freedom. We have filed several lawsuits over the right of Indians to use peyote and possess eagle feathers and the right of Indian prisoners to have sweat lodges and consult with their medicine men. The NIYC was involved in helping get the Indian Freedom of Religion Act passed by Congress. Recently, there has been an adverse court decision dealing with this legislation. The court ruled that the Indian Freedom of Religion Act had no legal force because it was only an advisory memo from Congress to the Department of the Interior. So, we have formed a national coalition of churches, civil rights organizations, and Indian groups to get legislation introduced to guarantee Indian religious freedom.

We are also interested in protecting Indian voting rights. We have finished an in-depth political information poll for the Third Congressional District of New Mexico. Indians constitute about a third of that district. We have carried out voter registration drives. We have registered 37,000 Indians in Southern Arizona and New Mexico. We encourage Indian people to run in local elections. School board and county commission elections often impact Indian life more than electing a congressman or even a president.

Gerald Wilkinson, Cherokee, executive director,
National Indian Youth Council

CHAPTER ONE

Self-Rule in the Past and the Future: An Overview

W. Roger Buffalohead

In our time, thoughtful people cannot search for a reasonable past without wondering if there will be a future in which to make use of it. In the scary times in which we live, with, to mention only two examples, the nuclear holocaust weighing on our minds and life-threatening chemicals and industrial waste polluting the air, the water, and the land we breathe, the future does look rather bleak. To many of us and to a growing number of young people in this country, a usable past seems like a frill when what we desperately need is a usable future.

There are a number of ways in which we can rethink the past and the future of Indian policy. For complex historical and contemporary reasons, the Indian Reorganization Act, indeed John Collier and the entire so-called Indian New Deal program, appear in a very different light today than fifty or even twenty-five years ago. Historians call this hindsight, the ability to see historical events through a different perspective than that of those who made or participated in the great and small events of history.

History is really nothing more than the present taking a look at itself through the past. Indians have two ways of doing this—through the oral tradition and through the written record. The problem is that the two ways of understanding the past seldom agree, making Indian history a kind of contest. To add to the problem, most Indian communities are kind of like Blanche DuBois in "A Streetcar Named Desire." They rely on the kindness of strangers to interpret their history.

[265]

In the case of John Collier and his Indian New Deal policies, the result is a split perspective which we must reconcile if we are ever to get a handle on the meaning of tribal self-government, tribal sovereignty, and self-determination. John Collier cannot be, at one and the same time, the patron saint of Indian self-determination and the man who disguised assimilation as self-government to make it easier for the federal government and white exploiters to manipulate Indians into signing away their last resources. In the belief that the big picture of tribal self-government's history might enable us to see more clearly the significance of the IRA, I am going to: (1) suggest a way of looking at the history that preceded the Indian Reorganization Act, (2) review some of the literature which followed, and finally, (3) look at what has been a developing consensus around the idea or the philosophy of Indian self-determination since the 1960s.

First, the big picture before 1934: contemporary tribal governments are the heirs of two historical and cultural traditions that fused together over time into distinct legal, political, and sociocultural systems within American society. Out of the tribal past came sovereign powers which pre-date the existence of the United States, and a way of life with ancient roots that make the five centuries of Indian-white relations only a brief moment in the history of this part of the world. At various times in the last five hundred years, trade, warfare, peaceful coexistence, and creative culture change have characterized Indian-white relations, but the larger and more powerful society eventually imposed its will, principles, and ideas on tribal societies. While self-serving, arrogant, and at times careless, this imposition came with restraints which acknowledged the sovereignty and land rights of native tribes. Such rights were based on the theory of natural laws and on the international agreements which existed between sovereign nations and they found their way into the United States Constitution. These legal rights with the apparatus established to carry out government-to-government relations form the cornerstone of Indian affairs.

From the beginning, tribal and American people saw their relationship very differently. Tribal societies thought in terms of a sharing and cooperative relationship—one which would let them live as they wanted to, with minimum interference from outsiders. Members of the larger society tended to see in the relationship a means to secure land and resources. When white settlement engulfed tribal societies, the relationship was transformed into a weapon or tool to remove, isolate, and eventually assimilate the native population into American society. By 1871, treaties were no longer made with Indian people, and the federal government exercised what we now know as plenary power over the lives of Indian people.

Earlier in some tribal groups, but by the last half of the nineteenth century in all Indian societies, American growth and development shattered the traditional competence of tribal people to make a living and sustain their own way of life. When traditional competence breaks down without an acceptable alternative, human tragedy fills the vacuum. When that tragedy is misunderstood, as it was in the larger society, and attributed to racial and cultural inferiority it can result in the psychological destruction of the people.

By the late nineteenth century, the economic and psychological resources of tribal societies were badly eroded, and Americans concluded that the Indian people were a dying or a vanishing race. The Dawes Allotment Act of 1887 was a Christian and humanitarian plan for a disappearing people. Still land rich in the eyes of non-Indians, tribal folk might be rescued from total oblivion by using their land to transform them into farmers with enough white ways, at least among the younger people, to save the nation from the embarrassment of a "savage and demoralized people" in its midst. In addition to being a Christian or humanitarian thing to do, the allotment policy had the happy effect of transferring an average of two million acres of Indian land per year to white ownership during the next forty-five years.

When the twentieth century began, most Americans who thought about Indians at all did so in the past tense. Like a photograph, the image of Indian culture was frozen in time. Yet, for Indians, the twentieth century was to become a time of recovering. Instead of a photograph, Indian life and culture was like a motion picture and the story line moved on, transcending the ending which American history seemed to have confirmed for Native Americans.

If we are going to understand the twentieth century and the role of the Indian Reorganization Act in it, we must realize that three different philosophies have attempted to guide and shape Indian affairs in this century. Underlying each of these philosophies is a set of controlling assumptions about the past, present, and future of Indian people. We have already examined the main features or outlines of the so-called assimilation policy. While it is fashionable these days to count coup on John Collier and to chip away at the philosophical views and principles underlying the Indian Reorganization Act, Collier did have a different view of Indians. It was taken from what he read about the British concept of indirect rule and what he knew about the Canadian government's use of that process among some tribes in that country. He was smarter than the Canadian authorities. When they went in to implement indirect rule among the Iroquois, they used the Royal Mounties to organize the councils and to oversee the elections.

The simple idea that Collier brought into Indian affairs was limited self-government. To understand how the Indian Reorganization Act has affected the last fifty years, one must understand that it was an attempt to strike a compromise between two competing philosophies— the idea of assimilation and the idea of limited self-government. As it wended its way through Congress, the Indian Reorganization Act had its wings clipped, but it emerged with enough momentum to be declared a New Deal for Indians. It was a piece of compromise legislation that satisfied neither side. The Indian Reorganization Act was immersed in controversy from the beginning.

John Collier failed to develop a strong consensus around limited self-government, or self-rule, in tribal America. The inability of Collier to develop such a consensus generated support for an older philosophy. Indian assimilation reemerged in the 1950s as the termination policy. It continues, down to the present time, to appear in certain forms and fashions as the final solution for Indians in this country. The Indian Reorganization Act also encouraged the development of another philosophical direction, this among Indian people themselves, which we now call the tribal sovereignty or the traditional government movement.

If we now take a brief look at the literature on the Indian New Deal, we will not find much consensus. There is widespread agreement that the Indian Reorganization Act of 1934 ranks along with the Indian Removal Act of 1830 and the Dawes Allotment Act of 1887 as a major turning point in national Indian policy. During the last fifty years, however, the Indian Reorganization Act has been called a New Deal and a raw deal for Indians, a Magna Charta and a classical case of internal colonialism, a communist plot and a conspiracy of capitalistic Jewish lawyers. It also has been characterized as a responsible, therapeutic promotion of democracy, and an anti-American, anti-Christian attempt to turn the clock back and preserve Indians as living museum pieces.

Viewpoints about tribal constitutions and tribal governments organized under the act have been just as contradictory. Depending on whom you read, the IRA constitutions and governments are either a compact, or covenant, with the federal government based upon Indian consent or instruments of cooptation and control by the secretary of interior. To other writers these same constitutions and governments are depressingly uniform and ignore Indian political traditions and values, or they are the modern tools for responsible representative democracy in tribal communities. Finally, tribal governments, both IRA and non-IRA, have been described both as puppets of the Bureau of Indian Affairs and as the true voice of Indian people.

The same sort of contradiction surrounds the general assessments that have been made of the IRA record. On the success side, one finds an impressive list of achievements, ranging from reversing the allotment policy to bringing Indian consent back into Indian affairs after the sixty-year hiatus that followed the discontinuance of treaty making in 1871. These successes are offset by an equally impressive list of failures, ranging from Collier's difficulty in relating to Indians to his inability to implement constitutions that reflected tribal values and traditions.

What can be made of all this contradiction? There are at least four things which can be made of it. From the perspective of the 1980s, it is clear that the Indian Reorganization Act had too little faith in Indian people and too much faith in the concept of limited self-government. There was disbelief that Indians could even organize constitutions without the BIA there to help them and to provide the model which was copied over and over again across the country. There also was a belief that Indian political values and traditions, Indian ways of decision making, were not as valuable as the representative democratic method. What do I mean by suggesting that the IRA had too much faith in the concept of limited self-government? Collier probably believed that his leadership and his team could in fact change the BIA and they did not. We are experiencing the same thing in Central America now with our government trying to impose a form of government on those countries that they apparently do not want and will not pursue. Indians were not numerous enough nor important enough for their wishes to matter very much, until recent times.

The second thing we can make of all this contradiction is that the Indian Reorganization Act faltered on the stumbling block of all national Indian policy—Indian political, economic, and cultural diversity. Those considering future policy should remember that we have never been able to come up with legislation which deals with more than two hundred tribes who do not see their future destiny or their present life in the same way. They each have unique histories. They each are, whether tiny or large, separate little communities within this society, and it requires years of research to even begin to understand the diversity among Indian people.

What else can we conclude from the contradiction? The IRA reconfirmed the nation's commitment to Indian treaty rights but found no acceptable way to exercise federal trust responsibility, except at the expense of Indian sovereignty. That has been and remains the central problem of the Indian Reorganization Act.

The fourth and final thing that we might conclude about this contradiction is that the Indian Reorganization Act was both a success and a failure. It was a success because it did some important things for Indian people. It reversed the allotment policy and moved the federal government into the position of land restoration and conservation. It also provided a cultural and educational framework which is pretty close to the one that we would like to have more fully implemented today, and it brought many lasting benefits to Indian people through economic and educational programs. It was a failure because the program that Collier presented and implemented did not really provide Indian people with the basic and fundamental thing that must support tribal sovereignty: economic self-determination. That, too, remains a central problem of our time.

Since the early 1960s, tribal governments have been attempting to work out a new consensus around the philosophy of Indian self-determination. Currently the consensus provides only a thin veneer over reservation communities deeply divided by competing groups who often work at cross purposes. In the last two decades, the Indian self-determination consensus has become dangerously dependent upon the federal dollar for its power and survival. It also has fought to enlarge the treaty rights and powers of tribal governments through court decisions, new federal Indian legislation, and negotiated Indian land settlements. Furthermore, this consensus has fended off anti-Indian thrusts at the local and national level and worked out compromises or stand-offs with confrontational groups, at home or in the broader Indian community, who are distrustful of tribal government and tribal leaders.

The genius of the self-determination consensus is that it has survived some very turbulent times in Indian affairs, enhanced the role and respectability of tribal governments in national and state policy decision making, and made some progress in developing the institutional structures for tribes to exercise greater control over their political, economic, and social life. The tragic flaw in the Indian self-determination consensus is that there is so little actual Indian self-determination in Indian country because the consensus rides on the destiny of national political and economic trends rather than on the will or needs of Indian people.

The fundamental dilemma created by tribal sovereignty or self-government within a dependency relationship with the United States government may always condition the relationship between Indian tribes and the federal government. But as Hartley White, a sage member of the Leech Lake Reservation business community in Minnesota, has put it, it is hard at times to tell whether Indian tribes are friendly or enemy governments to administrations in Washington, D.C. The purpose of looking at the Indian Reorganization Act and its effect on the last fifty years is to gain a better perspective on this fundamental problem in Indian affairs and to use our imagination, like John Collier did, to challenge the dogmas of our time and envison new ways for tribal governments to deal with the choices and challenges confronting Indian people and the larger society in the closing decades of the twentieth century.

When we consider that the flash of nuclear holocaust seems to be in our future and that life-threatening chemicals, overpopulation, and basic shortages in the resources needed to sustain life stalk the world, we might fairly ask what are the "wisest and ablest" in Indian country doing discussing the Indian Reorganization Act of 1934? When we add to that gloomy picture the contemporary philosophy that selfishness is a virtuous way to live in an absurd and uncontrollable world, the whole iceberg rather than the tip of 1980s American society floats into clear view. When we further add the Reagan administration, its preference for guns over butter, and the dear price that Indians and poor people in this country are paying for the frenzied restoration of the military-industrial complex, there does seem to be something out of focus or amiss in our reflection on the past.

Of all the people I have read in preparing for this paper, only John Collier seemed to have an answer. Collier believed that there was something special about Indian people. Their approach to life offered an alternative to the destructive effects of western culture on the human condition and on the earth upon which we live. For his views, Collier was charged with the sin of romanticism, a longing in urban industrial society for simpler times and the supposed virtues of small tribal societies left behind in the march of civilization and progress.

There were few people then, and there are few people now who took Collier's views about Indians very seriously. As pragmatic realists, with a stake in unlimited progress, they wrote his views off as romanticism. Yet it is interesting today, when the fruits of economic and technological progress seem to offer the possibility of human extinction and the ultimate ruin of the earth's ecology, that some thinking about how to save human life and the earth from destruction harks back to Collier's vision of Indian people and to some of the principles underlying the Indian Reorganization Act.

Whether you agree or disagree with E. F. Schumacher's economic theory, small is beautiful, there is a striking resemblance between Collier's economic program for Indians and what Schumacher has proposed as an alternative to gigantic economic enterprise. We should all recall that Collier encouraged cottage industries centered around arts and crafts, cooperative grocery stores, fishing enterprises, cattle associations, and other economic activities that, one might say, took as their priority the quality of Indian life on the land in which they lived. Collier's economic policies have always gotten a bum rap because of what happened among the Navajo, although what happened there was probably a fair assessment of Collier's failures as an administrator.

It was not Collier but later commissioners of Indian affairs and reservation Indian leaders looking for a quick fix to economic poverty who brought uranium mines and polluting coal development and many other economic enterprises to Indian reservations. These initiatives were supposed to have rescued tribal communities from chronic unemployment. Yet by no stretch of the truth do economic enterprises on reservations make up the reservation economy. The reservation economy *is* the welfare state, which the Reagan administration is now rolling back and which, until recently, provided the illusion that everything was getting better and better on Indian reservations when it was not.

In my state, I check in with the Minnesota Chippewa tribe and the Red Lake Reservation band and the Sioux communities quite frequently. On all those reservations, except the Sioux community which now has a world famous bingo parlor, the unemployment rate is anywhere between 50 percent and 80 percent. Many of the people there are demoralized by the lack of jobs. It is a critical time for those communities. In the state of Minnesota alone, 38 percent of the Indian households are headed by single females who make less than $8,000 a year.

There are several things we might consider as we look for guidelines for future policy. Tribes cannot have political self-determination without economic self-determination, and the federal government must realize that for most tribes the idea of self-sufficiency has not been achieved and will not be achieved without massive support from the federal government. Another problem that exists today is the so-called government-to-government relationship between the United States and all the different tribes. How is that to be carried out? How is the government to accept advice and recommendation from all of these tribes? Should we not be looking at some kind of forums, some kind of congresses, some way in which tribal views or advice that is bona fide and comes from those tribal communities, that reflects the needs of Indian people within those communities, can reach that vast bureaucracy in Washington, D.C.?

What about the matter of tribal constitutions? If the current tribal constitutions do not reflect Indian political beliefs and values, the question is whether the Department of Interior and the Bureau of Indian Affairs would approve amended constitutions for the IRA tribes. At last count, the Indian tribes organized under IRA totaled 127 in the United States exclusive of Alaska, and those who were not organized under IRA totaled 143. In Alaska, 70 groups were organized under IRA and 143 were not. These figures would not include those Indian groups which have won recent recognition from the federal government under the federal acknowledgement process. They would presumably have the right to organize uner Sections 16 and 17 of the Indian Reorganization Act, if that was their choice.

The point on tribal constitutions is that most of the tribes do not have IRA constitutions. If they want, they can change them any way they want them. The Red Lake Reservation has had a constitution since 1918. It has served the reservation very well in the twentieth century. Many tribes have constitutions or informal unwritten principles through which they operate. For those tribes who are organized under IRA, the ballgame is really in their court to change their constitutions and to force the Bureau to recognize those things that might be usable to them.

Information and communications are critical to tribal people in the 1980s. In considering the future, we must realize that tribal communities deserve and should seek the best technical information available to them. They must have adequate communication facilities to carry out modern tribal government. The whole information and communication system that now exists on reservations and in urban communities is based on the theory that the more information you have and can withhold from other groups, the more power that you will have over what goes on in Indian affairs.

Many problems surround 638 contracting, not the least of which is that unless tribes can find some way to negotiate better indirect cost rates they are going to go broke carrying out tribal contracting. There are at least twenty-six steps in the Bureau for approval of 638 contracts. That means that twenty-six administrators are creaming off a piece of the money that is supposedly going down to tribes, before it reaches us. It is like the old days in Indian education when something like $6,000 per child was appropriated and about $600 of that amount of money actually made its way to reservation communities.

We need to take a new look at Indian preference. Most of you know that the Indian Reorganization Act contained an Indian preference clause, but that has been pretty much supplanted by PL 95–561. The problem surrounding Indian preference has not. There is a parable about Indian preference that appeared in a book called *The Gift That Hurt the Indian.* I will let it speak for itself.

> A wealthy Indian bought a Lear jet and hired a competent pilot to go with it. The Indian was boss and owner; he knew it and the pilot knew it. The Indian knew, too, that he himself could not pilot the plane. He was too busy to learn. So he relied on the pilot. Everything went along fine. One day the Indian decided to "Indianize" his plane. He fired the pilot and hired an Indian, a cousin, who had been an aircraft observer in Korea. The new pilot was not without experience. He managed to get the plane off the ground. He also managed to fly it into a mountain. As the Indian boss-owner ascended heavenward to joint the feathered choir, he thought, "The reason for this unfortunate turn of affairs is clear—the fault is mine. Replacing the pilot was not enough, the plane itself should have been made by Indians."

The final future policy consideration that we should deal with is the question of the quality of life on Indian reservations. It seems to me that tribal governments exist for the purpose of improving the quality of life of their members and meeting basic human needs for health, education, welfare, and economic security. Now we can blame the BIA or the Reagan administration for all of our problems, or we can blame the party currently in power in tribal government for what is wrong with the way things are going at the local level. But we should only blame ourselves in the long run if we allow politics, misunderstanding, petty jealousies, personality conflicts, and all the other business that goes on in Indian affairs to rob the people in our communities of the best quality of life that we can provide them.

There is one final thing which needs to be discussed. Most of you know, and if you do not you should know, that thirty years ago a symposium to assess the Indian Reorganization Act was held in conjunction with the American Anthropological Association meeting in Tucson, Arizona. There are some interesting similarities and differences between the earlier symposium and the conference we held at Sun Valley— contrasts which seem to be worth pondering for a moment. The earlier symposium occurred in 1953, under the auspices of the American Anthropological Association, with students of Indian culture, including the famous Indian scholars Edward Dozier and D'Arcy McNickle, playing prominent roles in the proceedings. John Collier, of course, delivered the keynote address. Among the other distinguished people there were Ted Haas, Clarence Wesley, Joseph Garry, and several others whom you should all remember.

The 1983 conference was sponsored by the Institute of the American West, with a philosophical orientation toward humanistic studies. This change in sponsors is not entirely happenstance. It reflects a strain in relations between Indians and anthropologists which has deepened during the last thirty years. This falling out between old friends and allies is not unique to this country. It is part of a worldwide phenomenon where tribal and other colonial people have challenged academic experts' role as interpreters of non-western culture. In the rollback of colonialism across the world, anthropologists, rightly or wrongly, have been accused of lowering an ivory tower curtain around the exploitation and injustice suffered by subject or colonial peoples.

While too much can and has been made of what anthropologists did or did not do in Indian affairs, it is important for Indian people to consider how their own intellectual traditions might conflict with such traditions of the larger society. It seems to me that the anthropological reliance upon the scientific deductive method leads to a way of understanding reality through its fragments. The Indian intellectual tradition, on the other hand, has reflected a more holistic, integrative knowledge of the past. It may be that the scholarly differences that we need to explore have more to do with our ways of thinking, our intellectual traditions, and our ways of perceiving than with deliberate exploitation of one group by another.

At the symposium in 1953, the great philosopher, lawyer, and architect of the Indian Reorganization Act, Felix Cohen, died shortly before the meeting, and his presence was sorely missed. Theodore H. Haas, who had served as a chief counsel in the BIA and as an attorney and community government advisor for the Colorado River Relocation Camp for Japanese-Americans, took Cohen's place. He provided an historical background and analysis of the IRA which is still useful.

There were no, or few, Indian lawyers in 1953, none who were of that stature of Cohen and Haas or even working in the field of Indian affairs, and a big difference between then and now is that we have over two hundred Indian lawyers presumably working on the legal rights of Indian people. I think that the assessment today and the assessment then are going to remain pretty much the same, although there will be some difference in details. The really important thing is that tribes have to believe in themselves and keep a strong conviction that they can undo the tangled web of federal-Indian relations in such a way that it releases them to improve the quality of Indian life, allowing Indian people to rise up once more and fulfill their destiny in American culture. Perhaps if Collier had been right and had succeeded in what he set out to do, we Indian scholars and intellectuals would be discussing how we could help western culture save itself from destruction, rather than how we can save ourselves from western culture.

CHAPTER TWO

Federal Indian Policy Yesterday and Tomorrow

Suzan Shown Harjo, Russell Jim, Hazel W. Hertzberg,
Joe De La Cruz, Oren Lyons

The fundamental failure of American Indian policy throughout the twentieth century has been the continuing diversion of Indian property away from the economic benefit of Indian people. On the Quinault Reservation, people who own hundreds of thousands of dollars worth of timber cannot work their allotments themselves. They are obstructed by the Bureau of Indian Affairs. It will not provide them with the names and addresses of all the surrounding owners from whom they have to secure rights-of-way. The Bureau invoked the Federal Privacy Act as a basis for not telling them. But the BIA would contact those people if the land was bid to a non-Indian contractor. You cannot have sovereignty without some measure of underlying economic independence.

Hank Adams, Assiniboine, activist and writer

If a presidential commission is set up to study land claims, it has got to be a commission that is picked by tribal people. A short time ago, another commission to study economic development on reservations was established by President Reagan. The members of this commission had no interest in listening to the recommendations of Indian people. They set the agenda and wanted to talk about the realignment of the Bureau of Indian Affairs. The National Congress of American Indians and the National Tribal Chairman's Association refused to cooperate under those conditions.

Joe De La Cruz, Quinault, president of the
National Congress of American Indians

Suzan Shown Harjo

I am a member of the Cheyenne-Arapaho tribe of Oklahoma, which drafted an IRA constitution. This constitution has resulted in many drawbacks for the Cheyenne-Arapaho, but it has been most helpful in certain practical matters. When I served in the Department of the Interior during the Carter administration, I had the privilege of working with the Northern and Southern Cheyenne people in an effort to keep Bear Butte, a very important holy place, from being sold. Secretary Cecil Andrus was able to purchase this acreage for the Cheyenne and Arapaho tribes of Oklahoma because they were an IRA constituted entity.

When used as a tool, the IRA is very useful. As a law, the IRA can be changed if we decide that is desirable. So far, the fear of acceptable alternatives has prevented us from changing the IRA. The tragic lessons of history also make us cleave to whatever it is we have now.

We have historic inhibitions about change. It will be very difficult to alter the Indian Reorganization Act. Timing and strategy will be important. We will have to consider who is in Congress, who is in the executive branch, and who is in charge of our Indian governments. We will have to decide how to enter into coalitions that might bring us into conflict with other Indian people. And we do not want to be in conflict with other Indian people, especially on such an important issue as changing a major law such as the Indian Reorganization Act.

Many of the problems that Indian people have do not relate to the Indian Reorganization Act. They concern politics at home and politics in the broader society at the state and federal level. There are also problems that relate to the governing documents of our Indian governments, which we can change. After a full assessment on a nation by nation basis of whether or not we need the IRA and how we are going to change it if we do not, we may decide to scrap the whole project because we have other priorities.

Indian people have not really seen tough times yet, because we are not at war with other neighbors to the south who are engaged in Indian revolutions. We will have a terrible time when the first successful Indian revolution occurs. Then, we will have an Indian policy crisis in this country that will put termination to shame. We must develop our policies, internal structures, and directions and reestablish suitable forms of government before there is massive war in this hemisphere.

Internationally, the situation of American Indians has been, for the most part, a strong model for Indians in other countries. We have had a very strong legal position. But how will that change once we are in this kind of warfare?

Not enough attention has been given to the Indian activism of the 1960s and the 1970s. The American Indian Movement, the second battle at Wounded Knee, and the occupation of the BIA building brought about tremendous change in Indian country. These events altered the way Indian people are viewed and the way they look at themselves. We need to examine the effects of surveillance activities on many of us during that period—what effect it had on our lives and our hopes for the future.

We need to think about the kind of Indian economic development that is being allowed today by the Department of the Interior. Activities such as bingo add a unique dimension to the term "self-exploitation." They are a creative interpretation of the Indian trade and inter-course acts.

Finally, I would like to say that John Collier was an important man. He helped establish significant changes in Indian policy. But John Collier is not the important issue before us. The important issue is what kind of governments work for Indians today and what kind of governments will work for Indians tomorrow to bring about real Indian self-rule.

RUSSELL JIM

I have no magic formula for the future. I can only speak as a culturally oriented person. I am one of those Indians that drives an air-conditioned pickup and lives in an air-conditioned house. I take advantage of the means of comfort in contemporary society, but I also speak my own language and practice what has been taught to me as a way of life.

The Yakima chose not to join the IRA. My immediate family was directly involved in thwarting any attempts to impose this legislation upon the Yakima. Yet, we still survive as a tribe, people, and nation.

We are a sovereign people. Sovereignty is a word that shakes up communities because they misunderstand its implication. Sometimes even the tribes misunderstand what sovereignty means.

Many of you have read *Global Report Year 2000*. It is estimated that in the year 2000 there will be six billion people on this earth. There has never before been an onslaught on the environment such as there has been in the last four decades, and that environment is tied directly to the indigenous people of this land. We need to preserve our ecosystems from contamination so indigenous people can utilize those natural resources.

I constantly chastise those people and organizations that have set up roadblocks against the furtherance of my people. I have been especially critical of the Bureau of Indian Affairs. Perhaps the BIA is necessary to carry out the government's trust responsibility, but as far as I am concerned, there still is not a true definition of what trust responsibility means. When I look up the definitions of trust and responsibility in *Webster's Dictionary*, I come to the conclusion that the federal government has a fiduciary obligation to help me preserve what is mine. The government has the responsibility to honor our treaty rights for as long as the sun shall shine, the mountains stand, and the rivers flow.

HAZEL W. HERTZBERG

It is important to look at Indian affairs as part of a much broader process in our society. When we consider the Indian Reorganization Act, we should be asking ourselves what is characteristic of the IRA that is also characteristic of the entire New Deal? We also need to know, if the IRA was unique, in what way did it depart from the whole New Deal?

Those of you who are not historians may not realize that contemporary attacks on the Indian Reorganization Act were part of a much more general attack on the New Deal that came from both the left and the right. Among historians there is now a very strong reevaluation of the New Deal. So, it is not surprising that the New Deal is being reevaluated also in terms of Indian affairs.

When we examine termination, we ought to look beyond Indian affairs. We should ask ourselves what was happening in the broader society that might help to explain termination. Some of the trends which need to be explored in more depth are: the emphasis on local community and local self-government, and the reaction against big government in that era.

The relocation of Indians to cities was part of the movement of the general population in that period. When Indians were being relocated, many other Americans were relocating voluntarily to the suburbs. The movement of Indians to cities was part of a much broader demographic change that helps us to understand relocation itself. It is also important for us to look at the alternatives that seemed realistically open to both Indians and non-Indians at the time. It is all very well for us fifty years or a hundred years later to be telling the people of the past what they should have done. But I think we need a certain humility when making historical judgements.

In the period that we are in now, it is important to realize that tribal governments depend on some kind of conception of a public good that goes beyond the fortunes of individuals. And the idea of the public good in society as a whole is not in very good shape at the moment. I hope it is going to improve for both Indians and non-Indians.

A second point I would like to bring to your attention is the question of the criteria for success or failure in Indian policy. How do we tell that a policy has failed or succeeded? For a long time everybody said that the Dawes allotment policy was succeeding. Then, it turned out that it completely failed. The same thing happened with the Indian Reorganization Act. It is important to develop some ideas about how you judge whether a government policy has failed or succeeded. Do you know by today's standards; do you know by the hosts of people who sponsored the legislation? What are the criteria that you use? This problem is particularly difficult in Indian affairs because tribal groups are very different. If you look at the Navajo, you can say the Indian Reorganization Act failed, but if you look at the San Carlos Apache, maybe you can say it succeeded. So it is important in Indian policy to take a rather broad view.

A third point that I would like to make is that we need to know more about the role of Indian organizations. Both the Dawes allotment era and the IRA era produced a major Indian organization and a white organization. The white organization in the Dawes era was the Indian

Rights Association which formed in 1883. The Indian organization was the Society of American Indians. It was founded in 1911. Both groups generally supported the Dawes Act but increasingly became critical of it. The Association on American Indian Affairs was established in 1936. The National Congress of American Indians was organized in 1944 by D'Arcy McNickle and other people from the Chicago Area Office. All of these organizations, with the exception of the Society of American Indians, were important in the termination fights during the 1950s and beyond.

A fourth point that I want to discuss is the relationship of religious groups to major Indian legislation. Missionaries have been criticized for their role in Indian affairs, and they are very easy targets. But a lot of Indian people are very active in Christian churches. We need to look more carefully at how organized Christian movements were involved with major pieces of legislation such as the Indian Reorganization Act and the Self-Determination Act. They played an important role in mobilizing public opinion.

Another topic I want to mention is the question of what new forces were created by the various changes in Indian policy. It has been pointed out that the Office of Economic Opportunity created a managerial class which has not yet made its full impact, and there are now hundreds of Indian lawyers, doctors, teachers, professors, historians, and anthropologists. They are bound to have an important impact on Indian life.

We need to pay more attention in the future to economics when discussing Indian affairs. It is a very neglected subject. We talk about Indian poverty, but there has not been enough analysis of the economic conditions on reservations.

Another issue that deserves more attention and underlines almost all major Indian legislation, including the Indian Reorganization Act, is the question of assimilation versus cultural pluralism or separatism. This issue must be looked at much more analytically. If our grandparents were here, whether they were Indian or white, they would think that quite a few changes have taken place. We need to analyze those changes and what they mean for the present and future.

Finally, I just want to say a word about the role of history in all of this. History gives us a sense of perspective; it is a way of living beyond one's own life. But sometimes when we talk about things such as the Indian Reorganization Act, they seem very impersonal. We forget the pain and the anguish and the joy that is connected with almost all important events in human history.

JOE DE LA CRUZ

The Quinault people have had a continuing history of opposing United States policy. One topic that we have not adequately discussed is the fisheries dispute among the Indians in the Pacific Northwest. A lot of people think that this dispute started in the late 1950s and early 1960s. Actually, the federal government began pushing the Northwest Indians out of their fishing territories in the 1890s. When the tin can was invented in 1900, the American corporations and banking people started building canneries along the Pacific coast. The Indians were left with only small areas where they could fish.

The government attempted to regulate what was left of the Indian fisheries in 1923. Our Quinault people resisted and took their case to the domestic courts of the United States. They got a ruling that neither the United States nor the Bureau of Indian Affairs could manage fish on the Quinault Reservation. In February 1974, District Court Judge George H. Boldt ruled that tribes in the Pacific Northwest were entitled to 50 percent of the harvestable fish. The Quinault nation was determined to regulate its own affairs. We have had to struggle to develop our own technical capabilities and information systems to take advantage of the Boldt ruling and other favorable court decisions.

I do not like to hear that it is impossible for tribes to do something. We now have an administration that claims it wants to establish a government-to-government policy with the Indian tribes and Indian nations. A lot of people have asked, "What does that mean? Where is this going to lead us?" I believe strongly that if Indian people will adhere to some of the principles that came out of their treaties, they will survive these changes. Indian people must stick with three principles: (1) Indian governments and people possess original and inherent sovereignty, (2) specific Indian tribes and nations possess the inherent right to determine their own political futures, and (3) Indians have the right to pursue their political, social, and cultural development without outside interference.

I feel very strongly that if tribes work collectively they can establish a government-to-government policy with the United States. Our forefathers made treaties that created a nation-to-nation relationship. Some people may feel that this idea is unrealistic. But when a small tribe such as the Quinault can persuade the courts that it has jurisdiction to regulate and manage its fisheries, you can see that it is not impossible.

I have heard many comments about the problems and faults of tribal government. We do have many problems in tribal government, and we have many problems between tribal governments. It is up to the Indian people to develop their own mechanisms to resolve disputes. We have had some problems that came out of the Boldt decision concerning the allocation of fish amongst the tribes. There are twenty tribes on Puget Sound and the Washington coast and five tribes on the Columbia River that have to determine how the fish are going to be divided. That is a difficult question. But I feel that we have the leadership to work these things out.

Since President Ronald Reagan announced his so-called policy on government-to-government relations, several people have advised the administration on how this process should be developed. Recently I talked to the executive director of the National Congress of American Indians. He read me a letter from a group of people that call themselves "The National Indian Republicans." Some of these people were Democrats a year or two ago. But if they call themselves the National Indian Republicans, they have the ear of key people in the White House. I do not believe that one of them has ever lived on an Indian reservation, so we know that whatever policy or change comes about is not going to be something that Indian people and Indian tribes want.

Tribes need to be very fearful of what has happened in the last two-and-one-half years of this administration. Domestic programs and health services have been destroyed through the appropriation process. As Indian people, we must decide whether we want to be governed by the states, the United States, or our own tribal governments. When you look at the history of America, it seems clear that the states and the federal government, for the most part, have not made decisions that benefited Indian people. Therefore, I hope that Indians will try to resolve the disputes within their communities and work towards a consensus on where Indian country should be going.

OREN LYONS

What I have to say will be a reflection of my nation's point of view and should not be construed as speaking for other nations or people. We were one of those nations that did not accept the IRA. We rejected the IRA in a formal vote. It was one of the few times that our people voted in an alien process. One of the chiefs of the longhouse went from house to house. He said, "I know you do not like to vote. I know you are against voting, but if you vote once in your life, this is the time." The IRA was defeated by very few votes.

I am a faith keeper and a subchief of the Onondaga nation. I represent the Turtle Clan in the council. The Onondaga nation is the fire keeper for the Six Nations of Iroquois. Our position is that we are sovereign and independent nations. We have the right to continue our life as it was given to all of our people.

Today we have IRA governments, BIA governments, and traditional governments. The processes of Indian government are flexible. We have had to adapt to our white brothers and sisters or else disappear. We have always faced the problem of being separate and independent and trying to survive in a very dominating society that has interests and directions of its own.

We have recognized the equal status of non-Indians because they are a manifestation of the creation and demand respect. But that was not the perspective that came from the other side. Whites felt that they were superior and that we were uncivilized "tribes."

The basis of all the Indian nations, as I know them, is the family. At the center of the family is the woman. She is the central fire—the power of life. For thousands of years, Indian people developed methods of continuing a vibrant family life, but these methods were smashed and eradicated in a very short time. In their place institutions such as the IRA were substituted to restructure Indian society.

At one time, a beautiful cultural and social fabric, with tremendous varieties of design, was woven on this continent. Then, our brothers and sisters from overseas came over here and took apart that fabric strand by strand and restructured it. They have taken something beautiful and destroyed it.

You can tell the health and welfare of a nation by looking at its children and elders. If children are in despair, running about without control, and alienated from their families, then society is in great strife. If elders are separated from their families, not enjoying their last years, then you have a very sick society. If Indians accept this kind of society for their people they must bear the consequences.

Indian people should hold on to what they have. I cannot accept the Department of the Interior as an ultimate authority that oversees every decision we make. Self-determination under the federal government is a very limited self-determination. It is defined by what outsiders perceive to be good for you.

The Six Nations of Iroquois have attended international forums with members of other tribes. In 1977, we made a common statement before the United Nations at Geneva, Switzerland. The people at the United Nations did not know what to expect. They were very apprehensive when we sang songs and opened the session with a prayer, which is against the law of the United Nations. Then we began a very eloquent presentation of the history of the destruction of our people and culture. The people at the United Nations were profoundly moved. Even the interpreters stood up and clapped. That was a great occasion.

We have a lot of friends internationally, and we are concerned about the policies that the United States is now following in Central and South America. In 1981, we advised the president of the United States that we would not allow our young men to be drafted. If the Onondaga nation does not have authority to draft our own men, how can the United States have that authority? Most of all, we do not want our children shooting other Indians. We are not going to be part of that, because we are a separate sovereign nation.

The United States has many problems. There should be a forum where we can sit down and examine the future together. The future is bleak. It is going to require the counsel of our elders to help you, but they are dying off pretty fast as we become experts in the process of becoming American citizens. In that process, we are losing valuable knowledge of our own culture.

The Six Nations of Iroquois advocate a position that says land should be held in common, we should protect our children, and we should protect the future. We believe that it is necessary to make decisions for the seventh generation of the future. That is not very good economics, but you cannot make a profit on the heads of your grandchildren. If the United States continues on its present course, it will destroy both Indian and non-Indian people. If we destroy ourselves by our own folly, it is the working of natural law. When there are too many rabbits, they disappear. When lemmings overpopulate, they run into the sea. Human beings also may disappear. And it will mean nothing to the natural world, which is used to cries of anguish and pain. It is part of life.

CHAPTER THREE

Tribal Sovereignty:
Roots, Expectations, and Limits

R. David Edmunds, Robert Burnette, Hank Adams

John Marshall, in one of his landmark opinions, remarked on the arrogance of the "doctrine of discovery" which held that one European ship landing on the East Coast would entitle that sovereign to ownership of a vast territory of land. I do not know of a clearer case on the earth of this than the arctic region. I cannot think of a civilized argument why the native people, who live in this area, should not have the right to constitute an independent nation if that is their desire. They are the only ones who have adapted to the environment of the arctic. We really need to determine if large countries are justified in keeping these people under their jurisdiction.

Philip S. Deloria, Standing Rock Sioux,
director, American Indian Law Center

From 1951 until early 1970, the leaders of tribal governments knew about their treaties. They exercised as much authority and power as they could from those documents. But the term sovereignty was never used. We knew that we were part of the United States and that our people were subject to the plenary powers of Congress, and we knew that our constitutions and bylaws and charters were issued by the secretary of the interior. To exert pressure to obtain total tribal sovereignty would have meant directly opposing the United States of America and everything that it stood for. Indian tribes have used sovereignty as a goal for publicity purposes since 1971. This has attracted a lot of attention and made Europeans and other people begin to ask questions.

Robert Burnette, Rosebud Sioux, former director,
National Congress of American Indians

[289]

R. David Edmunds

I am not as optimistic about the issue of Indian sovereignty as some people. It depends upon how you define sovereignty and what makes a people sovereign. From my understanding of the term and the way it is generally used it means the ability to completely control one's own affairs regardless of intervention by outside powers. Given that sort of framework, I am pessimistic about restoring tribal sovereignty.

During the very earliest periods of Indian-white contact and surely before the European invasion of America, Indian people were sovereign. There is no doubt about it. They controlled all aspects of their lives. The unfortunate historical reality is that as the white frontier rolled westward Indian cultures were either overwhelmed or controlled to a certain extent by the federal government. Their sovereignty diminished. By 1871, the government recognized this, and it stopped making treaties with the tribes. The government then began to dictate to the tribes its decision to establish reservations and other aspects of tribal policy.

The government of the United States is really a government of pressure groups. It is the groups who have political power, especially economic power, that run this country. Until Native American people have a greater economic power base from which to build, their sovereignty is going to be very limited. You must have a viable economic base if you are going to influence a government that essentially functions in response to economics. That is the key issue. Sometimes, we hear people talk in mystical terms about sovereignty, but it does not put pork chops on the table.

There are many definitions of the word sovereignty in Indian America. It seems to me that the majority of Indians mean "the maximum amount of self-control for the Indian people under the existing system" when they use this term. I doubt whether there will ever be complete tribal sovereignty in the United States.

What we need to do is look at the different groups inside the United States who have a tremendous amount of influence on the federal government and on the economic structure in this country and at how they influence those particular structures. We are talking about pressure groups such as big industry, organized labor, arms manufacturers, and farmers. You can even point to certain racial ethnic minority groups in the late 1960s.

Blacks, for example, gained considerable sovereignty in the civil rights movements in the late 1960s and early 1970s. They gained substantially more control over their destinies than they had previous to that time. Now that does not mean, of course, that blacks as a group of people, exist free from government control.

Indian people will probably never be divorced from those kinds of controls. One of the interesting things about all of the groups that have been able to gain political and economic power is that they have done it through very sophisticated and centralized political organizations. That is where Indians have been at a big disadvantage. Indian organizations have not been able to match the economic and political power of groups that have opposed them. The nature of Indian people and the structure of tribal governments make it all but impossible to develop that particular type of response.

ROBERT BURNETTE

The issue of tribal sovereignty has been misused and abused by Indian leaders in the last few years. In the period when I was the executive director of the National Congress of American Indians and president of the Rosebud Sioux tribe, I had no use for the word sovereignty. I believe that tribes had legal sovereignty, but they certainly do not enjoy the benefits of sovereignty because they do not have an armed force with which to enforce it. If Indians had an army as big as the Soviet Union, they might be sovereign. But they do not have an army.

We are part of the United States of America. We are within its jurisdiction and subject to the plenary powers of Congress. So we are not, in a sense, sovereign, except that we do have treaties and the United States has usually tried to honor those treaties. The notion of tribal sovereignty is wishful thinking on the part of most modern day tribal leaders.

The talk about tribal sovereignty reveals the desire by Indians to exist in the midst of our tremendously complex nation. The United States is, for all practical purposes, an economic entity. If we cannot exist economically, then we are not going to exist at all. We are going to be overrun sooner or later. Unfortunately, when economic progress occurs on reservations you often attract a lot more people than you actually need, and you are taking another chance. So economic progress is a pretty dangerous thing if that is where the tribes want to go.

Not one tribe, in my estimation, has utilized economic progress to its real advantage. I believe that tribes could develop, if they wanted to, their coal resources and their oil and gas resources. They could joint venture those resources. It makes little sense to throw out a contract to ARCO, or whoever it may be, and let thousands of people come onto a reservation and establish a big town. Then, the Indians lose all the political powers that they have and all the rest that goes with it.

I hope that tribes will open their eyes and begin to deal with reality instead of crying and moaning about something that is happening to them. They need to *make* things happen their way. If they would do that, then whatever happened on a given reservation, they would be responsible and would have to deal with it. Expecting the United States to come in and do all your business and protect you is like wishing that all the gold in the Black Hills was in your back pocket. We have to do those things that are practical in government.

The War on Poverty did not just happen by accident. Somebody made it happen. Indians were part of that social justice movement. The Indian heirship bill did not lay down and die, we killed it. This is the way to do things. I have always tried to be one of those people who makes things happen in Indian country. From 1956 until 1964, I played a major part in deciding what was going to happen in the Indians' world. Expectations are one thing; achieving them is another thing.

The IRA, in my estimation, provides tribes with limitless opportunities. They are only limited by the boundaries of what one can accomplish in the financial, economic, and industrial world. The IRA provides a platform from which many tribes could spring and enter the economic system of the country. But once tribes show their economic ability, Congress will most likely move in and start limiting their actions. I know this because at one time we almost reached that point at Rosebud. We drew back because of it. We were afraid of termination. We could have done a lot more things, but we decided to wait and let everybody else catch up. Unfortunately, OEO came along, and everybody forgot where they were going except to chase federal dollars. But I still think there are virtually no limits on any of the tribes if they want to really move up.

HANK ADAMS

The IRA, in general, has been metaphorically America's twentieth century Ghost Dance for American Indians. And John Collier has been it metaphysical Wovoka. It is not very useful to celebrate the last fifty years under the flawed vision of John Collier. Instead, we should shed the Ghost Dance shirts, which have not afforded protection to the Indians at places such as Wounded Knee in 1973.

I first became involved in Indian affairs about twenty-five years ago. When I was fourteen years old, I went to a tribal council meeting with my stepfather on the Quinault Reservation. The Quinault were an IRA tribe from the standpoint of the Bureau of Indian Affairs, but they were also a non-IRA tribe from the standpoint of many tribal members. The Quinault had held two elections, one which rejected the IRA and one which accepted it. Even today, it remains an unresolved dispute between the tribe and the BIA as to whether the Quinault are an IRA tribe.

At the meeting that I first attended when I was fourteen, the tribe voted on the issue of extending state jurisdiction over the Quinault Reservation under Public Law 280. The vote was either thirty-eight to three or forty-two to one. There were no more than three persons in the tribe who favored going under state jurisdiction. The following Monday, the chairman of the tribe, the tribal claims attorney from Washington D.C., and the BIA superintendent met at the agency and petitioned the state of Washington to assume jurisdiction over the Quinault Reservation. That action was a violation of Quinault sovereignty, and it revealed a fundamental problem between Indians and the federal government. Invariably, external forces contrive to get what they want at the sacrifice of Indian people, Indian rights, and Indian sovereignty.

Shortly after that, the tribal chairman committed suicide. His suicide was caused, in part, by guilt for violating the tribe's governing institutions and the will of the Quinault people. He was spared the problem that he had created, but his people suffered under the effects of that action for more than a dozen years.

The roots of tribal sovereignty are written in antiquity, but for most people of the earth the concept of sovereignty is relatively new. Europeans and Americans formulated legal concepts of sovereignty during the later stages of the Enlightenment. One of its strongest expressions in a conceptual form came in 1758 in a book by Emmerich de Vattel, a Swiss jurist, called *The Law of Nations*. In that treatise were the concepts of government and sovereignty that were adopted by the United States in its Constitution. The Constitution also drew from some of the governmental forms that were employed by Indian nations on the East Coast, primarily the Iroquois confederacy, but also two tribes to the south, the Creek confederacy and the Cherokee nation.

When Chief Justice John Marshall began defining the rights of Indians under the Constitution of the United States, the Supreme Court used *The Law of Nations* as its basic legal authority. This book had drawn upon universal human experiences to formulate international law. It took into account the development of law that was found to exist in Persia and South America and the law that was found to exist among the American Indians.

During the Iranian hostage crisis, the Iranians said, "Why should we abide by international law when we had no hand in writing it?" They failed to recognize that they had a part in writing international law prior to the Enlightenment. Indians in the New World also made a contribution to the writing of *The Law of Nations*, and Indian experience played an important part in the law that the United States both recognized and was founded on.

One expression of sovereignty is the notion of equality among all men and nations. Another attribute of sovereignty is the authority over one's self at the personal level, or the sovereignty of the individual. Sovereignty also means the authority of people over themselves as a society or a nation free from external direction. That is basic. Beyond that, one of the utilitarian values of sovereignty is in forming the relationship that exists between one sovereign entity and another.

There is a tendency to think of sovereignty as being an absolute quality that exists. In reality, it is just a question of whether or not the sovereignty is completely there or has drained away in some part. In fact, sovereignty is a dynamic concept whether it exists at the individual level or whether it exists at some higher level, particularly at the level of nations.

CHAPTER FOUR

Indian Control of Indian Resources

Gordy High Eagle, Edward C. Johnson

*There are 129 timbered reservations in the United States. In 1981,
I learned, at a timber symposium in Spokane, that 580 million board feet of
timber had been recently removed from the Colville, Spokane, Yakima,
Quinault, and Makah reservations in the state of Washington. The tribes
or the individual Indians on those five reservations made an $11 million
profit. The state, in the jobs that were created and in other things, realized
$13 million in taxes. The exploiting timber companies made $157 million.
Yet, something is wrong when we still have 67 percent unemployment on
those reservations.*

Joe De La Cruz, Quinault, president of the
National Congress of American Indians

*If tribes are going to have meaningful self-rule, they must have eco-
nomic self-sufficiency. The reservations in the Dakotas have farming and
grazing lands with few minerals. If my own reservation at Rosebud is going
to maintain its sovereignty and identity, the people will have to sit down
with technical experts and determine the capacity of the reservation to
support human beings. They must find out how many people are left on
the remaining land. I am sure there are 50 to 75 percent more people on
the Rosebud Reservation than the resources of the land will support.*

Benjamin Reifel, Sioux, former congressman
from South Dakota, commissioner of
Indian affairs under President Gerald Ford

GORDY HIGH EAGLE

I am from the Nez Perce tribe in north central Idaho. What we need most of all is respect for our tribe from the city, county, state, and federal governments. They should give us the opportunity to control our resources within the boundaries of the reservation. If that happened, all the other things such as economic development would fall into place.

The Nez Perce Reservation contains approximately 750,000 acres, but we own only 90,000 checkerboarded acres because of land allotment and some other things. Most people know that we are a minority within the reservation, and we often come out on the short end of the stick in court cases and other matters.

Despite these problems we have made progress in certain areas, such as taxation, without having to go to court. We are trying to develop a track record to show that we have ability. We are weighing those things where we can gain control over our economic resources. We are farmers. We are also involved in the timber and fishing industry. The resources on our reservation are the same kind of resources utilized by all the people in the state of Idaho. We must begin to cooperate and work together to promote economic development.

We have a limestone deposit on our reservation, and we could have had a cement plant and mined limestone for one hundred years. We chose not to because one hundred years is not a very long time. We wanted to consider the people who are still unborn. We did not want to act hastily and lose control of that resource. What we are now doing is contracting out in the pulp market.

One of the things that the Nez Perce tribe has been working on is the state-wide fisheries management plan. We have used that vehicle to protect water quality. It takes us out of our existing reservation boundary into north central Idaho and the total Salmon River drainage area. We deal with approximately half of the state because of the fisheries issue. We have also looked at environmental damages in the national forest. We have been involved in suits against the secretary of commerce and the states of Oregon and Washington.

Article three of our 1855 treaty provides the right to hunt, fish, and gather roots and berries. That is basically what we are doing.

We have not been successful in mining, but we have been successful in stopping projects that are basically going to destroy the water quality of the streams and the spawning habitat of the salmon.

EDWARD C. JOHNSON

I believe that every tribe is concerned about the control of their natural resources. When I was the representative to the National Congress of American Indians for the Walker River Paiute tribe in Nevada, I was introduced to a consultant in Washington D.C. We developed a resource management proposal for the entire Walker River Indian Reservation during my two years as tribal chairman in 1978 and 1979.

Our reservation, which consists of five hundred square miles, is the second largest reservation in Nevada. We have a number of resources such as minerals and farm land. I was determined to develop a resource management proposal that looked at all of our assets.

We wanted to examine our human resources, the infrastructure of the reservation, business, education, and health. We were able to draft a resource management proposal because we were supported by the Equitable Insurance Company and its subsidiary, Equitable Environmental Health.

We received a great deal of support from Congress. At the Bureau of Indian Affairs, they said it was like a blizzard. Congressional letters were constantly being dumped on the Bureau of Indian Affairs.

We submitted a proposal under Public Law 93–638 to the Bureau of Indian Affairs, the Economic Development Administration, and the Department of Commerce. We felt that our reservation was an example of where the government could really do something without saying, "Your reservation is too big, and it would take billions of dollars for economic development." We proposed that these agencies operate under the Joint Funding Simplification Act, which Congress passed in the 1970s. One of the problems you have in developing a reservation is when you go to federal agencies they say, "We do not have any funds" or "Our funds do not cover that area." It was our intention to obtain widespread federal funding. We strongly believed that it was better to do something on a comprehensive rather than a helter-skelter basis.

We also asked the Colorado School of Mines to do a mineral resource inventory that included drilling. Previously, a number of mining companies had come on the Walker River Reservation to explore for minerals such as uranium, gold, and silver, but they never reported back to us; so we got a proposal from the Colorado School of Mines that we included in our resource management plan.

We were also interested in developing our water resources. The Paiute tribe was given water rights on the Walker River Reservation in 1859. In 1939, the court ruled that the Winters Right Doctrine, which protects treaty tribes' water rights, extended to executive order reservations. But the Ninth Circuit Court of Appeals refused to allot us future water rights. We are at the end of the Walker River. That meant that everybody above us had been getting water first before the 1939 decree. We had a reservoir built on our reservation in the 1930s to provide irrigation water. Before and after the reservoir was constructed was like the difference between night and day. As soon as the reservoir was finished, we could get water to our farming areas.

We wanted the Carter administration to adopt our resource management proposal. Unfortunately, the Carter administration never developed a comprehensive Indian policy. I think that was indicative of President Carter's interest in Indian affairs. President Carter just allowed things to go on as usual. He did not take a great interest in Indian matters and neither did his high level staff.

Ann Wexler, an assistant to the president, was the highest ranking woman in the Carter administration. Through Americans for Indian Opportunity and LaDonna Harris, we were able to convene a White House conference to review our resource management proposal. We met at the Theodore Roosevelt room in the White House. We were all sitting there when Ann Wexler walked in the room. Everyone stood up because the assistant to the president was conducting this conference. It was the consensus of this meeting that the federal government should fund this proposal and that the bureaucrats should work together.

After we left the White House, we were not able to contend with the bureaucrats, who knifed our proposal. The Carter administration was not strong. If it had been under the Nixon administration, we might have implemented the proposal and shown that we could engage in comprehensive planning on our reservation. Instead, two months after the White House meeting, we received a "kiss-off" letter from the Carter people. It said, "Please go down and talk to the Bureau of

Indian Affairs about this matter." The Carter administration was not willing to knock the heads of bureaucrats in order to do something for our reservation.

Because of our setback, some members of the tribal council are now proposing that individual members of the tribe stake out areas on the reservation and act as fronts for mining corporations who are interested in mineral exploration. Individual members of the tribe run our cattle association. Why not take a similar approach with the minerals? We have also hired an attorney to look at our future water rights. We have just completed a preliminary hydroelectric analysis on our reservoir to see whether it is possible to generate electricity. As in the past, we are now working on small economic projects.

If the Indian Claims Commission had given us adequate funds for our claim, we could have forgotten about the trust responsibility. With a billion dollars we could have done something for our reservation. We can protect our private land. All we want are the resources to develop it.

One of our problems is that we organized under the Indian Reorganization Act and drafted a constitution in 1937. The Bureau of Indian Affairs has to approve of everything that we do, such as amending our constitution and drawing up tribal ordinances. We accepted that method of government, but we do not have the funds to implement any kind of Indian control over the resources on our reservation. We can just go from one small project to another.

We have been able to protect our hospital even though the Phoenix Health Service wanted to knife it. Senator Edward Kennedy personally intervened and saved our Indian hospital. Kennedy called the head of Indian health in Washington D.C. and told him that if we did not complete our comprehensive health plan, he was going to call him before his Senate committee. This kind of intervention does not come too often, but it helped us obtain another grant to complete our Indian health plan. It had to be run out of the Sacramento Area Office because the Phoenix Area Office refused to give us another grant.

Indian control of Indian resources is important, but I do not believe that either Congress or President Ronald Reagan are willing to give us the necessary amount of money to adequately develop Indian resources. People sometimes say, "Money is not important." I disagree. Money is extremely important, especially when the government is spending billions of dollars in faraway places such as Nicaragua. Individual tribes need this kind of money to develop and protect their resources. Adequate federal funding is the key to Indian control of Indian resources.

CHAPTER FIVE

The Trust Obligation

Charles F. Wilkinson, LaDonna Harris, Steven Unger,
Helen Peterson, Benjamin Reifel

*Congress ultimately defines the trust relationship, which has changed
over time. Early on in our republic, Congress did not use the trust relationship to give courts jurisdiction over crimes committed on Indian reservations. Later, that became part of the trust relationship. In the 1970s, child
welfare became part of the trust obligation. In 1976, Congress gave a clear
statement in the area of the relationship of the Bureau of Indian Affairs to
tribal self-government. It said that the BIA should give as much leeway as
possible to tribal sovereignty.*

Benjamin Reifel, former congressman from
South Dakota and commissioner of Indian affairs

*The trust relationship implies or results in Indian tribes being less
than complete international sovereigns. Because the Navajo nation has a
trust relationship with the United States, it does not have the international
status of Mexico. The trust relationship has benefits for Indians, but it also
has a negative aspect that means there is a subsidiary relationship to
another sovereign. Consequently, Indian tribes have less than all the
powers of sovereign nations.*

Charles F. Wilkinson, professor of law, University of Oregon

[302]

CHARLES F. WILKINSON

By any standards, the trust obligation of the federal government is a sensitive and delicate issue. It seems to me that the trust obligation is sensitive and complex because it is so multifaceted. And we all appreciate that as a concept it is poorly understood. The trust has several dimensions: it has a moral and political dimension, it has historical roots and development, and it has a legal dimension. It is very important to assess the way the trust obligation is perceived by informed non-Indians who deal in Indian affairs, and the way in which it is perceived by Indians. Although legally the trust obligation exists between governments—the United States and Indian tribes—Indian people, properly in my judgment, view it as being somewhat in the nature of promises and guarantees being made to individual Indians.

I am extremely proud to say that I became involved in federal Indian law at the Native American Rights Fund under the tutelage of people such as Helen Peterson. I am a lawyer and intend to give a very brief statement about how Indian trust law is viewed by the United States courts in a domestic context. I will not attempt to assess the international dimensions of trust law, and I do not intend to suggest what is right or wrong about the way our court system has analyzed the trust.

There is no legitimate question that Indian lands and resources are held in trust and that the United States has a high fiduciary obligation. In my judgement, it is wrong to conclude that the trust does not extend to other areas. Beginning with the Cherokee Nation case in 1831, the Supreme Court has on numerous occasions indicated that the trust relationship extends to areas such as education, housing and health. If you read the early treaty negotiations, it is also clear that the content of the trust relationship goes beyond Indian land and resources.

Congress has a trust responsibility under the Constitution toward Indian tribes, but this trust obligation is not enforceable against Congress. It is impossible to sue Congress, but the courts have said that Congress has a moral obligation. It is most important as a matter of law not to denegrate the fact that Congress has a moral obligation towards Indians.

It should not matter that Congress can not be sued in court. We need to put the trust relationship in a broader context and realize that there are all kinds of areas in which Congress has obligations and duties that are not enforceable in court. For example, you cannot sue Congress over political questions, over membership, and in some cases over division of authority with the executive branch, but that does not mean that Congress does not have the obligation to act properly. If a representative appears with improper credentials, even though a suit cannot be filed, Congress has an obligation under the Constitution to act properly. Congress has broad authority over foreign affairs. It cannot be required to fund a military effort. But Congress has real obligations that are debatable. And lawsuits cannot be filed over national security issues. That does not mean they are not real issues that can be argued.

Over the years, Indian advocates have very effectively argued in front of Congress that the trust is a legal obligation. Sometimes the argument has not worked. But that does not mean the trust doctrine is not there.

When a statute is passed by Congress and authority is delegated to an administrative agency, the trust then becomes enforceable in court. We have had major decisions, particularly in the modern era, where courts have enforced the trust against the Indian Bureau, HUD, and what is now the Department of Education. Although Congress cannot be sued, administrative officials can be sued, and they become the trustee. So, the trust is definitely enforceable in court. No federal official can properly say that the trust is only a moral obligation that applies to Congress. Administrative officials have to act within the bounds of the trust.

The Boldt decision in 1974 was important. It reaffirmed Indian fishing rights and demonstrated the seriousness of the trust obligation. It ultimately led the Supreme Court to find that far-ranging Indian fishing rights existed in the northwestern part of the United States.

LaDonna Harris

I want to share an experience I have had in the past few months. Maybe it will help us understand that there are different ways of viewing what we feel and mean about the words trust obligation. Recently, Americans for Indian Opportunity held seminars on tribal governments.

In our first seminar we listened to a political scientist from Rutgers University who made a presentation on western political thought. His presentation and the discussion that followed convinced me that Indian people are philosophically more eastern than western, because we immediately came into philosophical conflict with the political scientist.

I believe that words such as trust, sovereignty, and genocide often mean different things to Indians and non-Indians. Indians have used the word trust both in a moral and political sense. For Indians, the trust obligation is not just with the land. We have used this concept in its broadest meaning to convince other federal agencies besides the Indian Bureau that they should serve Indians. For example, we have insisted that the Environmental Protection Agency has a trust obligation to Indian tribes. We are very passionate about the moral aspect of the trust obligation. It has become a very important political instrument in our struggle with Congress.

STEVEN UNGER

I would like to look at the trust obligation in terms of public policy. We need to remember that the president, the courts, and especially Congress are responsible for upholding the trust obligation. I would like to concentrate on Congress because it is the only branch of the government that is really responsive to what the American people want.

The trust obligation began when Congress acquired Indian land with treaties. A trust obligation also has evolved to provide health, education, and welfare services to Indian people. These services are mostly provided through the Snyder Act of the 1920s. This act simply says that the BIA shall use such moneys as Congress may from time to time appropriate, but there is no mention of any federal obligation to appropriate funds for Indian people.

In the mid–1970s, Congress carefully examined its obligations to American tribes. It set up the American Indian Policy Review Commission which looked at the federal government's historical and special legal relationship with American Indian people. Congress took this action because it wanted to formulate new policies and programs for the benefit of Indians.

In the mid to the late 1970s, there was a substantial innovation in the "Findings and Declaration of Policy" sections of bills passed by

Congress. For example, in Public Law 93–638, the Indian Self Determination and Educational Assistance Act (1975), Congress said that the prolonged federal domination of Indian services had served to retard rather than advance Indian progress. Congress also recognized the obligation of the United States to promote self-determination for Indian people by assuring maximum Indian participation in federal services such as education.

In 1976, Congress passed the Indian Health Care Improvement Act. In this legislation, Congress declared that special federal health services were required by the federal government's unique historical relationship with Indian people. Congress also declared as policy the legal obligation to provide the highest possible health care to American Indians.

Two years later, in legislation dealing with Indian child welfare, Congress provided an even more expansive view of its trust obligation. It assumed a general responsibility for the protection and preservation of Indian tribes and their resources. Congress also noted that no resource was more vital to the continued existence and integrity of Indian tribes than their children, and it promised as a trustee to protect children who were eligible for membership in an Indian tribe.

The Indian community colleges bill, which Congress passed, had language in it declaring that education was a trust responsibility, but President Reagan vetoed this bill. It is unlikely that Reagan's veto meant that there was no federal trust responsibility for education. Instead, the veto indicated that there was no trust responsibility for the Congress to provide community colleges on Indian reservations.

The concept of a trust responsibility played a major role in two other bills during the late 1970s. The first bill created the Department of Education, which President James E. Carter had proposed. This bill would have moved Indian schools out of the BIA into the new Department of Education. The bill was opposed by over ninety percent of the Indian tribes. They feared that moving the schools would weaken the government's trust responsibility for Indian education. The members of Congress were incredulous when tribes defended the BIA on that bill. It was a common perception in Congress that the BIA was the most incompetent agency in the American government. Tribal leaders produced some very interesting figures to demonstrate that the BIA did not have such a terrible record. For instance, the absentee rate in BIA schools was less than the absentee rate in New York City. One of the most critical arguments that Congress responded to was the new role of community controlled contract schools, which gave Indian communities, for the first time, the chance to control the education of their children.

The concept of the trust also can be seen in the various sunset bills that were proposed in the late 1970s. These bills basically said that every federal program would be allowed to run for periods of from five to ten years. After that specified period ended, no program would be reauthorized unless it could specifically justify itself. Several arguments were made before Congress concerning those bills. One of the most important was that Indian programs were different because of the trust obligation.

The trust is part of a moral obligation that the United States has assumed. We have to look at it in terms of congressional support for Indian programs. There is widespread agreement that the trust obligation pertains to Indian land and natural resources. There is also non-Indian support for doing charitable good works. Until about 1950, Congress used the term "gratuity appropriations" when it funded Indian health, education, and welfare programs. The Reagan administration has expanded this old Christian view of charity and extended it to corporations.

Another way that the people through Congress support programs for Indian tribes is in the sense of reparations. Because terrible wrongs have been done to Indian people, they believe that the United States has the responsibility to help these victims. This is analogous, in some ways, to the German nation paying reparations to Israel. There also are people who see a more liberal role for the government. They feel there is a governmental responsibility to help Indians under the social contract.

The moral obligation is more compelling, in many cases, than the legal obligation in terms of the way non-Indians can be moved to support Indian tribes. Congress is more willing than the courts to take a holistic view of the trust obligation. If the trust obligation protected only Indian land, would the trust be adequately discharged if the land survived and the Indian people died?

HELEN PETERSON

The manner in which the BIA and all the other federal agencies carry out the trust obligation depends a good deal upon how much money Congress is willing to appropriate. It is important that the general public understands the trust obligation, because the general public sends men and women to Congress, and they hold the trump cards.

I have struggled over many years trying to explain the trust obligation to other people. I have found it helpful to compare the BIA to the trust department of a bank. Americans know about the trust departments of banks, and they seem to understand that in the government of the United States there is a Bureau of Indian Affairs which corresponds to a bank's trust department.

It is important that potential friends of Indians understand very quickly what the trust relationship is and the BIA's responsibility for carrying it out. I do not think it is as important to separate out the moral, political, and legal aspects of the trust obligation, as it is to understand the Indians' dependence on the Congress of the United States. The vulnerability of Indians became apparent during the early 1950s when Congress adopted the policy of termination in House Resolution 108. Termination was above all else the ending of the trust on Indian land.

We hear a good deal about both genocide and the cultural survival of Indians. The general public is often confused about this. But a few things are crystal clear. People find it difficult to survive as a distinct culture without a land base. This explains the tenacity of the Jews and their determination to establish and maintain a homeland. It is not unique to Indians to know that it is important to hold on to a piece of this earth. We need to concentrate on making these simple truths and facts better understood among both Indian people and the general public.

There is also the question of tribal versus individual interests and ownership. I recall that during Glenn Emmons's administration, a memo was written which said that, since the passage of the Indian Reorganization Act, tribal interests had been held paramount to individual Indian interests. Emmons then promised that he would consider individual interests to be paramount or equal to that of the tribe. This is a delicate, painful, tough, and persistent issue that needs constructive resolution. But it is also important to realize that there is a clear trust responsibility under the IRA. This legislation indefinitely extended the trust on the land of IRA tribes. And the secretary of the interior periodically extends the trust periods on land owned by non-IRA tribes.

BENJAMIN REIFEL

The trust responsibility includes the legal obligation to protect Indian land resources. It also involves political and legislative areas. If the trust obligation is not met and a tribe loses all of its land, it may still be sovereign because the people are working together to obtain federal services on a government-to-government basis.

There have been instances where the government has increased Indian landholdings. I went around on the Pine Ridge Reservation with a tribal lawyer. We convinced the director of the Farmers Home Administration to loan the Pine Ridge Sioux $1 million to increase the amount of tribal land. That was important because all of the allotted land on the reservation will someday disappear. Most of these allotted lands are inherited on the basis of state law. There are pieces of land that have as many as 150 heirs in one quarter section.

The Indians should be united about the importance of having the government carry out its trust obligation, but we fight and fuss among ourselves on our own reservations. If we cannot cooperate at home, how do we unite regionally or nationally?

Why does the nation feel a moral obligation to provide us with services? I think there is a latent sense of guilt in the American white community. When I was in Congress, one of my colleagues said, "Why don't you appropriate enough money to take care of this problem?" We must find a way to take advantage of the latent sense of guilt that exists in the United States.

We are less than 1 million out of 220 million people. That means we have to cite the factual content of treaties instead of giving diatribes against the government. And we have to make an effort to find our friends. When I was in Congress, I got on the Interior and Insular Affairs Appropriations Committee. The first thing I did was get $5 million added to the budget for our school on the Rosebud Reservation. You have to know who you can go to in the House and Senate to get this kind of support. People such as Senator Barry Goldwater are important. Recently, Goldwater sent a letter to President Ronald Reagan. It said, if you are spending all these billions of dollars for other people, why don't we spend a little here at home for our first Americans.

If Indians want to preserve the trust obligation, they must discuss ways to keep their tribes together. We need to keep up our tribal enrollment so that we are more united as a people. It is a mistake to have full bloods fight mixed bloods and try to kick them off the rolls. This kind of factionalism goes on all the time.

You are an Indian no matter where you live. It is important that tribes adopt everybody who has some right because of blood ties. There are a lot of people from all over the United States who are not enrolled because of tribal politics. Once they are on the roll, they can say, "I am an Indian." And they can help persuade Congress to maintain its trust relationship.

Indians cannot depend on the Interior Department to uphold its moral trust obligation. A secretary of the interior may come along who does not feel obligated to extend the trust status on certain Indian lands. I would admonish all tribal leaders to help their people understand that it is important to maintain the political aspects of the trust obligation. We must persuade Congress to continue education, health, and other federal services. If we do not do that, gradually our sovereignty will erode, and at some point we will be ineffective.

Fifty years ago, when I was employed by the Indian Bureau, Indians were dying like flies from tuberculosis, trachoma, dysentery, and malnutrition. Now we are in good health. We have a breathing spell. Our young men and women are students in universities and colleges. There are hundreds of Indian lawyers to look after our interests. We must get together with our white friends, stop quarreling among ourselves, and examine the purpose of life in the United States of America.

CHAPTER SIX

What Indians Should Want:
Advice to the President

Joe De La Cruz, Philleo Nash, Suzan Shown Harjo,
Oren Lyons, Philip S. Deloria

*Existing tribal income simply can not maintain the standard of living
to adequately maintain our culture. What should we do? If a recommendation is made to the president, it should ask for enough money for
each reservation to honestly provide a standard of living that will support
tribal sovereignty and self-rule. Then, we can proudly say, this is our culture and we are taking care of ourselves.*

Benjamin Reifel, Sioux, former commissioner of
Indian affairs under President Gerald Ford

*If a president wanted to do the right thing, he would set up a five or
ten member staff in the Office of Management and Budget. It would
coordinate all federal budgets insofar as they served, or failed to serve,
Indian communities. In addition, this staff would enforce responsibility on
all federal agencies to provide services to Indian communities. It would
review the actions of all federal agencies and propose legislation if they had
an impact on Indian tribes and on the federal tribal relationship.*
*I would recommend that the president implement a system where
individual tribes plan budgets with the federal government over a ten to
fifteen year span rather than the eighteen month projection that they now
have. Then, discussions of funding capital investments on reservations
would be in the context of when and not whether they take place.*

Gary Orfield, Brookings Institution, professor of
political science, University of Chicago

[311]

We are suffering under cultural imperialism. In our schools, we have to use books that tell us how the Indians impeded progress, justice, and civilization. We are viewed as savages because we protected our country. I would like an entirely new curriculum developed for our schools, so our children would not have to read those kinds of things.

Edward C. Johnson, Northern Paiute,
tribal historian for the
Walker River Paiute Tribe

Looking back at the 1930s, I sometimes feel there is a legacy that comes from one of the major cultural events of that era. It is the Wizard's response in the Wizard of Oz. *When the cowardly lion needed courage, he got a medal. When the tin man needed a heart, he got a watch. When the scarecrow needed a brain, he was given a diploma. Recently, I heard a conversation by an Indian staff member in the House of Representatives. It was suggested that "What Indians need now is to build their own bureaucracy." This is in the same vein as if Indians went to a Wizard of Oz known as the commissioner of Indian affairs and said, "We need our future." He would say, "You do not need a future, you just need a budget."*

Indian people do have a future. With each new birth among us, we will have a child of promise. We must make certain that all of our children, born and unborn, fulfill their destiny.

Hank Adams, Assiniboine, activist, leader, and writer

JOE DE LA CRUZ

A few years ago, we asked for a meeting with former President James E. Carter. Indian people, with expertise in technical matters and federal Indian policy, had developed papers that we were going to carry to the president. Unfortunately, President Carter never showed up for this meeting, and it seemed that the people he sent in to represent him did not want to listen to us.

I doubt whether any president is interested in listening to the viewpoints of Indians. But Ronald Reagan recently has made an important statement regarding Indian affairs. One of the things he promised was to honor the concept of Indian self-determination. I believe that there are some things in Reagan's statement that we can pursue to get a proper perspective on federal Indian policy. It is up to the Indian people to take this initiative.

For the last year and a half, as president of the National Congress of American Indians, I have been working with tribal leaders who are members of the National Tribal Chairmen's Association. We have attempted to cooperate with this administration, and it has been very frustrating. At times, we have felt like fighting with all of our strength. It is very apparent that the president of the United States, even though he signs his name on policy statements, probably does not know that there are still Indians in America. It is very obvious that he does not know that there are Indians in Central America who are human beings.

It is my strong feeling that we have to establish a formal process where Indian people can develop an agenda that defines their relationship to the United States. These formal discussions would also enable us to see where we are going in the future. If President Reagan is truly interested in government-to-government relations, we will be able to make progress.

Not too long ago, people who resided on islands in the Pacific Ocean held talks aimed at redeveloping their relationship with the United States. They have managed to alter the paternalistic relationship that they once had with this country. These people are now in a commonwealth situation. We need to see if we want to go in that direction.

The Reagan administration has issued a statement on self-determination. We need to find out whether the federal agencies that deal with Indian affairs are following this policy. We also must ask Congress, "This is what the President has said; why are you not carrying it out?" Finally, Indians need to educate Congress and the American public about international convenants that focus on the rights of indigenous people.

PHILLEO NASH

I have advised presidents. Some of them took my advice and some did not. My principle advice to Harry Truman was that he should veto the Navajo-Hopi rehabilitation bill unless Congress took out section nine which would have put the Navajo and Hopi Indians under state jurisdiction in three states. President Truman agreed and he vetoed this bill. Congress later passed similar legislation without section nine.

In the 1960 election, a rather interesting thing happened. Both candidates were asked a series of penetrating questions about Indian affairs by both the National Congress of American Indians and by the Association on American Indian Affairs, and both candidates, in that year, committed themselves to improving federal Indian policy.

President John F. Kennedy was committed to appointing an Indian to head the Bureau of Indian Affairs. And he wanted to honor the provisions of Indian treaties. President Kennedy may have made some campaign promises that were inadvisable. He may have promised more than he could deliver, given the political reality of the country. Indian people do not want campaign promises. They want commitments that are obtainable.

We must recognize the symbolic importance of Indian treaties and the fact that they are part of organic law. Treaties are documents of great importance. They represent historical tradition and remind us of previous commitments. Presidents, Congress, and the courts are obliged to deal with the numerous and important organic acts in Indian affairs as serious documents.

President Kennedy did not give Congress a special message on Indian affairs. Instead, he had Secretary of the Interior Stewart Udall create a Task Force on Indian Affairs. I was a member of that task force. In our report, we recommended that termination should be ended. President Kennedy gave his stamp of approval to this recommendation, and subsequent presidents have not altered this policy.

I do not think that it is appropriate any longer for non-Indians to offer advice on behalf of Indians. But presidents that think they can get along without advice on Indian affairs will find out that they have made a serious mistake. It is a very important matter to listen to the viewpoints of other people. Presidents of the United States, for a long time, have been tested by where they stand on Indian affairs. It is an acid test, because other great moral and ethical issues are connected with the guilt that Americans feel about Indians. Indian people have traditionally looked to their "Great White Father." This is something that we can make fun of, especially when we watch western movies, but it had profound implications in the past, and it still does. I believe every president of the United States knows that.

I believe that there have been significant changes in Indian affairs in the last few years. The take-over of the Bureau of Indian Affairs was important. The politics of confrontation by what had been a docile and passive minority group was a considerable eye opener, shock, and awakening. Not long after the episode, the OEO began to strengthen its funding.

The American Indian Policy Review Commission's report was historic. It was similar to the Presidential Commission on Civil Rights set up by President Truman. The commission dealt with the issue of sovereignty directly and confrontationally. It resulted in a loss to Congress of both chairmen on the Interior Subcommittee on Indian Affairs.

It should not be too surprising, after the occupation of the BIA headquarters and the political aftermath of the commission report, that we do not have any chairman of the Interior Subcommittee on Indian Affairs. This committee goes back to the early days of the Congress. It has been a hard hitting committee that dealt with significant issues. Today, nobody wants to be chairman of the committee. This gives me an ominous feeling with regard to the future.

For better or for worse, I think the situation now exists where there could be the termination of the Indian Bureau. Historically, the commissioner of Indian affairs, the secretary of the interior, and the president have been instrumental in forming executive leadership in Indian affairs. Today we do not have a strong head of the BIA. We also lack the congressional leadership on Indian affairs committees that is necessary to formulate policy with the president and his staff. There is a floundering going on, and I do not see how it could be otherwise.

Indian tribes may be already a little further along than they think they are towards self-determination. This comes at a time when a weakened, demoralized, and nearly all Indian Bureau of Indian Affairs is more ineffectual and disappointing than it has ever been in its history. Indian people, their leaders, and their organizations must decide what to do about this situation. I wish you well. But I have a feeling of chaos, indecision, and fragmentation. I think 1986 is going to be a watershed year. I hope that you are successful.

SUZAN SHOWN HARJO

The only president who has ever known me was James Carter. I gave him advice concerning the advisability of having a meeting with traditional Indian elders and leaders. Instead, we met with Vice-President Walter Mondale. I promised that this meeting would last one-hour-and-a-half. It lasted three-and-a-half hours, and that was the last advice I ever gave a president.

My advice to President Ronald Reagan is to get out of town quick and do not fire any of the dim bulbs on your one-watt administration. Otherwise, we might have some light rather than heat brought to Indian policy, and we do not want that to happen. I believe that it would be very helpful to end the war against poor people that is underway by this administration. The president should also stop the confrontational policy towards our neighbors to the south and the destructive activities in relation to the environment and should adopt a positive public policy toward women. Furthermore, Reagan should halt the campaign from his office to convert the nation to Christianity. The president should follow the advice of Mark Twain who asked the missionaries to "leave the heathens alone and convert the Christians to Christianity."

President Reagan should also attend to other matters. He should adopt a conciliatory posture toward nuclear disarmament even though the reservations are not targets for annihilation. It would be nice for the president to set aside a day to honor Martin Luther King, especially as we approach the twentieth anniversary celebration of the poor peoples' march on Washington. I hope that the president will become serious about his policy to consult with Indian governmental leaders. I would order his staff to implement the part of the Indian Reorganization Act that requires the secretary of interior to advise tribal governments about the budget. President Reagan should call a moratorium on the budget cuts that are being proposed for Indians. He should stop trying to force Indians into negotiations on resource issues that need not take place at this moment. Finally, the president should issue a proposed executive order on Indian religious freedom.

I would like to comment on a point that has been made regarding the jurisdiction of the Indian Affairs Committee in Congress. For many years there were Congressional standing committees for Indian affairs.

Since the 1940s, the House Indian Affairs Subcommittee has handled these matters. In the early 1970s, serious problems arose because a chairman of the subcommittee had abused his position. Morris Udall, the chairman of the Interior Committee, talked to a number of us. He proposed a plan to handle Indian affairs within the committee as a whole rather than have an irresponsible subcommittee. Udall persuaded a number of people on the Interior Committee to floor manage individual bills, which relieved him of the burden of handling all Indian legislation.

For about ten years, I have advocated the idea of having a joint Senate and House committee that would not legislate but oversee Indian affairs. This would be successful only if there was a comparable jurisdictional set-up within the executive branch of government. As long as there is confusion in the executive branch, there will necessarily be jurisdictional confusion within Congress about how to handle Indian affairs. On the other hand, we do not want a committee that oversees Indian policy that is made up of people who do not really like Indians.

OREN LYONS

I am not afraid of a direct discussion of Indian affairs. Our traditional people have been giving advice to various presidents for sometime. We are concerned about the process of termination. Treaty rights have been ignored, and jurisdiction for Indian matters has moved down from the federal to state level. If this process is not stopped Indian tribes eventually will wind up as a municipality of some county government.

The Iroquois always talk about their treaties. There are 371 treaties. Today, we are faced with legislation that attempts to serve all the interests of these different entities. It is obvious that this approach does not work, because there is too much variety in tribal self-government.

There are serious problems today associated with economic development on Indian land. Many Indian nations look like Las Vegas. Why does Indian economic development have to revolve around gambling, bingo, and the sale of cigarettes and firecrackers? This kind of negative economic development results in twenty or thirty people fighting for a piece of the pie. It is based on quick profit with no concern for the effect it will have on Indian communities. In my judgement, this kind of tribal economy has harmed the Seneca and other close relatives. People have become very angry. There are bitter discussions about who is to get money. This is the unfortunate reality today on Indian land.

President Reagan has proposed that we should welcome further economic development. From past experience, what he means is "Open up your door and we will step in. Then, we will show you how it is done." Before long the house is empty, and the Indians are standing there wondering what happened.

The development of nuclear power threatens Indian people. In New Mexico and Arizona, where mining has taken place, Indian people are dying from exposure to radiation. My good friend, Larry Redshirt died of a broken heart and overwork when his wife aborted because she lived in an area where nuclear waste got on rabbits, the food, and everything else in the open pits. She twice delivered malformed children. That is another reality today on Indian land.

The Iroquois believe that a high level presidential commission should be created so Indians can sit down and really talk about a fair settlement of their land claims. The American people must understand that Indian people are not going to take money in lieu of lost lands. What Indians want is some of their land back.

Why are the American people so apprehensive when Indians talk about land claims? It is because they know they are all sitting on original Indian land. But would not everyone be happier if we resolved this issue? Given the international problems that we face, it would be much better to be allies than adversaries fighting on our home front.

Indian nations are intelligent. They can hold their own in any discussion of how to settle land claims. So, let us find a way to expand Indian territory. Indian nations would then be secure and their children would have a future. Our chiefs worry about what its going to happen when they are dead. They wonder, who is going to protect our children when we are gone?

The Iroquois want to continue as separate nations. We do not want to be like other Americans. We are proud of our culture and think that we can enhance your life. Indians and non-Indians can be friends and work together. We must talk to our congressmen. We have to tell the president of the United States, "This is enough!" Let us clean up our own house before trying to save the world.

I am worried when President Reagan says, "Well, the devil made me do it." We have faced this philosophy before. The pilgrims talked about the same thing. They said, "You Indians are devils!" So, when I hear a president calling the Russians "devils," I ask what does that mean? We have had experience with that kind of rhetoric. It means trouble, and we must get beyond that kind of thinking. The future is in the hands of the American people.

Philip S. Deloria

I would like to identify some issues that might be worthy of consideration by Ronald Reagan or any other president. From my brief experience in helping to found the World Council of Indigenous Peoples, I learned that a fundamental issue is the relationship between industrial societies and tribal peoples. All around the world, village and tribal people are seeking to hold on to their land and their identity, but they are being forced off the land and into cities because of the needs of industrial societies. The economic promises that are implicit in plans for world development simply do not have the artithmetic to back them up. There are not going to be enough jobs created in light industry to employ everybody in Rio de Janeiro, Mexico City, or other large cities that are absorbing tribal and village people. In many respects there is a time bomb that is ticking.

That leads to some fundamental issues that have to be clarified for American society. In America, as I see it, the conflict has never really been between cultures. Those clashes have been only surface manifestations of a deeper problem. The real issue in this country has been over the control of land and natural resources and the relationship of Indians to the economy.

Historically, Indian policy has been largely bipartisan. For example, both termination and self-determination received bipartisan support. It is not going to be enough for both candidates in the next election, or the election after that, to make the same kind of campaign promises about self-determination and respect for treaties.

From recent Supreme Court opinions, it appears that the fundamental view of this society is that Indians do not belong in this economic system and their resources should be used and developed by somebody else. The Supreme Court has now invented the notion that federal agencies have a trust responsibility to their constituent groups that is comparable in the law to the federal trust responsibility for Indians. This is an astounding and drastic judicial viewpoint. It deserves a great public outcry.

The tools for the solution to many Indian problems already exist. The will and the spirit of Indian tribes must be harnessed to bring about political and economic advancement. And Indian communities have to realize that they are the only ones that can decide how to do this. The federal government also has the tools to coordinate the federal resources available to tribes, in order to achieve economic results. But the bipartisan will to do this has been lacking. Neither political party has had its feet held to the fire. They still think that Indians are willing to settle for platitudes.

The Carter administration, in my experience, was constantly in a state of public embarrassment. Whatever it did with respect to Indians simply added more embarrassment to an already humiliating four years. The Reagan administration seems to lack the capacity for embarrassment. This indifference to criticism greatly effects our strategies for changing the policies of this administration.

I agree that we should ask President Reagan to stop his war on poor people. But he did not stumble into that war and the poor people did not attack him. Officials in the Reagan administration made a calculated decision to follow this course of action, and they are not embarrased about it. Until there is a strong public consensus in this country which says that the nation will no longer tolerate such a public policy, Indians will continue to pay the price of poverty for continuing to be Indians. Reorganizing the Bureau of Indian Affairs is not going to have the slightest effect on ending this war.

The basic issue that Indians face is are we going to use our own resources, or is somebody else going to use them? The answer, for the last two hundred years, has been very clear. Somebody else is going to use our resources. I do not see the slightest indication that there is any demand for this process to change except from Indians and a few of our friends.

We showed, in response to the termination policy, that we can lobby very effectively against something. Our record since that time of demonstrating that we could lobby effectively for something has been less dramatic. There is an apparent absence of a will in the American political community to find a solution to our problems. So we must define the answers ourselves and keep pushing until something begins to happen. But we still will need public support. I am not ready to say what Indians want in specific details. But, in general, it is clear that Indians do not want to be poor anymore. The economic and political issues involved in the control of our resources are paramount and are most often ignored in the federal policies. There are still vast resources in the government to help us, but they are not being mobilized and targeted by federal officials.

Since the early 1970s, tribes have begun to face the need to act as governments that regulate and tax. In the process, we have created a set of issues with respect to federal, state, and municipal governments that were beyond the wildest imagination of people twenty years ago. A whole new set of issues has to be confronted. It involves the development of institutions and the implementation of political philosophies in a very short time. That is an almost impossible task, but we are going to have to do it. In order to be successful, we must stave off attempts to interfere with and abolish our governments.

Nobody went in and abolished the city of Cleveland when it almost went bankrupt under the direction of a youthful mayor. But tribes are constantly faced with the reminder, that in the view of much of the society, we are transitional governments. This makes it very difficult for us, over the long haul, to implement plans. We can not make even one percent of the false starts and the mistakes that every other government in this country is entitled to, as a matter or right, because they have a permanent existence.

Most people are not aware of the enormous growth and power of the Office of Management and Budget in the federal government. It no longer just deals with management issues or adding up numbers and giving them to the president. The OMB is a major policy-making force in America. Every person that works for OMB, in theory, speaks for the president. The levels at which Indian policy questions are decided in the OMB are so low that no one who is appointed by the president even knows they take place, unless they are very major issues.

The OMB is an unaccountable bureaucracy that essentially has the freedom to impose its policy preferences on Indians. There is no due process or access to policy formulation on the part of Indians. This situation happens in every administration.

We must find a way to break through that bureaucratic barrier and establish the permanency of Indian societies and governments in this system. This must not be done at the price of our continued poverty. We have to discover how to work our way out of poverty and still be permanent. That involves a conceptual framework that simply has not been developed, and we have to do it very quickly.

Contributors

HANK ADAMS, Assiniboine, Activist Leader, Writer.

VIRGINIA BEAVERT, Executive Secretary, General Council of the Yakima Tribe.

RAMONA BENNETT, Puyallup, Former Tribal Council Member, Fishing Rights Advocate.

ROBERT L. BENNETT, Oneida, Commissioner of Indian Affairs under President Lyndon B. Johnson.

EDWARD BOYER, Fort Hall Shoshone-Bannock.

W. ROGER BUFFALOHEAD, Ponca, Project Director, MIGIZI Communications Project.

ROBERT BURNETTE, Rosebud Sioux, Former Director, National Congress of American Indians (passed away September 10, 1984).

LUCY KRAMER COHEN, Wife of Felix S. Cohen, Director of the Association on American Indian Affairs.

RUPERT COSTO, Cahuilla, President of the American Indian Historical Society.

JOE DE LA CRUZ, Quinault, President of the National Congress of American Indians.

ADA DEER, Menominee, Office of Native American Studies, University of Wisconsin.

PHILIP S. DELORIA, Standing Rock Sioux, Director, American Indian Law Center.

GORDY HIGH EAGLE, Nez Perce.

LARRY ECHOHAWK, Pawnee, Idaho State Legislator, Attorney for the Fort Hall Tribes.

[323]

R. David Edmunds, Cherokee, Professor of History, Texas Christian University.

Fred Eggan, Anthropologist.

Gerald One Feather, Oglala Sioux, Past Tribal President, Present Police Commissioner.

E. Reeseman Fryer, Former General Superintendent for the Navajo Reservation, Assistant Commissioner of Indian Affairs under President John F. Kennedy.

Tim Giago, Editor and Publisher of the *Lakota Times*.

Suzan Shown Harjo, Cheyenne and Creek, Executive Director of the National Congress of American Indians.

LaDonna Harris, Comanche, Former Candidate for United States Vice President, Currently with Americans for Indian Opportunity.

E. Richard Hart, Former Director of the Institute of the American West, Present Director of the Institute of the North American West.

Hazel W. Hertzberg, Professor of History and Education, Teachers College, Columbia University.

Graham Holmes, Former United States Attorney for the Bureau of Indian Affairs; Former Superintendent, Area Director, and Assistant Commissioner of Indian Affairs.

Lenada James, Shoshone-Bannock, Indian Rights Activist.

Russell Jim, Yakima, Leader in the Northwest.

Edward C. Johnson, Northern Paiute, Director/Curator of the Stewart Indian Museum Association, Tribal Historian and Former Tribal Chairman for the Walker River Paiute Tribe.

Alvin M. Josephy, Jr., President of the National Council of the Institute of the American West, Author.

Ted Katcheak, Alaskan Native, Co-Chairman of the United Tribes of Alaska.

Oren Lyons, Onondaga, Artist and Tribal Council Member.

Arthur Manning, Shoshone-Paiute, Leader and Former Council Member of the Duck Valley Shoshone-Paiute.

Francis McKinley, Ute, Former Tribal Chairman at the Uintah-Ouray Reservation..

Alexander (Sandy) MacNabb, Micmac, Acting Commissioner of Indian Affairs under President Richard M. Nixon.

Don Mitchell, Alaska Federation of Natives.

Philleo Nash, Commissioner of Indian Affairs under President John F. Kennedy, Former Lieutenant Governor of Wisconsin.

JAMES E. OFFICER, Professor of Anthropology, University of Arizona, Associate Commissioner of Indian Affairs under Presidents John F. Kennedy and Lyndon B. Johnson.

FLOYD A. O'NEIL, Director, American West Center, University of Utah.

GARY ORFIELD, Brookings Institution, Professor of Political Science, University of Chicago.

ALFONSO ORTIZ, San Juan Pueblo, Professor of Anthropology, University of New Mexico.

JOHN PAINTER, History Professor, Northern State College, Aberdeen, South Dakota.

EARL OLD PERSON, Blackfeet, Chairman of the Blackfeet Tribe.

HELEN PETERSON, Oglala Sioux, Former Executive Director of the National Congress of American Indians.

KENNETH R. PHILP, Professor of History, University of Texas at Arlington.

BENJAMIN REIFEL, Sioux, Former Congressman from South Dakota, Commissioner of Indian Affairs under President Gerald R. Ford.

ELMER SAVILLA, Director, National Tribal Chairmen's Association.

HELEN M. SCHIERBECK, Lumbee, Director of the United Indians of America.

MARY ELLEN SLOAN, Counsel for the Southern Paiutes.

SOL TAX, Professor of Anthropology, University of Chicago.

ROBERT TREPP, Oklahoma Creek.

STEVEN UNGER, Executive Director of the Association on American Indian Affairs.

CHARLOTTE LLOYD WALKUP (Charlotte Tuttle Westwood from 1934 to 1940), Associate of Felix S. Cohen, Worked in the Solicitor's Office Assisting with the Drafting of IRA Constitutions.

DAVE WARREN, Santa Clara Pueblo, Expert on Indian Art and Cultural Education, United States Representative to the Inter-American Indian Institute.

WILCOMB WASHBURN, Smithsonian Institution.

CLARENCE WESLEY, San Carlos Apache, Former Tribal Chairman.

CHARLES F. WILKINSON, Professor of Law, University of Oregon.

GERALD WILKINSON, Cherokee-Catawba, Executive Director, National Indian Youth Council.

Recent Indian-White Relations: A Bibliography

Compiled by
Gregory C. Thompson with assistance from
Anthony Godfrey, Margery Ward, and Kathryn MacKay

Abbott, George W. "The American Indian, Federal Citizen and State Citizen." *Federal Bar Journal* 20 (1960) : 248–260.

Ablon, Joan. "American Indian Relocation: Problems of Dependency and Management in the City." *Phylon* 26 (1965) : 362–371.

Akwesasne Notes. B.I.A., I'm Not Your Indian Any More. Mohawk Nation via Roosevelttown, New York, 1973.

———. Mohawk Nation via Roosevelttown, New York. Various Issues.

———. *Voices from Wounded Knee, 1973.* Mohawk Nation via Roosevelttown, New York, 1974.

American Indian Policy Review Commission. *Final Report.* Washington, D.C.: Government Printing Office, 1977.

Announcements. Native American Rights Fund, Boulder, Colorado. Various issues.

Bach, Arthur L. "Administration of Indian Resources in the United States, 1933–1941." Ph.D. dissertation, University of Iowa, 1942.

Berkhofer, Robert F., Jr. *The White Man's Indian: Images of the American Indian from Columbus to the Present.* New York: Alfred A. Knopf Company, 1978.

Berthrong, Donald J. *The American Indian: From Pacifism to Activism.* St. Charles, Missouri: Forum Press, 1973.

Blaine, Peter. *Papagos and Politics.* Tucson: Arizona Historical Society, 1981.

Boender, Debra R. "Glenn Emmons of Gallup." Master's thesis, University of Mexico, 1976.

Boyce, George A. *"When Navajos Had Too Many Sheep": the 1940s.* San Francisco: Indian Historian Press, 1974.

Brody, J. J. *Indian Painters and White Patrons.* Albuquerque: University of New Mexico Press, 1971.

Bromert, Roger. "The Sioux and the Indian CCC." *South Dakota History* 8 (Fall 1978) : 340–356.

———. "The Sioux and the Indian New Deal, 1933–1934." Ph.D. dissertation, University of Toledo, 1980.

Brophy, William A., and Aberle, Sophie E., comps. *The Indian; America's Unfinished Business: Report of the Commission on the Rights, Liberties and Responsibilities of the American Indian.* Norman: University of Oklahoma, 1966.

Burnette, Robert and Koster, John. *The Road To Wounded Knee.* New York: Bantam Books, 1974.

Burt, Larry W. *Tribalism in Crisis: Federal Indian Policy, 1953–1961.* Albuquerque: University of New Mexico Press, 1982.

Burton, Henrietta Kolshorn. *The Re-establishment of the Indians in Their Pueblo Life Through the Revival of Their Traditional Crafts: A Study in Home Extension Education.* New York: Columbia University Bureau of Publications, 1936.

Butler, Raymond V. "The Bureau of Indian Affairs: Activities Since 1945." *Annals of the Academy of Political and Social Science* 436 (1978) : 50–60.

Cohen, Felix S. *The Legal Conscience: Selected Papers of Felix S. Cohen.* Edited by Lucy Kramer Cohen. New Haven: Yale University Press, 1960.

———. "The Erosion of Indian Rights, 1950–1953: A Case Study in Bureaucracy." *Yale Law Journal* 62 (February 1953) : 348–390.

———. *Handbook of Federal Indian Law.* Washington D.C.: Government Printing Office, 1942; reprint ed., Albuquerque: University of New Mexico Press, 1976.

Collier, John. *From Every Zenith: A Memoir and Some Essays on Life and Thought.* Denver: Sage Books, 1963.

———. "United States Indian Administration as a Laboratory of Ethnic Relations." *Social Research* 12 (September 1945) : 265–303.

———. *Indians of the Americas.* New York: New American Library, 1947.

———. *On The Gleaming Way.* Denver: Sage Books, 1962.

Colton, Mary-Russell F. "Wanted—A Market for Indian Art." *Southern California Business* (October 1930).

Costo, Rupert, and Henry, Jeannette. *Indian Treaties: Two Centuries of Dishonor.* San Francisco: The Indian Historian Press, 1977.

Dale, Edward Everett. *The Indians of the Southwest; A Century of Development Under the United States.* Norman: University of Oklahoma Press, 1949.

Debo, Angie. *And Still the Waters Run.* Princeton: Princeton University Press, 1940.

—————. *The Five Civilized Tribes of Oklahoma: Report on Social and Economic Conditions.* Philadelphia: Indian Rights Association, 1951.

—————. *A History of the Indians of the United States.* Norman: University of Oklahoma Press, 1970.

Deer, Ada. "Menominee Restoration: How the Good Guys Won." *Journal of Intergroup Relations* 3 (1974): 41–50.

Deloria, Vine, Jr., and Lytle, Clifford M. *American Indians, American Justice.* Austin: University of Texas Press, 1983.

—————. *The Nations Within: The Past and Future of American Indian Sovereignty.* New York: Pantheon Books, 1984.

Deloria, Vine Jr. *Behind the Trail of Broken Treaties: An Indian Declaration of Independence.* New York: Delacorte Press, 1974.

—————. *Custer Died for Your Sins: An Indian Manifesto.* New York: Macmillan Company, 1969.

—————. *God is Red.* New York: Grosset and Dunlap, 1973.

Dippie, Brian W. *The Vanishing American: White Attitudes and U.S. Indian Policy.* Middletown, Conn.: Wesleyan University Press, 1982.

Dobyns, Henry F. "The Indian Reorganization Act and Federal Withdrawal." *Applied Anthropology* 7 (Spring 1948): 35–44.

Downes, Randolph. "A Crusade For Indian Reform, 1922–1934." *Mississippi Valley Historical Review* 32 (December 1945): 331–354.

Dunn, Dorothy. *American Indian Painting.* University of New Mexico Press, 1968.

Erving, Robert. "New Indian Art." *El Palacio* 76, (Spring 1969).

Fixico, Donald L. "Termination and Relocation: Federal Indian Policy in the 1950s." Ph.D. dissertation, University of Oklahoma, 1980.

Freeman, J. Leiper. "The New Deal for Indians: A Study in Bureau-Committee Relations in American Government." Ph.D. dissertation, Princeton University, 1952.

Getches, David H., Rosenfelt, Daniel M., and Wilkinson, Charles F. *Federal Indian Law: Cases and Materials on Federal Indian Law.* St. Paul, Minneapolis: West Publishing Company, 1979.

Gibson, Arrell Morgan. *The American Indian: Prehistory to the Present.* Lexington, Mass.: D.C. Heath & Co., 1980.

Gilbert, William H., and Taylor, John L. "Indian Land Questions." *Arizona Law Review* 8 (1966):102–131.

Gower, Clavin W. "The CCC Indian Division: Aid for Depressed Americans." *Minnesota History* 43 (Spring 1972): 3–13.

Gundlach, James H., Reid, Nelson P., and Roberts, Alden E. "Native American Indian Migration and Relocation." *Pacific Sociological Review* 21 (1978): 117–127.

Haas, Theodore H. "The Legal Aspects of Indian Affairs from 1887 to 1957." *Annals of the American Academy of Political and Social Science* 311 (May 1957): 12–22.

———. *Ten Years of Tribal Government Under I.R.A.* Washington, D.C.: U.S. Department of the Interior, 1947.

Haase, Larry J. "Termination and Assimilation: Federal Indian Policy, 1934 to 1961." Ph.D. dissertation, Washington State University, 1974.

Hagan, William T. "Tribalism Rejuvenated: The Native American Since the Era of Termination." *Western Historical Quarterly* 12 (January 1981): 6–16.

Harnoncourt, Rene. "North American Indian Arts." *Magazine of Art* 32 (March 1939): 164–67.

Harnoncourt, Rene, and Douglas, Frederic H. *Indian Art of the United States.* New York: Museum of Modern Art, 1941; reprint ed., New York: Arno Press, 1969.

Hauptman, Laurence M. *The Iroquois and the New Deal.* Syracuse: Syracuse University Press, 1981.

Hendrickson, Kenneth E., ed. *Hard Times in Oklahoma: The Depression Years.* Oklahoma City: Oklahoma Historical Society, 1983.

Hertzberg, Hazel W. *The Search for an American Indian Identity: Modern Pan-Indian Movements.* Syracuse: Syracuse University Press, 1971.

———. "Reaganomics on the Reservation." *The New Republic*, November 22, 1982, pp. 15–18.

Herzberg, Stephen. "The Menominee Indians: From Treaty to Termination." *Wisconsin Magazine of History* 60 (1977): 267–329.

Highwater, Jamake. *Song from the Earth: American Indian Painting.* Boston: New York Graphic Society, 1976.

Hodge, Frederick Webb, LaFarge, Oliver, and Spinden, Herbert, J., eds. *Introduction to American Indian Art: To Accompany the First*

Exposition of American Indian Art Selected Entirely with Consideration of Esthetic Value. New York: Exposition of Indian Tribal Arts, Inc., 1931; reprint ed., Glorieta, New Mexico: Rio Grande Press, 1970.

The Indian Historian. American Indian Historical Society, San Francisco. Various Issues.

Indian Natural Resources. Association on American Indian Affairs, New York. Various Issues.

Iverson, Peter. *The Navajo Nation.* Westport, Conn.: Greenwood Press, 1981.

Josephy, Alvin M., Jr. *Now That the Buffalo's Gone: A Study of Today's American Indians.* New York: Alfred A. Knopf, 1982.

————. ed. *Red Power: The American Indians' Fight for Freedom.* New York: American Heritage Press, 1971.

Kelly, Lawrence C. "Anthropology and Anthropologists in the Indian New Deal." *Journal of the Behavioral Sciences* 16 (January 1980): 6–24.

————. *The Assault on Assimilation: John Collier and the Origins of Indian Policy Reform.* Albuquerque: University of New Mexico Press, 1983.

————. "Choosing the New Deal Indian Commissioner: Ickes vs. Collier." *New Mexico Historical Review* 49 (October 1974): 269–288.

————. "The Indian Reorganization Act: The Dream and the Reality." *Pacific Historical Review* 44 (August 1975): 291–312.

————. "John Collier and the Indian New Deal: An Assessment." In *Indian-White Relations: a Persistent Paradox.* Edited by Jane F. Smith and Robert M. Kvasnicka. Washington, D.C.: Howard University Press, 1976.

————. "John Collier and the Pueblo Lands Board Act." *New Mexico Historical Review* 58 (January 1983): 5–34.

————. *The Navajo Indians and Federal Indian Policy, 1900–1935.* Tucson: University of Arizona Press, 1968.

Kelly, William H., ed. *Indian Affairs and the Indian Reorganization Act: The Twenty Year Record.* Tucson: University of Arizona Press, 1954.

Kickingbird, Kirke, and Ducheneaux, Karen. *One Hundred Million Acres.* New York: Macmillan, 1973.

Kinney, J. P. *Facing Indian Facts.* Laurens, New York: Press of the Village Printer, 1973.

Knack, Martha C., and Stewart, Omer C. *As Long As the River Shall Run: An Ethnohistory of Pyramid Lake Indian Reservation.* Berkeley: University of California Press, 1984.

Koppes, Clayton R. "From New Deal to Termination: Liberalism and Indian Policy, 1933–1953." *Pacific Historical Review* 46 (November 1977): 543–566.

Kunitz, Stephen J. "The Social Philosophy of John Collier." *Ethnohistory* 18 (Summer 1971): 213–39.

Kvasnicka, Robert M., and Viola, Herman J., eds. *The Commissioners of Indian Affairs, 1824–1977.* Lincoln: University of Nebraska Press, 1979,

La Farge, Oliver. "The Enduring Indian." *Scientific American* 202 February 1960): 37–44.

———. "Termination of Federal Supervision: Disintegration and the American Indian." *Annals of the American Academy of Political and Social Science* 311 (May 1975): 56–70.

Levitan, Sar A. and Johnston, William B. *Indian Giving: Federal Programs for Native Americans.* Baltimore: Johns Hopkins Press, 1975.

Marden, David. "Anthropologists and Federal Indian Policy Prior to 1940." *Indian Historian* 5 (Winter 1972): 19–26.

McNickle, D'Arcy, and Fey, Harold E. *Indians and Other Americans: Two Ways of Life Meet.* New York: Harper and Row Publishers, 1959.

McNickle, D'Arcy. *Indian Man: A Life of Oliver La Farge.* Bloomington: Indiana University Press, 1971.

———. *Native American Tribalism: Indian Survivals and Renewals.* New York: Oxford University Press, 1973.

Mekeel, Scudder. "An Appraisal of the Indian Reorganization Act." *American Anthropologist* 46 (April–June 1944): 209–217.

Meriam, Lewis, ed. *The Problems of Indian Administration.* Baltimore: Johns Hopkins Press, Institute for Government Research, 1928.

Nash, Jay Brain. *The New Deal for the Indians: A Survey of the Workings of the Indian Reorganization Act of 1934.* New York: Academy Press, 1938.

Officer, James. "The Bureau of Indian Affairs Since 1945: An Assessment." *Annals of the American Academy of Political and Social Science* 436 (1978): 61–72.

Orfield, Gary. *A Study of the Termination Policy.* Denver: National Congress of American Indians, 1965.

Ourada, Patricia. *The Menominee Indians: A History*. Norman: University of Oklahoma Press, 1979.

Parman, Donald L. "The Indian and the Civil Conservation Corps." *Pacific Historical Review* 40 (February 1971): 39–56.

——. *The Navajos and the New Deal*. New Haven: Yale University Press, 1976.

Peroff, Nicholas. *Menominee Drums, Tribal Termination and Restoration, 1954–1974*. Norman: University of Oklahoma Press, 1982.

Philp, Kenneth R. "Herbert Hoover's New Era: a False Dawn for the American Indian, 1929–32." *Rocky Mountain Social Science Journal* 9 (April 1972): 53–60.

——. "John Collier and the American Indian, 1920–1945." In *Essays on Radicalism in Contemporary America*. Edited by Leon B. Blair. Austin: University of Texas Press, 1972.

——. "John Collier and the Controversy Over the Wheeler-Howard Bill." In *Indian-White Relations: A Persistent Paradox*. Edited by Jane F. Smith and Robert M. Kvasnicka. Washington, D.C.: Howard University Press, 1976.

——. *John Collier's Crusade for Indian Reform, 1920–1945*. Tucson: University of Arizona Press, 1977.

——. "John Collier and the Indians of the Americas: The Dream and the Reality." *Prologue* 11 (Spring 1979): 5–21.

——. "The New Deal and Alaskan Natives, 1936–1945." *Pacific Historical Review* 50 (August 1981): 309–327.

——. "Termination: a Legacy of the Indian New Deal." *Western Historical Quarterly* 14 (April 1983): 165–180.

Prucha, Francis Paul. "American Indian Policy In The Twentieth Century." *Western Historical Quarterly* 15 (January 1984): 5–18.

——, ed. *A Bibliographical Guide to the History of Indian-White Relations in the U.S*. Chicago: University of Chicago Press, 1977.

——, ed. *Documents of United States Indian Policy*. Lincoln: University of Nebraska Press, 1975.

——. *The Great Father*. Lincoln: University of Nebraska Press, 1984.

Quinton, B. T. "Oklahoma Tribes, the Great Depression and the Indian Bureau." *Mid-America* 49 (January 1967): 29–43.

Rusco, Elmer. "The Organization of the Te-Moak Bands of Western Shoshone." *Nevada Historical Society Quarterly* 25 (Fall 1982): 179.

Schifter, Richard. "Trends in Federal Indian Administration." *South Dakota Law Review* 15 (1970): 1–21.

Schrader, Robert Fay. *The Indian Arts & Crafts Board: An Aspect of New Deal Indian Policy*. Albuquerque: University of New Mexico Press, 1983.

Schusky, Ernest L. *The Right to be Indian*. N.P., 1965.

Shames, Deborah, ed. *Freedom With Reservation: The Menominee Struggle to Save Their Land and People*. Madison: National Committee to Save the Menominee People and Forest, 1972.

Smith, Michael T. "The Wheeler-Howard Act of 1934: The Indian New Deal." *Journal of the West* 10 (July 1971): 521–534.

Snodgrass, Jeanne A. *American Indian Painters: a Biographical Directory*. New York: Museum of American Indian, 1968.

Snodgrass, Marjorie P. *Economic Development of American Indians and Eskimos 1930 Through 1967: A Bibliography*. Washington, D.C.: Bureau of Indian Affairs, 1968.

Sorkin, Alan L. *American Indians and Federal Aid*. Washington, D.C.: Brookings Institution, 1971.

———. "American Indians Industrialize to Combat Poverty." *Monthly Labor Review* (March 1969): 19–25.

———. "The Economic and Social Status of the American Indian, 1940–1970." *Nebraska Journal of Economics* 22 (Spring 1974): 33–50.

Stefon, Frederick J. "The Irony of Termination: 1943–1958." *Indian Historian* 11 (Summer 1978): 3–14.

Stein, Gary. "Tribal Self-Government and the Indian Organization Act of 1934." *Michigan Law Review* 70 (April 1972): 955–986.

Steiner, Stan. *The New Indians*. New York: Delta, 1968.

Steward, Julian. "The Limitations of Applied Anthropology: The Case of the Indian New Deal." *Journal of the American Anthropological Society* 1 (Fall 1969): 1–17.

Stuart, Paul. "United States Indian Policy: From the Dawes Act to the American Indian Policy Review Commission." *Social Service Review* 51 (1977): 451–453.

Szasz, Margaret. *Education and the American Indian: The Road to Self-Determination, 1928–1973*. Albuquerque: University of New Mexico, 1974.

Taylor, Graham D. "Anthropologists, Reformers, and the Indian New Deal." *Prologue* 7 (Fall 1975): 151–162.

———. *The New Deal and American Indian Tribalism: The Administration of the Indian Reorganization Act, 1934–45*. Lincoln: University of Nebraska Press, 1980.

————. "The Tribal Alternative to Bureaucracy: The Indian New Deal, 1933–1945." *Journal of the West* 13 (January 1974): 128–142.

Taylor, Theodore W. *American Indian Policy*. Mt. Airy, Maryland: Lomond Publications, 1983.

————. *The States and Their Indian Citizens*. Washington, D.C.: U.S. Department of the Interior, 1972.

Tyler, S. Lyman. *A History of Indian Policy*. Washington, D.C.: U.S. Department of the Interior, 1973.

————. *Indian Affairs: A Work Paper on Termination with an Attempt to Show Its Antecedents*. Provo, Utah: Institute of American Studies, 1964.

U.S. Commission on Civil Rights. *Indian Tribes: A Continuing Quest for Survival*. Washington, D.C.: Government Printing Office, 1981.

Underal, James S. "On the Road Toward Termination: The Pyramid Lake Paiutes and the Indian Controversy of the 1950s." Ph.D. dissertation, Columbia University, 1977.

Vaillant, George C. *Indian Arts in North America*. New York: Harper and Brothers, 1939.

Waddell, Jack A., and Watson, O. Michael, eds. *The American Indian In Urban Society*. Boston: Little, Brown, and Company, 1971.

Washburn, Wilcomb E. *Red Man's Land/White Man's Law*. New York: Scribners Sons, 1971.

————. *The American Indian and the United States: A Documentary History*. Volume 3. New York: Random House, 1973.

Watkins, Arthur. "Termination of Federal Supervision: The Removal of Restriction Over Indian Property and Person." *Annals of the American Academy of Political and Social Science* 311 (May 1957): 47–55.

Weeks, Charles J. "The Eastern Cherokee and the New Deal." *North Carolina Historical Review* 53 (July 1976): 303–319.

White, Richard. *The Roots of Dependency*. Lincoln: University of Nebraska Press, 1983.

White, Robert A. "American Indian Crisis." *Social Order* 11 (May 1961): 201–211.

Wilkinson, Charles F. "Perspectives on Water and Energy in the American West and in Indian Country." *South Dakota Law Review* 26 (Summer 1981): 393–404.

Wilkinson, Charles F., and Biggs, Eric R. "The Evolution of the Termination Policy." *American Indian Law Review* 5 (1977): 139–184.

Wilson, Edmund. *Apologies to the Iroquois.* New York: Random House, 1966.

Wright, Peter M. "John Collier and the Oklahoma Indian Welfare Act of 1936." *Chronicles of Oklahoma* 50 (Autumn 1972): 347–371.

Zimmerman, William, Jr. "Economic Status of Indians in the United States." *Journal of Religious Thought* 7 (Summer 1950).

———. "The Role of the Bureau of Indian Affairs Since 1933." *Annals of the American Academy of Political and Social Science* 311 (May 1957): 31–40.

Index

Adams, Hank, 235, 239–242, 293–295
Affiliated Tribes of Northwest Indians, 181
Agua Caliente Band of California, 122
Alabama-Coushatta Indians of Texas, 124–125
Alaska Federation of Natives, 13
Alaska Native Claims Settlement Act, 13, 23, 109
Alaska Reorganization Act of 1936, 109
Alaska natives, 18, 59
Alcatraz Island occupation, 172–173, 230, 235–236
Alinsky, Saul, 233
Allotment policy, 16, 22, 39, 87, 297
American Indian Chicago Conference, 211
American Indian Day, 12
American Indian Defense Association, 35, 37, 71
American Indian Federation, 59–60
American Indian Movement (AIM), 4, 173, 203, 241, 280
American Indian Policy Review Commission, 23, 305, 315
Anderson, Clinton P., 127
Andrus, Cecil, 279
Anthropology and anthropologists, 62, 98–100, 133, 157–158, 244, 275–276
Arizona State University, 220
Assimilation policy, 6, 8, 30–33, 36–37, 48, 61, 89, 132–134, 148, 175–176, 229, 268, 283
Association on American Indian Affairs, 217–218, 283, 314

Ayres, Roy, 50

Beatty, Willard, 20–21, 43, 60–61
Benedict, Ruth, 9, 98–99
Bennett, Ramona, 234–237
Bennett, Robert L., 23, 83–86, 162–164, 169, 194, 209–211, 224–225
Bigman, Max, 4
Blackfeet Reservation and Indians, 52, 107, 253–254
Boas, Franz, 71
Bronson, Ruth, 169
Brophy, William A., 118, 119–120, 165
Bruce, Louis, 23, 194, 213–214, 230, 233, 241
Bruner, Joseph, 4, 60, 103
Buffalohead, W. Roger, 155–156
Bureau of American Ethnology, 62
Bureau of Indian Affairs, 105, 130–132; abolition of, 116, 315; Applied Anthropology Unit, 62; bureaucracy and organization, 4, 7, 63, 95–97, 122–123, 196–198, 259, 320; Indian employment preference, 18, 23, 75, 274–275; Indian Organization Division, 81–82; occupation of offices, 215, 230; paternalism, 4, 7, 15, 18, 22, 44, 82
Burke, Charles H., 37
Burnette Robert, 104–108, 149, 211–212, 226–227, 291–293
Bursum Bill of 1922, 35, 69

California Indians, 50–51, 114–115, 124–125, 127